GREAT WEST

LINES & LANDSCAPES

Business and Pleasure, Heritage and History

ALAN BENNETT

RUNPAST
PUBLISHING

Contents

This book is dedicated to my mother, Doris May Bennett.

Foreword

The Great Western Railway has long attracted the public's imagination – it was surely no accident that 'Great Western' was one of the first of the old company names revived by the privatized train operators. Quite what today's 20- or 30-somethings make of it isn't clear, but to a slightly older generation, far too young to have known the original company before nationalization, the name still conjures up all sorts of pleasant and evocative images thanks to the continuance into the 1960s of the GWR's marketing techniques by the Western Region of British Railways. The company always sold the seaside heavily, particularly in the West Country, although the archetypal gentle English countryside of the Cotswolds and the near West, and the often rougher beauties of Wales, Ireland, Cornwall and the English upland moors were also important. Nor was the Great Western's appeal restricted to those who did not have to deal with the often unpleasant and dangerous realities of railway work. Nearly four decades after the company's demise, the very last of its former employees – by then nearing retirement after a lifetime with BR – were still keen to impress on me, a raw operations management trainee in South Wales, that the Great Western's way of doing things was, if not invariably, then at least usually, the best.

Image is one thing, and reality another. In truth the Great Western did have a lot going for it, not least the places it served. In this nature and circumstance had dealt the company a strong hand. Yet the desirability of the places it served was not inherent in them: it had to be created. It was in this process of making places desirable that the Great Western and its successor, the Western Region, excelled during the first six decades of the 20th century and which Alan Bennett so skilfully reveals and dissects. He shows the GWR as a company of contrasts, perhaps even paradoxes. On the one hand, a thoroughly modern business enterprise, willing to use all the up-to-date techniques of marketing and publicity in pursuit of profit: on the other, the deliberate promotion of an often traditional, conservative sense of place, history and identity in which the railway, when it appeared at all, had to be finessed as part of the 'natural' order. In particular the Great Western both drew upon and contributed to a tradition of feelings and half-consciously articulated senses of what it meant to be English. This was true even when it was Wales, Ireland and Cornwall that were being marketed, for these were all presented as Celtic places: as contrasts to, and thus confirmations of, Englishness. There was though a great deal of subtlety and flexibility in all of this, so that the GWR was able to appeal to public – and potential passengers – as diverse as the English middle class in search of improving experiences and north Americans of Anglo-Saxon extraction intent on discovering their 'roots' as well as the urban masses wanting a good time at the seaside. Even the industrial heartlands of South Wales and the English Midlands, hugely important sources of revenue from freight traffic, were brought within the ambit of traditional Englishness.

This is not then a book in the usual run of railway histories. Yet it is in an important sense a book with railways at its focus, for without the GWR as a means of transporting people from urban 'centre' to rural 'fringe' the travel literature and posters examined here makes no sense at all as a collective body. Alan Bennett's meticulous original research and considerable scholarship means we can all appreciate how the Great Western Railway made itself part of the English way of life.

Colin Divall
Institute of Railway Studies, York

Introduction

This work examines the extensive literature produced by the Great Western Railway primarily over the first forty years of the twentieth century but with particular reference to the inter-war era when the output was most prolific and the content and style at its most challenging and dynamic. The intention is to set the GWR's promotional works into their contemporary context – social, economic, political and cultural – and thereby indicate the central, structural role of publicity for a modern, enterprising railway company. When removed from the heavily nostalgic perspectives in which they are largely perceived today, the GWR's literary initiatives can be appreciated, not only for their carefully considered commercial value in promoting tourism, but also as a significant register of cultural activity and focus. The content and, in particular, the style of these publications revealed a great deal in terms of the company's approach to issues such as that of empire, of Englishness, rural and industrial experience, perspectives on leisure and recreation, and to attitudes to history and the past, to the significance of landscape and, collectively, to notions of citizenship.

Some idea of the GWR's importance may be had from its role in the Travel Association of Great Britain. Beckerson argues that the 'Come To Britain Movement', dating from 1926,[1] and, later, reformulated as 'The Travel Association of Great Britain and Ireland' was "one of the first groups to draw attention to the economic benefits of foreign visitors to the U.K... It was a key plank in the strategy of the Travel Association."[2] The role of the railway companies and, specifically, the contribution of the GWR, in developing the potential of the Travel Association through innovative marketing, was considerable and should be noted. Felix Pole was the only general manager from the four railway companies to attend the first meeting of the provisional committee of the Travel Association on 26 February 1929.[3] The company, for example, played a prominent role in the campaign for fiscal reform in terms of prohibitive taxes on visitors to Britain and advocated the extension of rateable levies, nationally and locally, to provide for increased tourist marketing and amenities.[4] The Travel Association's efforts to encourage foreign tourists, particularly Americans, to visit Britain emphasised themes of common ethnic origin and shared cultural experience. This approach was also prominent within the GWR literature where there was also a related initiative, thematically, by way of an appeal to Irish-American interests through literary and poster works on Southern Ireland.

The GWR's literary and visual representations drew heavily upon the concept of 'departure', that is, the qualitative, distinction between daily or accepted routine and that of a special experience. Departure could assume an historical form, a particular location, an aesthetic appreciation (as with the Celtic sublime) or the sheer, exuberant pleasures of the seaside, for example, as an important dimension of 'departure', GWR marketing also stressed the experience of the journey itself in its various forms, as a spectacle, an adventure and often as a unique and glamourous event, in the general context of service, en-route, as reflected in matters of speed, safety, efficiency and modernity. These were brought together in 'prestige advertising',[5] a dimension of place marketing not widely recognised by historians beyond the present-day context of nostalgic representation or that as evidence for technical-engineering interests. The broader social and cultural significance of the experience and impact of the journey itself has not been developed to any considerable extent, despite the fact that railway literature generally, and, indeed, poster work, drew particular attention to this essential element of company identity.

Extended and serious consideration of issues such as those indicated above can, however, be seen in the literature relating to railway posters. Here, analysis focuses on questions of imagery, composition, style, etc., looking beyond the popular, present-day agenda of nostalgia and whimsy. For example, Beverley Cole and Richard Durack, 1992,[6] and Tony Hillman and Beverley Cole, 1999,[7] analyse poster work in its historical, social and cultural context, seeing it as a dynamic expression of specific periods, and places and, indeed, their projected and desired characterisations. The language and protocol evident in, for example, the GWR's hierarchically-formulated approach to its holiday resorts (Chapter Two), in its recognition of places of pilgrimage (Chapter Three); in its approach to landscape of great aesthetic acclaim (Chapters Three and Four) and, again, in its correlation of commercial activity and the interests of empire and nation through its internationally-based freight services (Chapter Five), reflects the direct interaction that existed between the railway and the wider community generally.

In its appeal to the 'English Speaking Peoples' of the world at large, and its association with the Empire Marketing Board, each in their own way statements of the direct recognition of what the company called "the brethren of the Mystic Tie" and Britain as the "Mother Country," the GWR revealed its deeply held and complex cultural interests. These were, in turn, grounded and intensified in the company's evident celebration of rural, historical England – the characteristic pastoral landscape of the 'South Country' and its traditional imagery of thatched cottages, deep lanes, orchards, and cattle grazing on hot, still afternoons: the landscape of the ploughman, the shepherd and the smithy, and, inevitably, the local branch line as an intrinsic element of the local community and symbol of stability. This pastoral idyll is, of course, predominant in terms of imagery and associations favoured by the latter-day preservation movement, as evident on the West Somerset,the South Devon and the Severn Valley Railways. Nostalgic representations, however, lock the GWR into an overwhelmingly rural and seemingly static, timeless identity, impervious to the process of history and, therefore, the impact of change. But when considered clearly in the context of the inter-war era, however, the GWR was anything but static and timeless. It was a dynamic organisation committed to progress and change apparent in every aspect of railway business, not least, that of marketing. Amongst its many interests the company probably achieved its greatest success in terms of popular perception in its development of the 'Holiday Line' imagery – one vital dimension of the overall GWR identity considered here.

REFERENCES – INTRODUCTION

1: John Beckerson. Making Leisure Pay: the Business of Tourist Marketing in Great Britain 1880-1950. Journal of Business. P5.

2: Ibid P6.

3: The British Travel Association 1929-1969. British Tourist Authority, London 1970, PP2-3, P6 for reference to Local Authorities (Publicity) Act 1931, enabling halfpenny in the pound levy for promotion of "commercial, historical, scenic, recreational, curative or climatic" amenities.

4: G.W.R. Magazine. Britain's Increased Tourist Traffic, October 1935, P540.

5: G.E. Orton. Railway Publicity. G.W.R (London) Lecture and Debating Society, October 1934. P5.

6: Beverley Cole and Richard Durack. Railway Posters 1923-1947. National railway Museum, Laurence King, London 1992.

7: Beverley Cole and Tony Hillman. South For Sunshine, Southern Railway Publicity and Posters 1923 to 1947. National Railway Museum, Capital Transport, London 1999.

Table 3

Table 3

CORNISH RIVIERA EXPRESS

RESTAURANT CAR SERVICE

LONDON, PLYMOUTH, TRURO and PENZANCE

WEEK DAYS and SUNDAYS

	E	S	SUNDAYS (Commences 16th July)	SUNDAYS (Runs until 9th July)
London (Paddington) dep	am 10A30	am 10A30	am 10A30	am 10A30
Plymouth .. arr	pm 2 30	..	pm 3 25	pm 3 35
Liskeard .. "	..	..	..	4 16
Par.. .. .. "	3 32	..	..	4 45
St. Austell .. "	..	..	..	4 57
Truro .. .. "	4 3	pm 4 33	4 57	5 20
Redruth .. "	..	..	5 20	5 44
Camborne .. "	..	..	5 30	5 53
Gwinear Road "	4 32	..	..	..
Hayle .. .. "	..	..	5 40	6 3
St. Erth .. "	4 42	5 17	5 48	6 9
Penzance .. "	4 55	5 30	6 0	6 25

	E	S	SUNS.
Penzance .. dep	am 10A 0	am 10B 0	am 9A45
St. Erth .. "	10A10	..	9A55
Gwinear Road "	10A22	10B22	..
Camborne .. "	..	..	10A11
Truro .. .. "	10A52	10 52	10 38
Par.. .. .. "	11A22	..	11 10
Plymouth .. "	pm 12A30	pm 12A30	pm 12A20
Exeter (St. David's) "	..	..	1 50
London (Paddington) arr	4 40	5 20	5 30

A—Seats can be reserved in advance on payment of a fee of 2s. 0d. per seat (see page 23).

B—Passengers travelling beyond Plymouth are required to hold Regulation Tickets (see page 47), see also Note "A".

E—Except Saturdays. S—Saturdays only.

54

THE CORNISH RIVIERA

As an Ideal Winter

HEALTH AND PLEASURE RESORT.

How to go there and What to see there.

Top: *Timetable for Cornish Riviera Express, Summer 1961.*

Here and right: *Front Cover of 'The Cornish Riviera' first edition of January 1904.*

CHAPTER ONE

IMAGERY AND ENTERPRISE

The Great Western Railway began as a project to link London and Bristol. Authorised on 31 August 1835 the railway opened in stages to Bristol, where through services operated on the broad gauge, 7'0¼, began on 30 June 1841. Isambard Kingdom Brunel was appointed as engineer. Together with his specific duties as railway engineer Brunel also envisaged a related, innovative scheme to link the GWR with wider international perspectives. He suggested that the company could take advantage of the dramatic potential in steamship development, as exemplified in his own vessel, the 'Great Western', to promote associated maritime interests. Under Brunel's scheme, Bristol could become the railhead for Atlantic passenger traffic; in effect, a prestigious London-New York service.[1] On the railway itself the Bristol and Exeter company extended westward, once again, opening in stages to Exeter on 1 May 1844. Thereafter, moving west over much more difficult terrain, the South Devon Railway linked Exeter and Plymouth, opening throughout in April 1849. From Plymouth westward, the Cornwall Railway ran to Truro, opening in May 1859, where it met the standard gauge West Cornwall Railway opened between Truro and Penzance in August 1852. This network became the GWR main line from Paddington to Penzance which by 1889 had been incorporated into the Great Western fold and was thereafter gradually improved and, in terms of company policy and identity, clearly Great Westernised.

Elsewhere, Birmingham was reached from Paddington, via Oxford and Banbury by 1852; Wolverhampton and Shrewsbury, in 1854. South Wales was linked with London in 1850 but this entailed a circuitous route via Gloucester and thence to Swindon, midway between Paddington and Bristol. The opening of the Severn Tunnel in January 1886 transformed this situation, offering direct communication between Bristol, Newport and Cardiff. The 1890s saw considerable development in GWR affairs. Identified as 'The Great Awakening,'[2] these included the removal of the broad gauge in May 1892, the introduction of improved train services and plans for several new routes, identified here in Chapter One. In a further related form, 1904 marked the beginning of the company's distinctive publicity drive with the publication of the 'The Cornish Riviera'[3] and, with the lucrative North American market a priority, 'Historic Sites and Scenes of England.'[4]

The early years of the twentieth century also saw extensive progress in terms of technical expertise and the creation of a modern, highly efficient railway network. Prior to World War One the management invested heavily in the development of its trunk routes.[5] The major initiatives here comprised: the Badminton, South Wales Direct Line, avoiding Bath and Bristol, this being in conjunction with the development of Fishguard Harbour and then lucrative Trans-Atlantic and Irish traffic, the Badminton line opening in 1903; the new route from Reading to Taunton - the West of England main line - opening in 1906, directly improving access and overall standards of service in tourist traffic to the West of England; the Birmingham-Cheltenham line, opened in 1908 giving direct access from the South Wales ports to the Midlands; and the Great Western/Great Central Joint Railway (1910) providing a much improved direct link between Paddington and Birmingham via High Wycombe and Bicester. All such investment contributed directly to the interests of tourism and operational efficiency as in the enlargement and extensive rebuilding of key stations, for example, Westbury, Newbury, Bristol Temple Meads, Taunton, Newton Abbot, Cardiff, helping consolidate the essential corporate identity and the attendant prestige vital to the GWR's public image – as a progressive, self-confident organisation. The Great Western's commercial and operational ascendancy in the West of England had been effectively acknowledged by the rival London and South-Western Railway in 1909. Minutes of a meeting between the GWR Chairman, Viscount Churchill, and Sir Charles Scotter, Chairman, LSWR, recorded the latter's considered pursuit of "amalgamation and total absorption" with and by the GWR ... "that the GWR should in other words, buy them up and manage the whole concern from Paddington."[6] Set against the LSWR's static commercial returns over the five-year period to 1910, the GWR enjoyed an annual increase of five per-cent at competitive points on their respective systems.

There were also major achievements in terms of mechanical engineering. G.J. Churchward, Chief Mechanical Engineer to the Company, 1902-1922, gave the Great Western a fleet of modern standardised locomotives, the product of advanced, innovatory designs that put the GWR to the forefront of performance. Churchward also gave Great Western locomotive design an almost instant 'family' identity that the layman could easily recognise thus underlining the crucial concept of corporate identity. Combining efficiency with elegance, the Swindon tapered boiler, copper-capped chimney, gleaming, polished brasswork and brunswick green livery was calculated to give GWR locomotives a dignity and overall sense of distinction that was vital to the promotion of public image.

Churchward set the pattern for future development. His successors, C.B. Collett in 1922, and F.W. Hawksworth in 1944, followed his example, producing modified designs based on trusted Churchward principles. The best known locomotives of the GWR between the World Wars – the 'Castles', 'Kings', 'Halls', 'Granges', 'Manors' and, post-war, the 'Counties' – exemplified the essential Churchward design, with their unmistakable Swindon parentage, much enhanced by means of a carefully considered naming policy. Resonant of order, authority and prestige, the class names were intended to reflect a hierarchically-inspired celebration of Englishness, a perspective exploited in the company's sale publications, as in 'GWR Engines, Names, Numbers, Types and Classes' 1938. 'The "King" of Railway Locomotives', 1928, 'Caerphilly Castle', 1924 or 'Locomotives of the Great Western Railway', 1929.[7] A range of jigsaw puzzles reinforced the thematic focus. But in as far as the GWR relied on its essentially tried and trusted Churchward principles into the 1940's, locomotive design and development clearly reflected the company's essentially conservative nature, very different from that of the LMS, LNER and the SR, who were much more innovative in this specific area. Collett's rolling stock, however, gave the GWR such definitive designs as the Ocean Liner saloons of 1931, named after members of the Royal Family, and the famous Centenary Stock of 1935. Both were redolent of confidence, authority and prestige in their dimension and luxurious interiors. There was also the considerable technological achievement, together with the attendant publicity, of the famous 'Cheltenham Flyer' of 1932. Culturally, this train was important, conferring substantial international acclaim upon the GWR, as W.G. Chapman recorded in the company's publication 'The Cheltenham Flyer', 1934:

> I need not tell you that 'Cheltenham Flyer' has made a name for herself all over the world. Americans, Chinese, Frenchmen, Germans, Indians and visitors from other countries have made a great point of including a trip on the world's fastest train in their itineraries.[8]

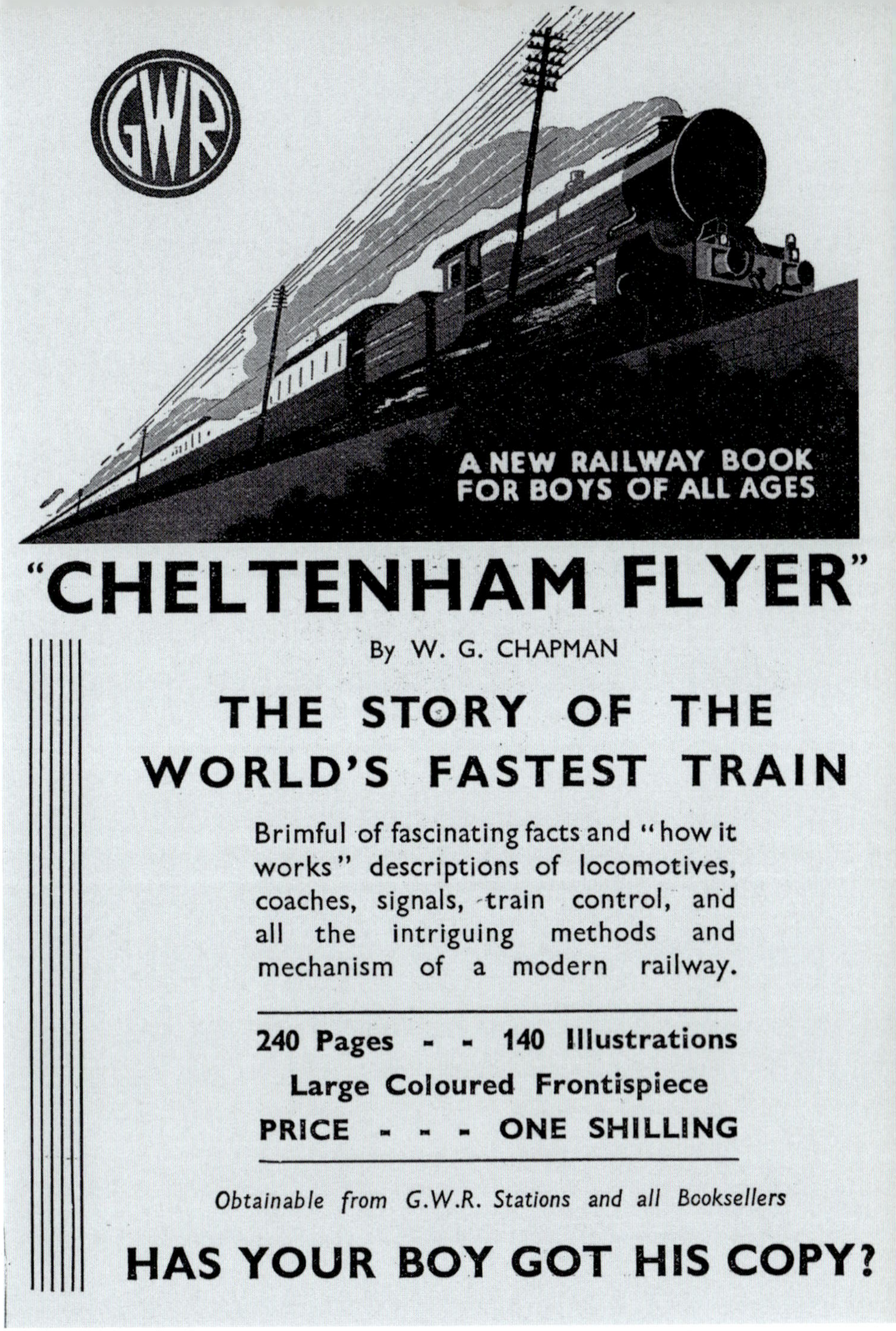

The 1938 edition of 'GWR Engines, Names, Numbers, Types and Classes.' Pictorial covers were provided from 1932 onward, the final edition appearing in 1946. Author's collection

Advertisement for W G Chapman's 'The Cheltenham Flyer' 1934, placed in Holiday Haunts. Author's collection

The details here of Great Western enterprise in engineering achievement and standards of service indicate the extent to which the company was aware of the need to consistently integrate technology and public image. It was this recognition and achievement, when allied to a received rural, historical imagery, the effective marriage of technology and historic cultural identity, that gave the GWR its most powerful and enduring appeal in terms of its public perception. This conflation of technology and the literary, historical and aesthetic qualities of Great Western experience was implicit and, often, conspicuously explicit, as in the literary perspective of the 'Through the Window' trilogy of 1924-1926.[9] These books offered a unique experience of landscape, tradition, aesthetic perception and GWR enterprise, in the collective concept of 'The Journey.'[10]

'Through the Window' focused on the spectacular attraction of the landscape, the history and cultural heritage that could be enjoyed from the passing train, as in the Paddington-Penzance journey. The journey westward was described as "an adventure and experience ... having something of the fascination of foreign travel."[11] The content and style of the 'Through the Window' trilogy represented a real attempt to link different locations and larger regions, South-West with North-West and Wales and Southern Ireland with London. Overall, a metropolitan-provincial-rural configuration. 'Through the Window' served to identify the specific character of a given region/county whilst relating it structurally to the many other, similar or contrasting, locations across the GWR system. The constituent parts of the network were, thereby, presented in terms indicative of an organic relationship with Paddington, as Head Office and the company's commercial, organisational hub.

The Literary Record

Of the four railway companies in the inter-war era – the Great Western Railway, the Southern Railway, the London and North Eastern Railway and the London Midland Scottish Railway – and amongst the numerous pre-grouped companies in the first two decades of the twentieth century, the Great Western was the most prolific and the most innovative in terms of the literary record. It was also a prime mover in the development of joint publicity schemes between railway and resort, and between companies for national and, particularly, international trade. At this point, however, it is necessary to stress that the literary work formed part of the GWR's much larger, comprehensive publicity initiative wherein all means at its disposal were employed to enhance its public image. As will be examined below, the guiding principle was, as one senior official remarked in 1929, "to create in the minds of the public a desire to visit the places situated on our system."[12] Press reports, posters and works of literature were devoted to that end but, whilst the literature, in particular, suggested an identifiable thematic focus and imagery, no formal statement identifying a systematic company policy on content and style is evident.

The literary record began, effectively, in 1904 with the publication of three books: 'The Cornish Riviera', the company's first major work, 'Historic Sites and Scenes of England' directed expressly at the American market and 'Southern Ireland, Its Lakes and Landscapes' directed at an Anglo-American audience. Many more regional and county-based works followed: 'South Wales, The Country of Castles', 1905; 'North Wales, The British Tyrol', 1906; 'Devon, The Shore of the Sea Kings', 1906; 'Wilts, Somerset and Dorset, Wonderful Wessex', 1908; 'Rural London, The Chalfont Country and the Thames Valley', 1909; and 'Beautiful Brittany', also 1909. These works went into many editions and remained largely unaltered until the late twenties when they were replaced by new titles with evidently up-dated perspectives, written by popular, modern authors of the day.

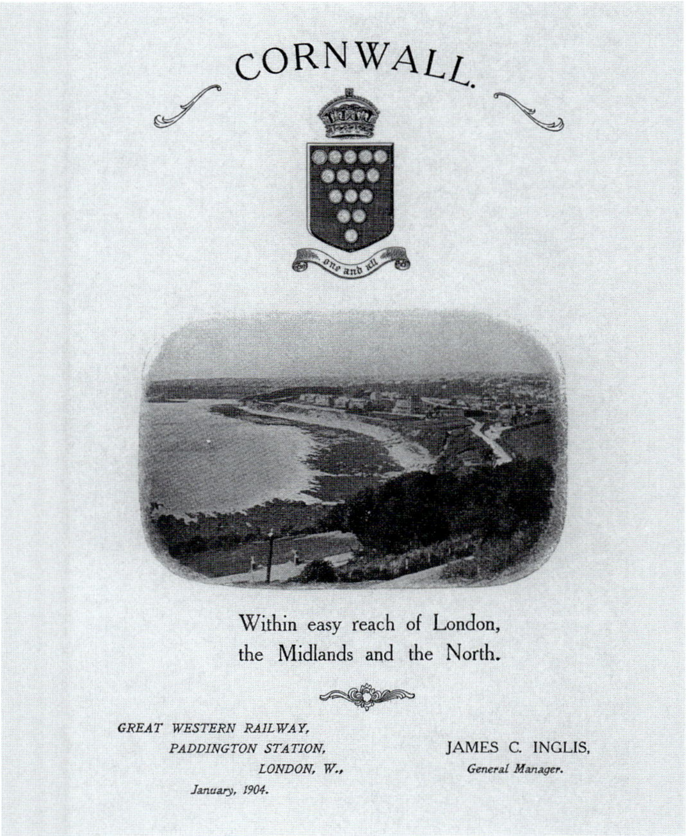
CORNWALL.

one and all

Within easy reach of London, the Midlands and the North.

GREAT WESTERN RAILWAY,
PADDINGTON STATION,
LONDON, W.,
January, 1904.

JAMES C. INGLIS,
General Manager.

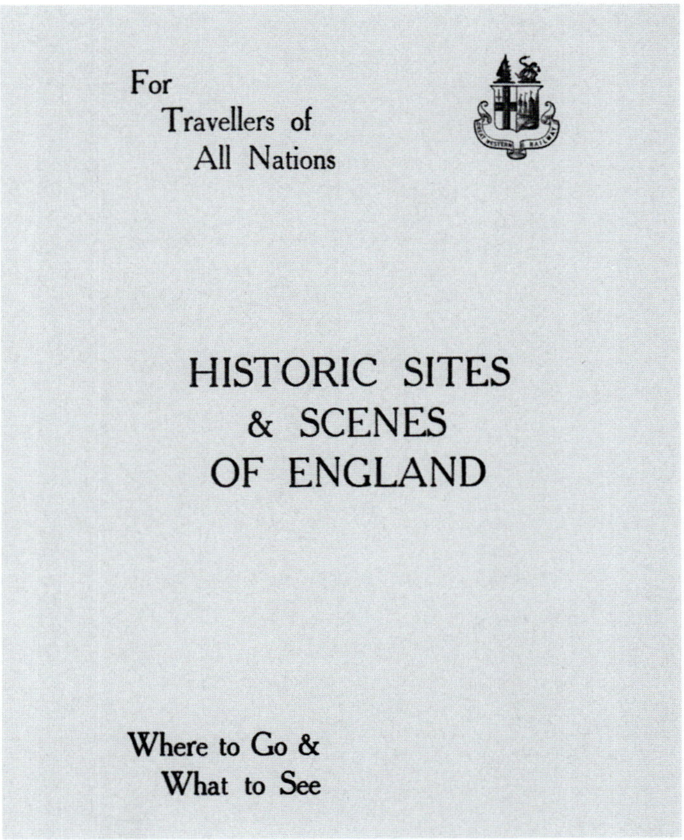
For
Travellers of
All Nations

HISTORIC SITES
& SCENES
OF ENGLAND

Where to Go &
What to See

Title page; 'Cornish Riviera' 1904.

Front cover 'Historic Sites and Scenes of England' July 1904.

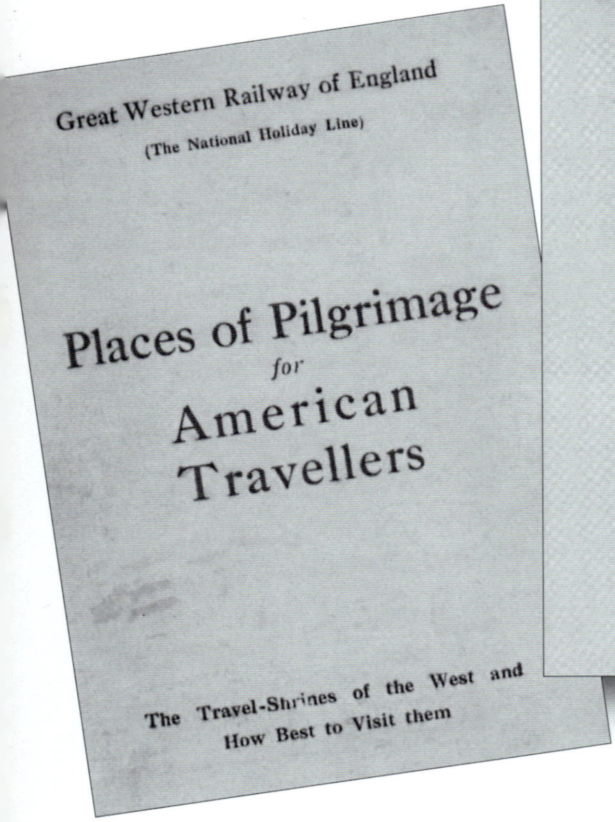

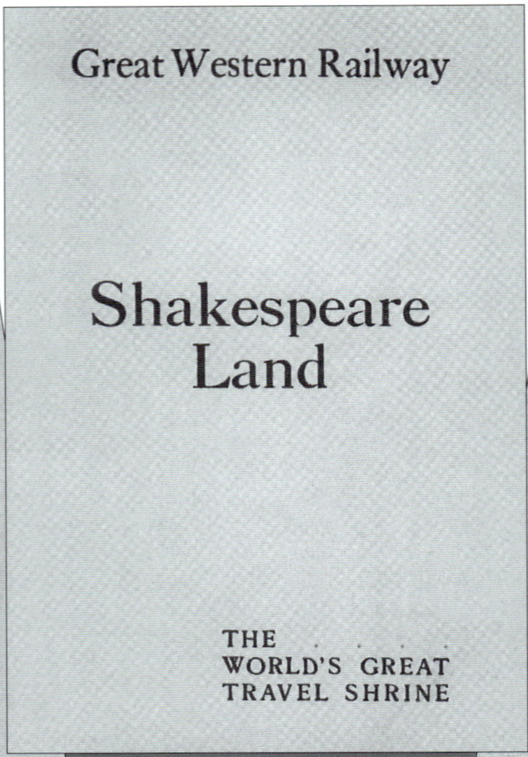

G.W.R. PUBLICATIONS.

One of the best ways of preparing for a holiday is to read about the countryside in which it is to be spent. A knowledge of its people and their history, as well as of its scenic beauties and other attractions, leads to greater enjoyment and more lasting appreciation. G.W.R. Publications are well written by authoritative writers, and are attractively produced at low prices.

THE CORNISH RIVIERA. By S. P. B. MAIS. A fascinating volume by the well-known broadcaster and travel writer, offering a wealth of information in a characteristically entertaining manner. 160 pages, 96 illustrations, and 12 maps.

GLORIOUS DEVON. By S. P. B. MAIS. Every corner of the county has been explored, and its manifold attractions are delightfully described in this book. 143 pages, 96 illustrations, and 12 maps.

Price 1/– each. Paper covers.

SOMERSET. By MAXWELL FRASER. The distinctive charm of "Smiling Somerset" is aptly revealed in this beautifully produced volume. 300 pages, richly illustrated.

Price 1/– Paper covers. 2/6 bound in cloth.

SOUTHERN IRELAND. By MAXWELL FRASER. A comprehensive Guide to a delightful holiday district. Illustrated in photogravure, with a map.

Price 6d.

ABBEYS. By the late M. R. JAMES, Litt.D., F.S.A., F.B.A., Provost of Eton, with a chapter on "Monastic Life and Buildings," by Professor Hamilton Thompson, M.A., D.Litt., F.S.A. A magnificent volume, which makes a delightful gift for both the general reader and the student. 164 pages, richly illustrated with photographs, drawings, and many plans.

Price 5/–, bound in quarter cloth.

HOLIDAY HAUNTS. The G.W.R. Official Guide to Holiday Resorts in England, Wales, Channel Islands and Isle of Man, including special introductory chapters by S. P. B. MAIS, and descriptive text by MAXWELL FRASER, F.R.G.S. Nearly 1,000 pages, over 320 photogravure illustrations, and 8,000 addresses of holiday accommodation.

Price 6d.

BOOKS FOR RAMBLERS. By HUGH E. PAGE.

A series of useful booklets dealing with some of the finest rambling country in the British Isles. Mr. Page is a well-known authority on rambling, and each of these handy volumes describes, in detail, 20 or 25 delightful rambles, illustrated with photographs or drawings, and a clear sketch map of each route.

RAMBLES IN THE CHILTERN COUNTRY.
RAMBLES IN SHAKESPEARELAND AND THE COTSWOLDS.
RAMBLES AROUND THE CAMBRIAN COAST.
RAMBLES AND WALKING TOURS IN SOMERSET.
RAMBLES IN THE WYE VALLEY.
RAMBLES IN SOUTH DEVON — enlarged edition, *to be published for the Summer Season, 1939.*

Price 6d. each volume.

These publications can be obtained from G.W.R. Stations and Offices, Booksellers, or from the Superintendent of the Line, G.W.R., Paddington Station, London, W.2.

G.W.R. PUBLICATIONS.

The popular "Boys of All Ages" series: three interesting books about the Great Western Railway. By W. G. CHAPMAN.

LOCO'S OF THE ROYAL ROAD. A century of G.W.R. Locomotives, from the tiny "North Star" to the mighty "Kings" of to-day. With a four-fold diagram in full colour. 232 pages, 144 illustrations.

TRACK TOPICS. All about the Railway Track—its construction and maintenance—Bridges, Tunnels, Viaducts and the like. How Brunel built the G.W.R., and how it is maintained to-day. 260 pages, 168 illustrations.

CHELTENHAM FLYER. The story of Britain's record-breaking train, with many interesting descriptions of Locomotives, Coaches, Signals, Automatic Train Control and other operating features. Folding coloured frontispiece. 240 pages, 140 illustrations.

Price 1/– each.

G.W.R. ENGINES. Names, numbers, classes and types of G.W.R. locomotives. New and enlarged edition.

Price 1/–.

THROUGH THE WINDOW. An attractive booklet which shows, in simple diagrammatic form, the features of interest to be seen from the carriage window while journeying between Paddington and Penzance, Torquay and Newquay. With numerous illustrations.

To be published for the Summer Season 1939.

Price 6d.

OFFICIAL G.W.R. TIMETABLES. Complete edition (issued July and September), **6d.** Pocket editions for London–Reading, also Birmingham–Worcester districts, **2d.** each.

JIG-SAW PUZZLES.

G.W.R. Jig-Saw puzzles are strongly made of 3-ply wood, and have achieved widespread popularity.

Price 2/6 each (about 200 pieces):

Historic Totnes.	**Locomotives Old and New.**
The Model Railway.	**The Romans at Caerleon.**
Royal Route to the West.	**Cornwall—preparing for a catch.**
G.W.R. Locomotives in the making.	**Windsor Castle from the Air.**

Price 5/– each (about 400 pieces):

Drake Goes West.	**Oxford (Brasenose College).**
Stratford-on-Avon.	

PICTORIAL POSTERS.

Copies of pictorial posters issued by the Company can be supplied, when available, by the Superintendent of the Line, as follows:—

Double-Royal size (25 in. × 40 in.) . . . . . 2/6 each.
Quad-Royal size (50 in. × 40 in.) . . . . . 5/- „

G.W.R. Books and Puzzles can be obtained from G.W.R. Stations and Offices, or from the Superintendent of the Line, G.W.R., Paddington Station, London, W.2.

All these early publications were written by A.M. Broadley, whose work was informed by an extremely detailed and informed literary reference. Broadley related landscape to the Classical And English literary tradition evoking the perspectives of Shakespeare, Milton, Dryden, for example in a construction of received 'High Culture', a projection aimed at confirming the exclusive nature of its educated, informed audience. The perspective was, accordingly, that of a prevailing metropolitan-urban provenance, as in the company's clear identification with the prestigious ambience and protocol of the winter health resort: the English and, particularly, the Cornish Riviera. The initial representation of Cornwall was primarily that of the National Winter Health and Pleasure Resort.[13] Its principal focus was with its equable climate and restorative properties. Numerous references to climate and to comparative statistics with Mediterranean locations, including a complete chapter on meteorological data and medical endorsements from reputable doctors set the agenda and focus, underlining Cornwall's detailed and practical advantages as a winter resort over foreign locations. Similarly, Broadley's 'Devon. The Shire Of The Sea Kings' identified that county as "one of the great holiday haunts of the Empire."[14]

Broadley's works from the pre-World War One era, were the basis, indeed, the texts, for a series of 'Handy Aid' booklets covering all regional locations and perspectives across the GWR system. Looking to celebrate outstanding literary, historical or aesthetic attractions, these publications were pocket-editions to inform the visitor en-route or on location and included such titles as: 'Sunny Cornwall, England's Mediterranean Region; Devon, The Lovely Land of the Mayflower; The Wye Valley (two volumes), Shakespeare-Land' and 'Places of Pilgrimage for American Travellers'. The 'Handy Aids' series, although an adaptation of Broadley's early works, was essentially an initiative of the inter-war era. Selected titles did appear as early as 1913 but the full range was closely identified with the managerial initiatives of the Great Western's Managing Director, Felix Pole, who headed the company from 1921 to 1929.

Formerly the editor of the GWR Magazine for ten years up to 1919, Pole, as General Manager, identified publicity as fundamental to the GWR's interests. It was during his term of management that the company made its most significant progress in relation to content, style and focus within the literary work and achieved its greatest output and sales. Literary works, however, were by no means the only vehicle of publicity. Poster production, in particular, was prolific, if essentially conservative in its style and thematic range.[15] There were also official photographs celebrating the company's identification with historic sites, the landscape of rural-traditional England and the romantic, sublime perspectives of Cornwall, Wales and Southern Ireland. Lantern-slides and film-strips were also available for hire, often carrying the familiar titles marking the best known literary works, listed above. The lantern slides were estimated to comprise more than one hundred sets and were accompanied by printed lecture notes. Given the estimated 1200 to 1500 applications from libraries, clubs and educational interests generally, the GWR observed, "as every class of person is a potential traveller, we have taken full advantage of this form of publicity."[16]

Left, above: *Front covers – 'Places of Pilgrimage for American Travellers' 1924 ed., Shakespeare Land, 1924 ed., both in 'Handy Aid' series, and 'The Wye Valley' Vol II, 1924 ed.*

Left, below: *List of GWR publications as advertised in 'Holiday Haunts' 1939.* Author's collection

This was said as part of an authoritative statement on the work and the role of the Publicity Department delivered in October 1934. Under the Proceedings of the Great Western Railway (London) Lecture and Debating Society, Mr. G.E. Orton, Commercial Assistant To The Superintendent Of The Line, gave a lecture entitled: "Railway Publicity."[17] This was one of several papers on publicity presented to the Debating Society during the inter-war period and, as in Orton's case, the papers were the work of well-regarded authorities. Orton had been with the GWR for some thirty years. His responsibilities included those of

Below: *Advertisement for Lantern Lectures included in 'Holiday Haunts' 1934.*

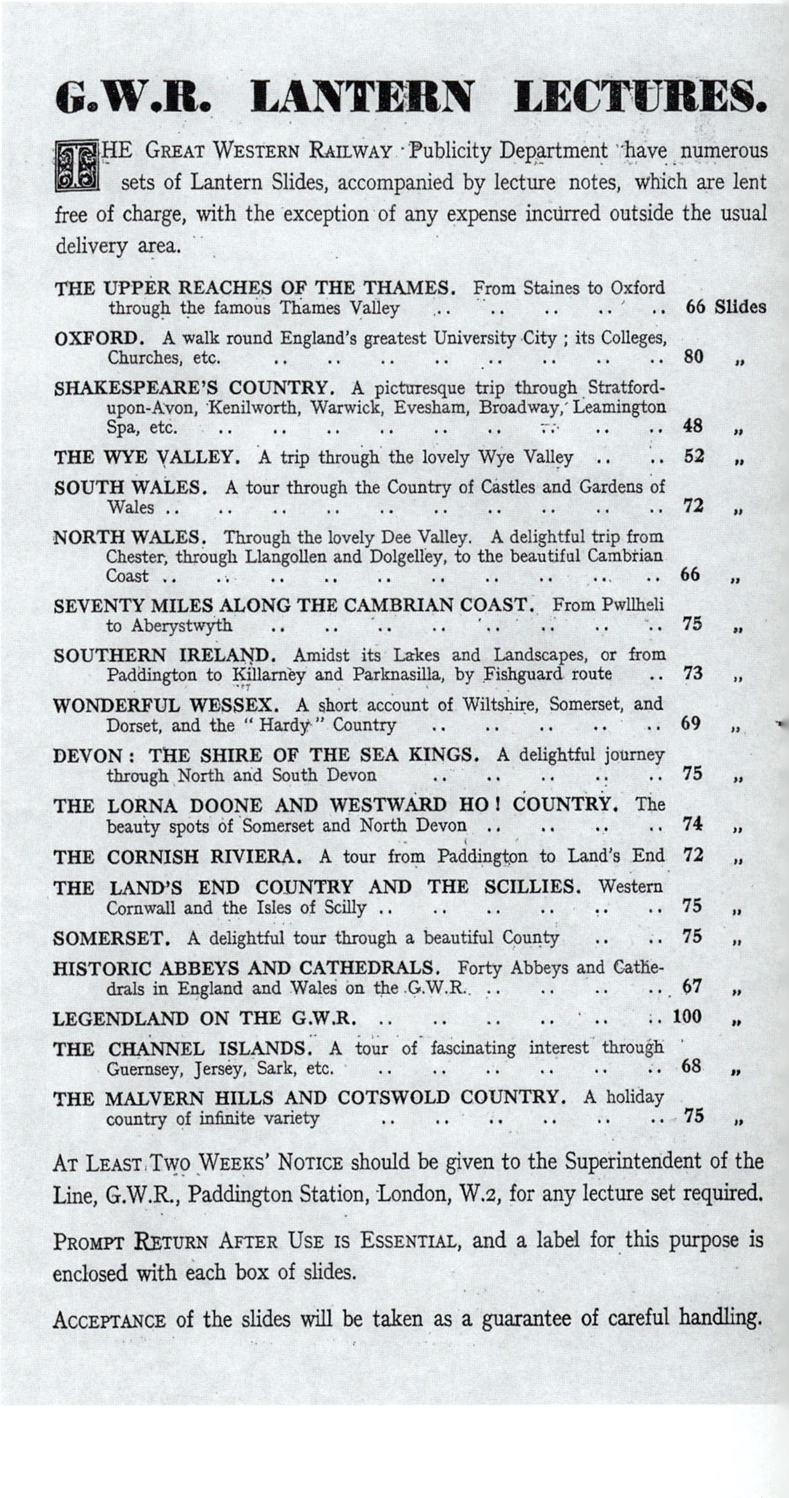

G.W.R. LANTERN LECTURES.

THE GREAT WESTERN RAILWAY Publicity Department have numerous sets of Lantern Slides, accompanied by lecture notes, which are lent free of charge, with the exception of any expense incurred outside the usual delivery area.

THE UPPER REACHES OF THE THAMES. From Staines to Oxford through the famous Thames Valley	66 Slides
OXFORD. A walk round England's greatest University City ; its Colleges, Churches, etc.	80 „
SHAKESPEARE'S COUNTRY. A picturesque trip through Stratford-upon-Avon, Kenilworth, Warwick, Evesham, Broadway, Leamington Spa, etc.	48 „
THE WYE VALLEY. A trip through the lovely Wye Valley	52 „
SOUTH WALES. A tour through the Country of Castles and Gardens of Wales	72 „
NORTH WALES. Through the lovely Dee Valley. A delightful trip from Chester, through Llangollen and Dolgelley, to the beautiful Cambrian Coast	66 „
SEVENTY MILES ALONG THE CAMBRIAN COAST. From Pwllheli to Aberystwyth	75 „
SOUTHERN IRELAND. Amidst its Lakes and Landscapes, or from Paddington to Killarney and Parknasilla, by Fishguard route	73 „
WONDERFUL WESSEX. A short account of Wiltshire, Somerset, and Dorset, and the " Hardy " Country	69 „
DEVON : THE SHIRE OF THE SEA KINGS. A delightful journey through North and South Devon	75 „
THE LORNA DOONE AND WESTWARD HO ! COUNTRY. The beauty spots of Somerset and North Devon	74 „
THE CORNISH RIVIERA. A tour from Paddington to Land's End	72 „
THE LAND'S END COUNTRY AND THE SCILLIES. Western Cornwall and the Isles of Scilly	75 „
SOMERSET. A delightful tour through a beautiful County	75 „
HISTORIC ABBEYS AND CATHEDRALS. Forty Abbeys and Cathedrals in England and Wales on the G.W.R.	67 „
LEGENDLAND ON THE G.W.R.	100 „
THE CHANNEL ISLANDS. A tour of fascinating interest through Guernsey, Jersey, Sark, etc.	68 „
THE MALVERN HILLS AND COTSWOLD COUNTRY. A holiday country of infinite variety	75 „

AT LEAST TWO WEEKS' NOTICE should be given to the Superintendent of the Line, G.W.R., Paddington Station, London, W.2, for any lecture set required.

PROMPT RETURN AFTER USE IS ESSENTIAL, and a label for this purpose is enclosed with each box of slides.

ACCEPTANCE of the slides will be taken as a guarantee of careful handling.

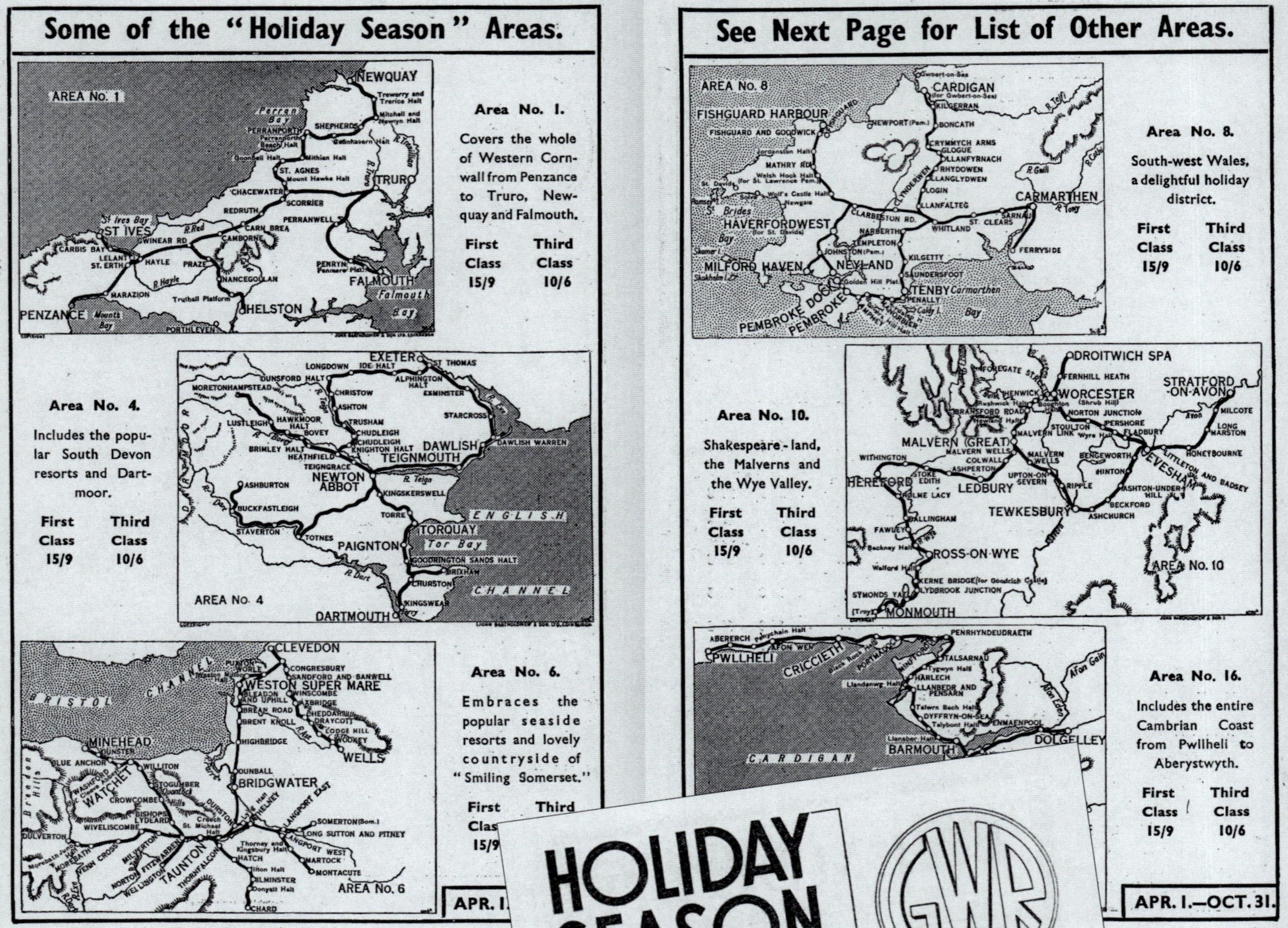

Advertisement: Holiday Season Tickets included in 'Holiday Haunts' 1935.

Holiday Season Tickets, covering prime tourist locations, 'Holiday Haunts' 1935.

Assistant Publicity Agent and, in 1929, General Agent in the USA and Canada; in 1932, Assistant Commercial Advertising and Publicity Agent; in 1933, GWR Publicity Agent and, in 1934, Commercial Assistant to the Superintendent of the Line.[18]

Orton began by stressing the differences between railway publicity and that of any other business, large or small. His was not the position "of the publicity manager of a commodity who has but a single and well-defined product to advertise."[19] He therefore emphasised that it was the duty of the publicity officer to prioritise and that, given the GWR's focus on press advertisements, almost 50 per cent of the expenditure in the Press went to advertising excursion arrangements. Newspaper advertisements were always central to the company's policy and practice, a factor underlined by Felix Pole, who, as General Manager, identified press coverage as one source of invaluable 'propaganda'. Orton revealed that the GWR ran some "25,000 [excursions] per annum, necessitating the regular weekly use of about 250 newspapers."[21] This "essential excursion advertising" was distinguished from what was termed "general advertising."[20] The latter comprised: "Train Service, Territory" – the popular holiday locations – "Travel Literature, Special Services" – season-holiday tickets, parcels, freight, docks interests – and "Prestige Advertising", as in high standards of infrastructure, rolling stock, signalling and safety measures "giving us an undertaking second to none in efficiency."[22] Moreover "no fewer than 41 varieties of illustrated folders, totalling in numbers printed, 1,142,000, which are in addition to 38 varieties of menus, totalling 440,000, advertising our holiday season tickets, are distributed to hotels in the districts where the tickets applied."[23] Distribution and general dissemination of information covered hotels, libraries, railway agents, local/regional authorities and, indeed, all incoming liners (see Chapter Five).

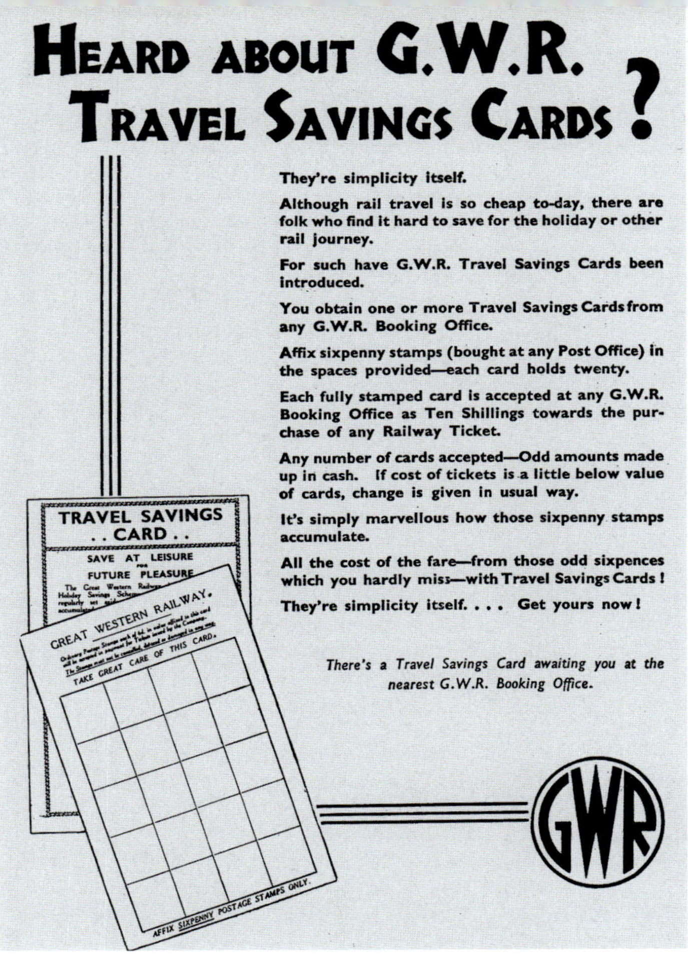

Advertisement for Land Cruises, 1934 season 'Holiday Haunts'.

List and details of Camping Coaches advertised in successive editions of 'Holiday Haunts' from 1935.

Advertisement for Travel Savings Cards carried in 'Holiday Haunts' 1938.

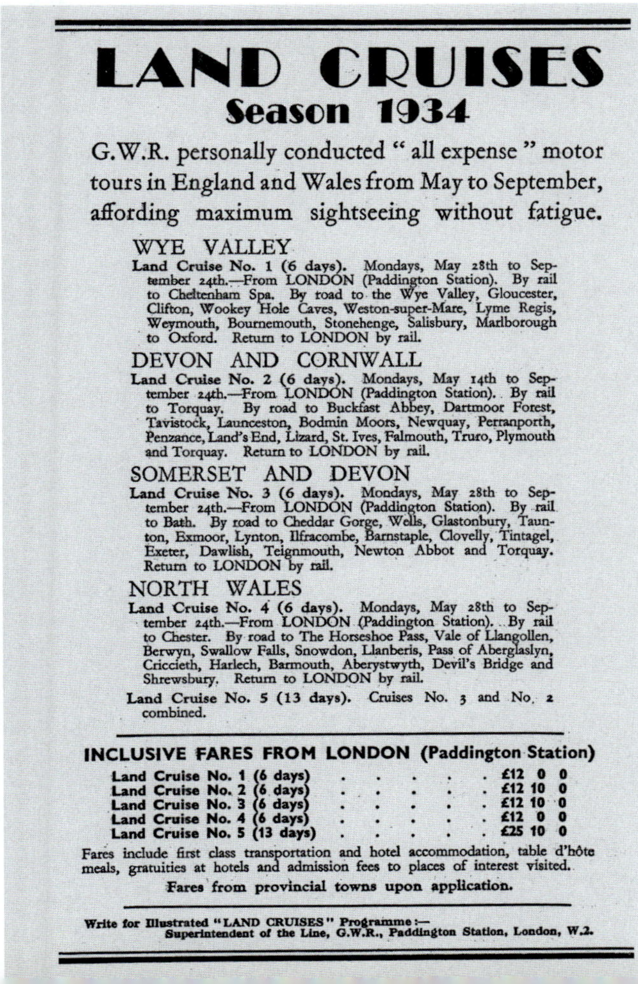

LAND CRUISES

Season 1934

G.W.R. personally conducted " all expense " motor tours in England and Wales from May to September, affording maximum sightseeing without fatigue.

WYE VALLEY

Land Cruise No. 1 (6 days). Mondays, May 28th to September 24th.—From LONDON (Paddington Station). By rail to Cheltenham Spa. By road to the Wye Valley, Gloucester, Clifton, Wookey Hole Caves, Weston-super-Mare, Lyme Regis, Weymouth, Bournemouth, Stonehenge, Salisbury, Marlborough to Oxford. Return to LONDON by rail.

DEVON AND CORNWALL

Land Cruise No. 2 (6 days). Mondays, May 14th to September 24th.—From LONDON (Paddington Station). By rail to Torquay. By road to Buckfast Abbey, Dartmoor Forest, Tavistock, Launceston, Bodmin Moors, Newquay, Perranporth, Penzance, Land's End, Lizard, St. Ives, Falmouth, Truro, Plymouth and Torquay. Return to LONDON by rail.

SOMERSET AND DEVON

Land Cruise No. 3 (6 days). Mondays, May 28th to September 24th.—From LONDON (Paddington Station). By rail to Bath. By road to Cheddar Gorge, Wells, Glastonbury, Taunton, Exmoor, Lynton, Ilfracombe, Barnstaple, Clovelly, Tintagel, Exeter, Dawlish, Teignmouth, Newton Abbot and Torquay. Return to LONDON by rail.

NORTH WALES

Land Cruise No. 4 (6 days). Mondays, May 28th to September 24th.—From LONDON (Paddington Station). By rail to Chester. By road to The Horseshoe Pass, Vale of Llangollen, Berwyn, Swallow Falls, Snowdon, Llanberis, Pass of Aberglaslyn, Criccieth, Harlech, Barmouth, Aberystwyth, Devil's Bridge and Shrewsbury. Return to LONDON by rail.

Land Cruise No. 5 (13 days). Cruises No. 3 and No. 2 combined.

INCLUSIVE FARES FROM LONDON (Paddington Station)

Land Cruise No. 1 (6 days)	**£12 0 0**
Land Cruise No. 2 (6 days)	**£12 10 0**
Land Cruise No. 3 (6 days)	**£12 10 0**
Land Cruise No. 4 (6 days)	**£12 0 0**
Land Cruise No. 5 (13 days)	**£25 10 0**

Fares include first class transportation and hotel accommodation, table d'hôte meals, gratuities at hotels and admission fees to places of interest visited.

Fares from provincial towns upon application.

Write for Illustrated "LAND CRUISES" Programme :— Superintendent of the Line, G.W.R., Paddington Station, London, W.2.

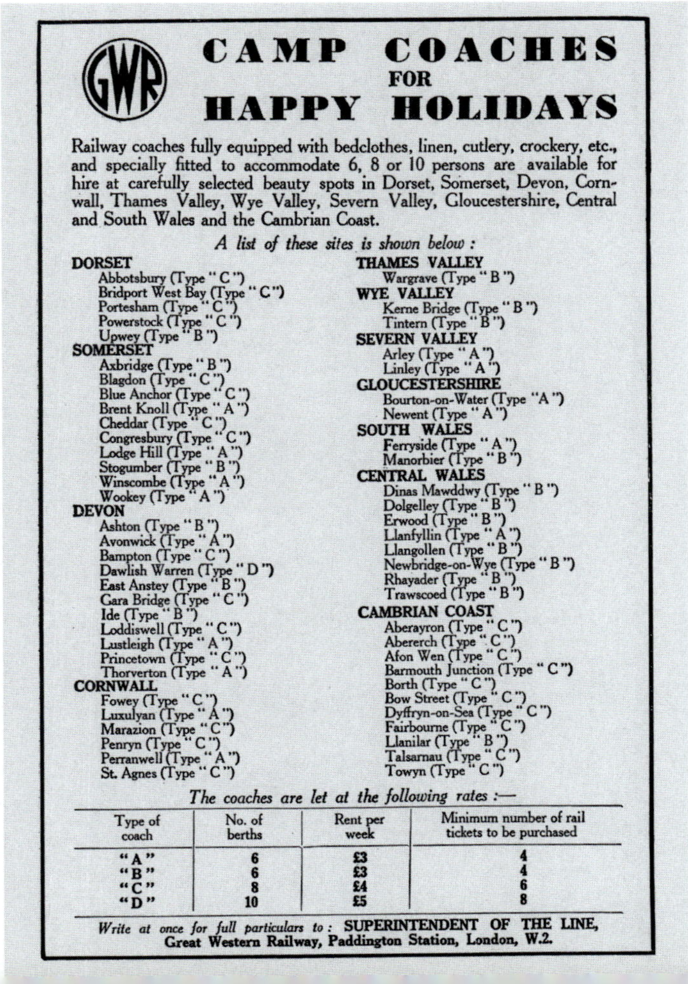

GWR

CAMP COACHES FOR HAPPY HOLIDAYS

Railway coaches fully equipped with bedclothes, linen, cutlery, crockery, etc., and specially fitted to accommodate 6, 8 or 10 persons are available for hire at carefully selected beauty spots in Dorset, Somerset, Devon, Cornwall, Thames Valley, Wye Valley, Severn Valley, Gloucestershire, Central and South Wales and the Cambrian Coast.

A list of these sites is shown below :

DORSET
Abbotsbury (Type " C ")
Bridport West Bay (Type " C ")
Portesham (Type " C ")
Powerstock (Type " C ")
Upwey (Type " B ")

SOMERSET
Axbridge (Type " B ")
Blagdon (Type " C ")
Blue Anchor (Type " C ")
Brent Knoll (Type " A ")
Cheddar (Type " C ")
Congresbury (Type " C ")
Lodge Hill (Type " A ")
Stogumber (Type " B ")
Winscombe (Type " A ")
Wookey (Type " A ")

DEVON
Ashton (Type " B ")
Avonwick (Type " A ")
Bampton (Type " C ")
Dawlish Warren (Type " D ")
East Anstey (Type " B ")
Gara Bridge (Type " C ")
Ide (Type " B ")
Loddiswell (Type " C ")
Lustleigh (Type " A ")
Princetown (Type " C ")
Thorverton (Type " A ")

CORNWALL
Fowey (Type " C ")
Luxulyan (Type " A ")
Marazion (Type " C ")
Penryn (Type " C ")
Perranwell (Type " A ")
St. Agnes (Type " C ")

THAMES VALLEY
Wargrave (Type " B ")

WYE VALLEY
Kerne Bridge (Type " B ")
Tintern (Type " B ")

SEVERN VALLEY
Arley (Type " A ")
Linley (Type " A ")

GLOUCESTERSHIRE
Bourton-on-Water (Type " A ")
Newent (Type " A ")

SOUTH WALES
Ferryside (Type " A ")
Manorbier (Type " B ")

CENTRAL WALES
Dinas Mawddwy (Type " B ")
Dolgelley (Type " B ")
Erwood (Type " B ")
Llanfyllin (Type " A ")
Llangollen (Type " B ")
Newbridge-on-Wye (Type " B ")
Rhayader (Type " B ")
Trawscoed (Type " B ")

CAMBRIAN COAST
Aberayron (Type " C ")
Abererch (Type " C ")
Afon Wen (Type " C ")
Barmouth Junction (Type " C ")
Borth (Type " C ")
Bow Street (Type " C ")
Dyffryn-on-Sea (Type " C ")
Fairbourne (Type " C ")
Llanilar (Type " B ")
Talsarnau (Type " C ")
Towyn (Type " C ")

The coaches are let at the following rates :—

Type of coach	No. of berths	Rent per week	Minimum number of rail tickets to be purchased
"A"	6	£3	4
"B"	6	£3	4
"C"	8	£4	6
"D"	10	£5	8

Write at once for full particulars to : **SUPERINTENDENT OF THE LINE, Great Western Railway, Paddington Station, London, W.2.**

A significant organisational feature, distinct to the GWR, was also underlined. Passenger enquiries were handled by the public information bureau which was attached to the publicity department. Orton considered this arrangement to offer the best possible service and, therefore, publicity. Detailed replies to enquiries, supplemented by information on wider-related publicity initiatives, represented advantages for all concerned which, in Orton's opinion, could not be over-estimated. He also drew attention to the work of the Press Bureau. The latter, operating within the Publicity Department, gathered newsworthy items from across the company for effective free publication in the national or regional press. There were also arrangements within the divisions whereby the divisional officers supplied their local papers with useful news items and engaged with correspondence columns on the company's behalf. This was intended to underline the presence and active role of the railway within the community.

In its range of marketing initiatives the GWR reflects parallels with the Empire Marketing Board, to which it gave considerable support. Indeed, Major M.J.M. Dewar, appointed as GWR Publicity Officer in 1934, had been head of outdoor publicity for the E.M.B. and, previously, on the headquarters staff of the British Empire Exhibition at Wembley, 1924-25.[24] The broadly educational agenda revealed by both parties in the provision of jigsaws and games, puzzles, competitions, visits, films and exhibitions, had considerable commercial-cultural resonance which was intended to encourage an active sense of participation in, and identification with, their respective interests. Both were well aware of the potential in fostering a sense of citizenship amongst children. The GWR utilised its extensive supply of network and regional maps which, correlated with the commercial and topographical detail – ports, industries, histories and topography – in the unifying factor of transport, were recommended to schools. Such amenities were also available to community outlets, as in the broad educational context of newspapers, illustrated talks and the popularist company handbooks and brochures which were distributed free of charge. Orton's identification of the central role of the national and regional-local press in reaching a mass-market readership and his recognition of the immediate and dramatic properties of the poster, suggests that the overall impact of these dimensions of marketing was always likely to be greater than that of the formal literary works. Reference to the twenties and to the later thirties confirms this perspective. Details from lecture papers for 1925 and 1929 are considered below, whilst for the latter half of the 1930s, the GWR produced no substantial literary works. Focusing instead upon booklets, standardised brochures and press announcements, the Coronation Year, 1937, occasioned an intense distribution of these various forms of advertising.

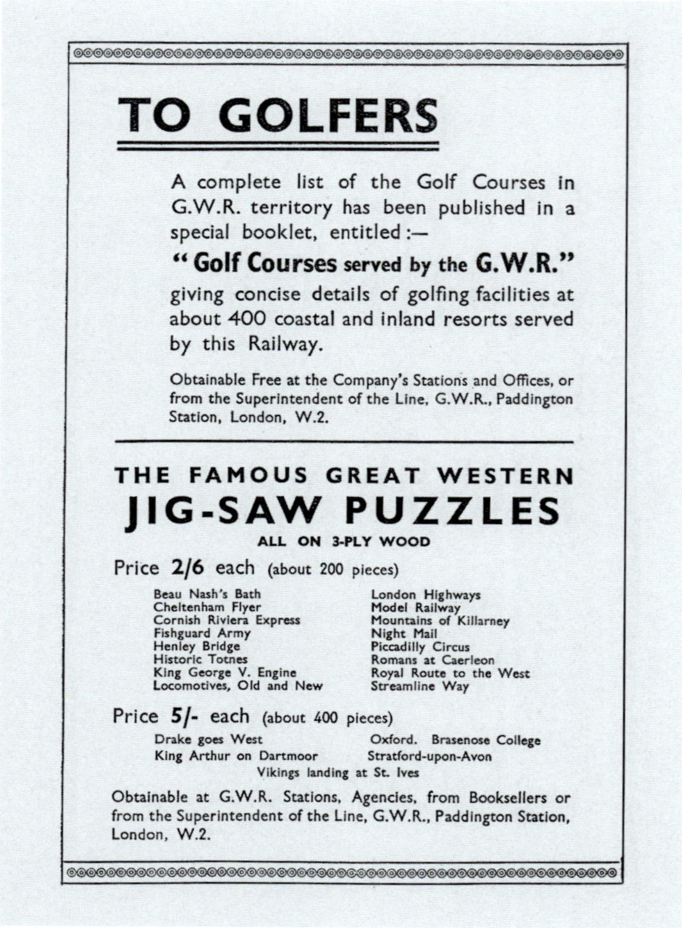

Advertisement for Golfers and the availability of Jig-Saw Puzzles celebrating outstanding locations, events and services identified with the GWR. 'Holiday Haunts' 1935.

Publicity had been a prominent issue for the GWR Lecture and Debating Society during the twenties. At the meeting of 5th February 1925, Mr. D. Richards presented a paper: "Advertising – with Special Reference to Railway Publicity"[25] As a former employee of the GWR, Richards went on to become Assistant to the General Manager of the Isle of Wight Central Railway. Thereafter, he pursued a career in commercial advertising and, as an advertising consultant with a railway background, Richards was recognised as an authoritative contributor to the GWR Society. He identified the national and regional/local press as the central vehicle for publicity, stressing this in relation to the poster, as a matter of record. "The poster in any field of advertising must always be complementary to the press", as the latter was considered to deliver a much larger measure of real and useful publicity."[26] Orton, however, (in 1925) whilst endorsing the Press as "first in importance every time,"[27] and conceding that the GWR's poster work in some cases was "not of much advertising value", did consider that the poster was improving considerably. He also pointed out that poster campaigns were invariably accompanied by Press announcements[28] but also observed that the GWR could and should do more to advertise freight services, to bring them more in line with passenger promotions. (This latter dimension was addressed in the creation of the Commercial Advertising Department, in January 1931,[29] leading to the publication of 'The Best Location', in 1932. See Chapter Five).

Mr. Goodricke of the LNER publicity department, likewise, endorsed the pre-eminent role of the Press but also identified literary works and, specifically, those of the GWR, as "one of three fundamental items in any scheme."[30]

> With regard to literature, an extensive series of books is issued by every railway company; the Great Western excel themselves in that respect and I am sure that it has proved a most profitable investment from the railway standpoint. The books do good in clubs and enquiry offices and those highly-rented establishments we have in large cities like London. Literature is the backbone of our efforts.[31]

The 1929 document: "Railway Advertising. Is it on the right lines?" – GWR (London) Lecture and Debating Society, January 1929 – took the form of a debate between C.S. Lock, Press Officer in the Publicity Department (Affirmative) and A.C. Pickford of the Goods Department, Pontypridd (Negative).[32] Lock offered useful statements of policy, beginning here with the emphasis upon literature and its context as developed from the 1925 paper. Under the heading; 'Development Of Territory Served By The Company,' he emphasised the press/poster campaign and, subsequently, the literary initiatives.

MOVING?

Then Move Cheaply, Speedily and Safely

The G.W.R. will estimate for the House to House conveyance of your Household effects, including the services of packing and unpacking by experts.

A typical G.W.R. Removal.

A Road-Rail Container, identical to a Furniture Lift Van, is brought to your Door, your Furniture packed in it by experienced packers. Conveyed to the station, the container, transferred to rail, is carried to destination by Express Freight Train. On arrival the container is delivered to your new residence and the Furniture unloaded and placed in position. If required, arrangements can be made for the laying of linoleum and carpets, picture hanging and other similar services, while Insurance against risks associated with removing can be effected at exceptionally low rates. Finally, families removing by rail secure 33⅓% reduction on rail fares to the new residence. Removals in the same locality are also efficiently executed, direct by road.

The Local G.W.R. Agent will give you full particulars, or post this coupon :—

THE CHIEF GOODS MANAGER, REMOVALS DEPARTMENT,
GREAT WESTERN RAILWAY, PADDINGTON STATION, LONDON, W.2.

I am moving my household from..

to..

Please send a representative at.. A.M. / P.M.

on...to inspect and quote for the removal.

Name..

Address...

....

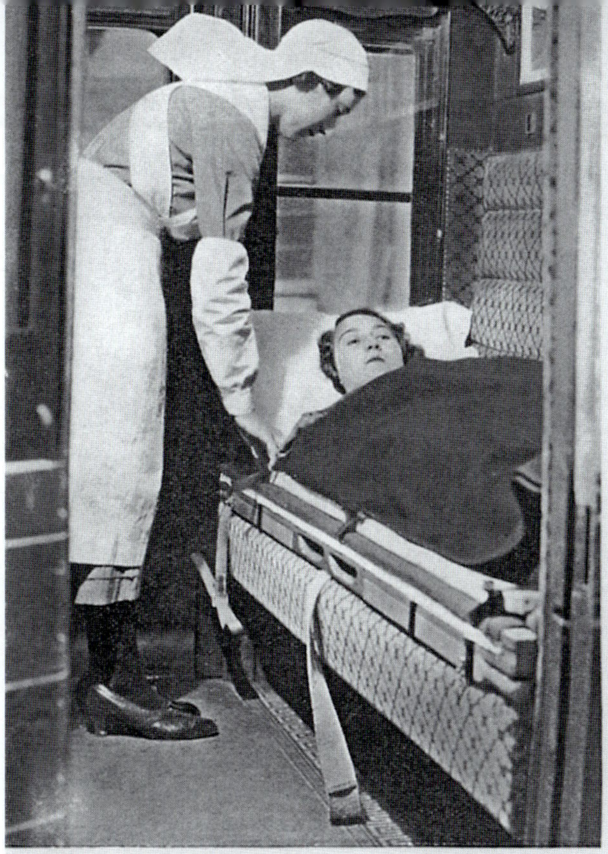

Comfortable Travel for Invalids

A REAL "BED-TO-BED" SERVICE

The Great Western Railway has paid considerable attention to the problems of invalids travelling by rail.

A new type of stretcher has now been designed which can be placed within the train compartment. By its use the patient makes the throughout journey between home and hospital lying on the stretcher.

This "bed-to-bed" service overcomes many travel difficulties and very materially adds to the comfort of invalids who need to travel lying down.

FULL DETAILS OF THIS FACILITY MAY BE OBTAINED FROM G.W.R. STATION MASTERS.

Advertisement: House Removals, emphasising the role and impact of the Road-Rail Container and the related services involved. 'Holiday Haunts' 1934.

Notice of special services available for invalids. This was prominent in the company's 'Winter Resorts' publication (1935 edition) which catered in many respects for those seeking a health resort within an overall medically-led context.

> ... in order to stimulate travel it has been the policy of the Company for a quarter of a century to endeavour to create in the minds of the public a desire to visit the places situated upon our system.... It was obviously to the Company's advantage to encourage this desire, especially in relation to the holiday habit and, in doing so, to encourage as great a part of this new traffic as possible to its system ...
> Consequently, Press announcements backed up by poster displays were undertaken, calling attention to the advantages of Cornwall, for example, as a holiday resort, and so successful was this effort that later Devon, Somerset, North and South Wales and other districts were given representation and a stimulus given to holiday traffic in general. This advertising created a big demand for literature and consequently a number of publications dealing with the various districts were issued.[33]

Lock identified excursion traffic as advertised in the Press as a source of much enhanced revenue: He also emphasised 'Overseas Advertising' principally the USA and the representation of the Summer and Winter Resorts in England as valuable revenue earners, the latter countering the strenuous efforts on the part of Continental resorts. Of the excursion traffic, figures were given from 1923 to 1927, inclusive: "1923, total figure, 26 million; 1924, total figure 30 million; 1925, total figure, 39 million; 1926, total figure, 38 million; 1927, total figure, 49 million. Comparative figures for the thirties reflect 'peaks', in 1936 and 1937, of 48 and 49 million respectively.[34]

The American market (See Chapter Five) was considered essential as this statement of development in the twenties reveals.

> It is computed that half a million Americans visited England last year, an increase of 25 per cent on the 1927 figure. Their interests are, of course, centred in the historic and beauty spots of this country and the Company is indeed fortunate in having a number of the most important of these on its system. We have thus a very direct interest in going "all out" for this traffic. We expend considerable sums on Press advertising and literature distributed in America and we have good reason to say that the results are on the upgrade. An index of some value is given by passengers landing at Plymouth. In 1913, the great boom year before the war, the total number of passengers disembarking at Plymouth was 27,000; in 1925 the number was 27,000; in 1927, 34,000; in 1928, over 36,000. This shows an increase of 2,000 in 1928 over 1927 – and 9,000 over both 1925 and 1913.[35]

Felix Pole put great emphasis upon the American market and duly despatched company representatives to the USA in 1925 to promote 'The Historic and Scenic Line of England.' 'The Handbook for Travellers from Overseas', 1926[36] effectively, the USA and Canada, advertised its General Agent at 315 Fifth Avenue, New York, highlighting "particulars of the railway arrangements for the convenience of overseas travellers arriving and departing from the Ports of Plymouth, Bristol, Liverpool and Cobh (Queenstown)"[37]. The handbook also included details of GWR literary works – both the free guidebooks and the larger retail selection, these, of course, being available aboard ship, en-route to England.

Pickford, however, whilst acknowledging these developments, identified various shortcomings. He called for more detailed and dynamic presentation in the Press, stressing the need to "attract attention, arouse interest and compel action."[38] His verdict on the current practice was that it "lacks appeal and directness; and neglects opportunities."[39] On passenger services he concluded: "The people we must influence are those who seldom, if ever, travel."[40] Pickford called for an extension of excursion fares "and other privileges"[41], that is the identification of particular types of passenger service – business, personal or pleasure – and of the real need to publicise them more effectively. Railway posters he considered to be "either too scenic or overloaded with detail,"[42] but 'Holiday Haunts' was singled out for praise, not least, for the fact, as he saw it, of comparative performance – "Its excellence serves but to

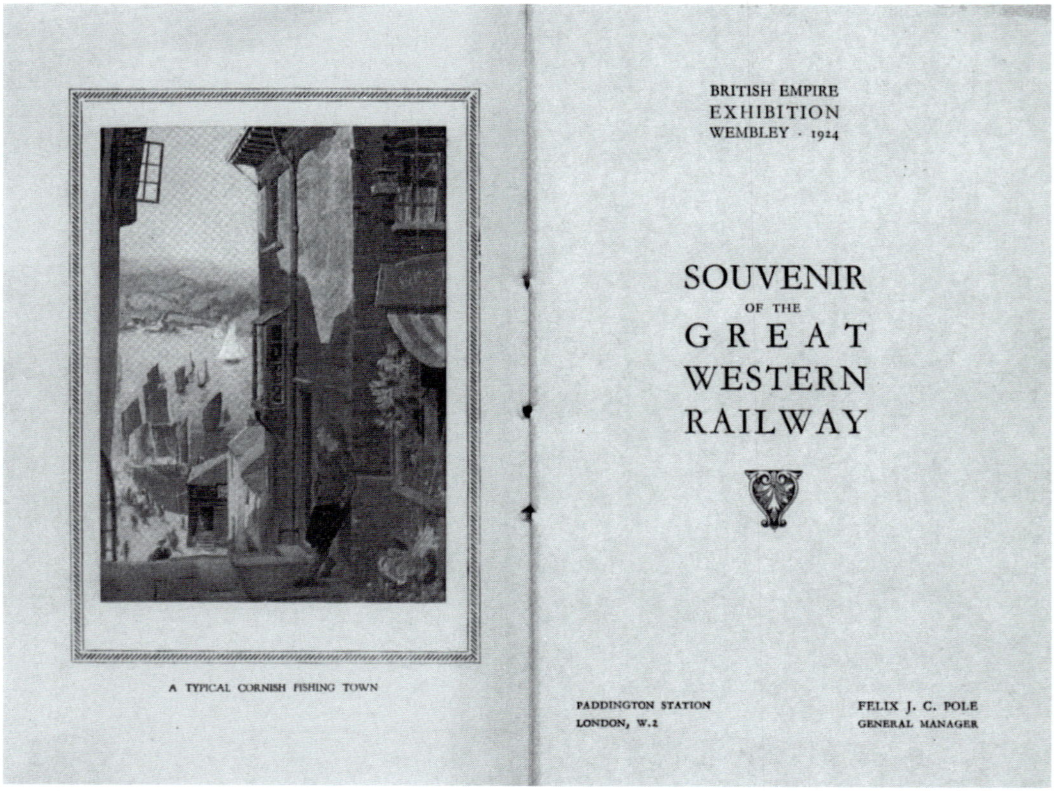

Left: *Title Page, 'Souvenir of the Great Western Railway. British Empire Exhibition, Wembley' 1924.* Author's collection

Opposite: *Front cover of the American-orientated booklet celebrating the Centenary and Pageant of the Baltimore and Ohio Railroad. The publication included details on Britain's commercial and cultural standing particularly in relation to the GWR, 1927.* Author's collection

GREAT WESTERN RAILWAY
OF ENGLAND
1837····1927

The Quickest Route
NEW YORK TO LONDON
via PLYMOUTH

exemplify the weakness of other phases, for it must not be forgotten that no part of advertising is complete in itself. Each is dependent upon, and complementary to, the other."[43] The GWR Magazine, by comparison, whilst having "a very appreciable public demand apart from the circulation amongst employees"[44] was subject to a severe handicap. Pickford posed the question: "Could one conceive of a more dull, lifeless-looking cover for such an interesting book?"[45] His question serves to bring us back to the company's concern to up-date and generally overhaul the presentation, style and format of its literature during the early post-Grouping period.

During the twenties, under the direction of Felix Pole, the company had begun to revise its literary work, particularly the early material by A.M. Broadley, with its exclusive, literary agenda, and to introduce new publications reflecting shifting perspectives in matters of recreation and leisure – the expectations and protocol of the holiday. This was reflected in the GWR's literary style, its content and presentation. 'Sunny Cornwall, England's Mediterranean Region,'[46] provides an example. "A Wonderful Summerland: England's Atlantic Seaboard", a section within this book, emphasised the theme of choice and, therein, the distinctive variety of experience. It expressed the infinitive: to go, to see, to feel, to smell, etc., highlighting the role of the senses and of active participation – a characteristically Great Western approach of the inter-war years, and the conflation of cultural-commercial interests. The content represented something of a bridge between the older concept of the holiday as a structured, formalised educational experience and the later, more relaxed, recreational emphasis, based around more varied, active pursuits. The inter-war years saw considerable evidence of the shifting perspective towards the more democratic and much less formal style of tourism to meet all requirements, consistent with the progressive context of 'citizenship' and reflected in the increasing range of participatory activities available.[47]

'The Cornish Riviera' and 'Glorious Devon', totally new publications in an equally new format, appeared in 1928. They comprised 167 pages and 151 pages respectively: 'Somerset' comprised 186 pages, with all three publications celebrating the rural-historical, aesthetic and seaside perspectives. They were also lavishly illustrated and, like the photographic plates in the company's 'Holiday Haunts' annual handbook, were the work of the Engineering Department. These new books were the work of S.P.B. Mais, an extremely popular travel-writer of the period, who also wrote for the Southern Railway.[48] These two volumes, together with Maxwell Fraser's 'Somerset', 1934, became major literary works of GWR literature and definitive reference books for the West of England.[49] All three were published in hardback format initially and in paperback by the mid-thirties. Mais, with his experience as leader-writer to the Daily Telegraph, was considered a good choice for these books. As a free-lance writer he had many books to his credit with various publishing houses on historical-topographical studies relating to British, European and overseas locations. His popular and partisanly narrative style, deeply descriptive and historically inclined, was totally removed from what by that time was Broadley's ponderous, remote terms of reference. The GWR also benefitted in its association with Mais, given his work with the BBC as a broadcaster. Mais' evening presentations of an historical-topographical character enhanced his reputation nationally and, as indeed Stanley Baldwin had found, the apparently direct, seemingly personal contact with the listener paid dividends in terms of communication and 'message'.

Maxwell Fraser was the GWR's most accomplished and prolific author. Appointed to the GWR by Felix Pole, she was the daughter of W.H. Fraser, who had been the company's publicity agent from 1924 to 1931 and, previously, a long-term member of staff. Maxwell Fraser was a Fellow of the Royal Geographical Society and, from 1930, was the editor of the company handbook, 'Holiday Haunts'. She undertook the task of

Left, below: *Opening chapter, page one, 'The Cornish Riviera', SPB Mais, 1928.* Author's collection
Right, below: *Sample page indicating format and style: opening Chapter IV. 'Somerset' Maxwell Fraser 1934.*

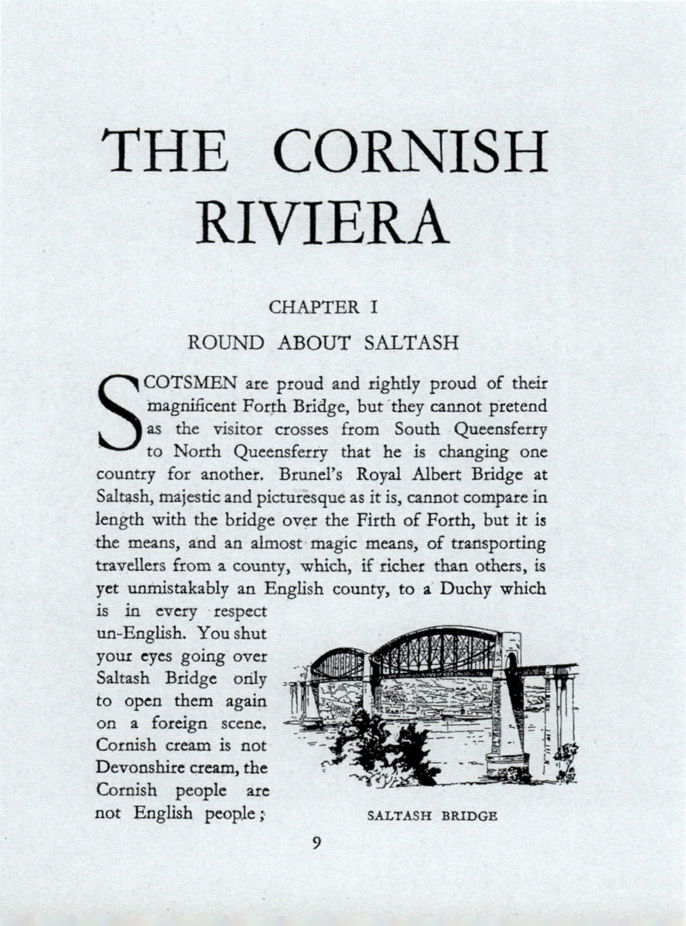
THE CORNISH RIVIERA

CHAPTER I

ROUND ABOUT SALTASH

SCOTSMEN are proud and rightly proud of their magnificent Forth Bridge, but they cannot pretend as the visitor crosses from South Queensferry to North Queensferry that he is changing one country for another. Brunel's Royal Albert Bridge at Saltash, majestic and picturesque as it is, cannot compare in length with the bridge over the Firth of Forth, but it is the means, and an almost magic means, of transporting travellers from a county, which, if richer than others, is yet unmistakably an English county, to a Duchy which is in every respect un-English. You shut your eyes going over Saltash Bridge only to open them again on a foreign scene. Cornish cream is not Devonshire cream, the Cornish people are not English people;

SALTASH BRIDGE

9

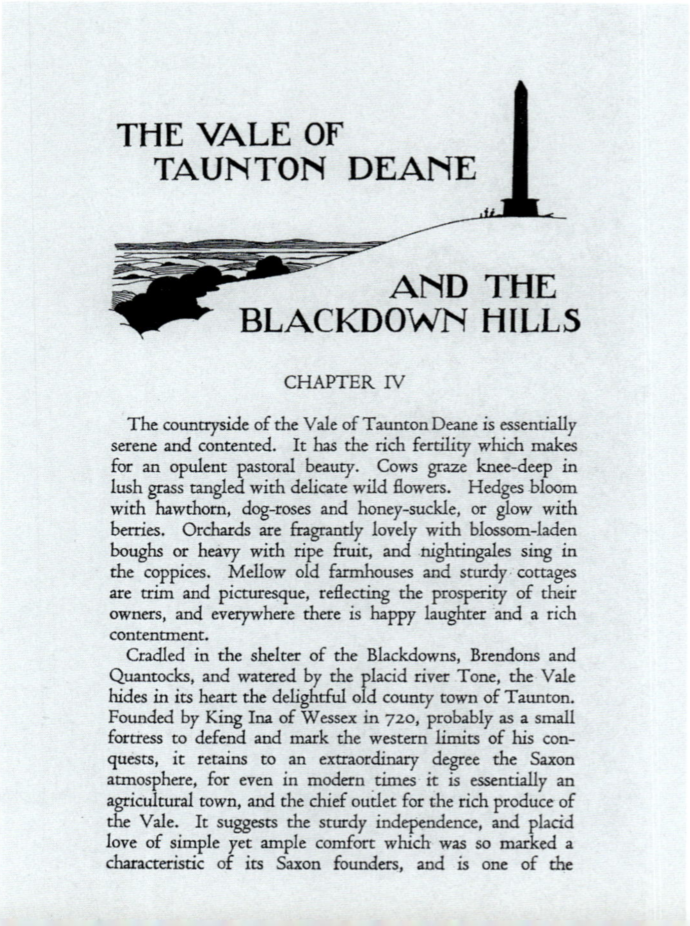
THE VALE OF TAUNTON DEANE AND THE BLACKDOWN HILLS

CHAPTER IV

The countryside of the Vale of Taunton Deane is essentially serene and contented. It has the rich fertility which makes for an opulent pastoral beauty. Cows graze knee-deep in lush grass tangled with delicate wild flowers. Hedges bloom with hawthorn, dog-roses and honey-suckle, or glow with berries. Orchards are fragrantly lovely with blossom-laden boughs or heavy with ripe fruit, and nightingales sing in the coppices. Mellow old farmhouses and sturdy cottages are trim and picturesque, reflecting the prosperity of their owners, and everywhere there is happy laughter and a rich contentment.

Cradled in the shelter of the Blackdowns, Brendons and Quantocks, and watered by the placid river Tone, the Vale hides in its heart the delightful old county town of Taunton. Founded by King Ina of Wessex in 720, probably as a small fortress to defend and mark the western limits of his conquests, it retains to an extraordinary degree the Saxon atmosphere, for even in modern times it is essentially an agricultural town, and the chief outlet for the rich produce of the Vale. It suggests the sturdy independence, and placid love of simple yet ample comfort which was so marked a characteristic of its Saxon founders, and is one of the

extensively rewriting it to reflect changing styles and interests and, significantly, reorganised its format. 'Holiday Haunts' had previously listed each county within the company's system in alphabetical order. Fraser introduced a regional format comprising seven sections: 'London and the Southern Counties; The Cornish Riviera; Glorious Devon; Somerset, Dorset and the Channel Islands; North Wales; South Wales and Monmouthshire; the Midland Counties and the Isle of Man.' This had the effect of enhancing the regional identities whilst clearly contextualising them within the overall Great Western system, making the handbook much easier to consult. Within the individual county-based entries there was also an extensive register of accommodation, covering the full range of hotels and boarding houses, together with details on amenities, 'remarks' as to disposition and service and the distance from the nearest station. Advertisements for specific towns, generally, full-page format, were incorporated with the participation of the resorts – Town Clerk, Information Bureau or the GWR's own contact point, as at Teignmouth, for example.

In its comprehensive character the company handbook represented a commercial-cultural document, the latter being established in terms of Maxwell Fraser's literary style and historical-aesthetic perspectives. Tenby, in Pembrokeshire offers a fitting illustration.

> Few seaside towns so large and popular as Tenby have such charm and individuality. Great cliffs stretch out on either hand, their recesses stained with deep purple shadows and their buttresses picked out by golden sunlight. Beyond the Northern cliff a great headland, nebulous in the distance, colours the horizon with a darker shade of blue and defines the meeting of azure sky with sapphire sea. Tenby stands on a headland above two great bays. The vast sweep of the tawny gold North Sands, cradled in the encircling cliffs, stretches with a satin smoothness only broken by a fantastically shaped rock, which becomes an island at high tide. The South Sands stretch for miles along the coast, which is indented with countless caves and bathing coves.[56]

This extract is interesting in that it functioned on various levels. It was, simultaneously, a commercial, cultural, aesthetic and political statement. Tenby is recognised as a 'large and popular' resort, thus fulfilling its commercial role within the GWR's context of 'care-free democracies', but the aesthetic structuring of landscape incorporates a more complex and, within the inclusive agenda of 'Holiday Haunts', a paradoxically differentiated yet graduated cultural representation. The various 'levels' in appreciation are apparent in the structure and imagery of the passage and, as such, represent the concept of progressive revelation as understood in citizenship and identification of landscape in relation to personal and national-cultural identity. Conceived in broad terms as an educative context, as discussed, above, the political dimension is apparent. As an aesthetic statement, the passage reflects the company's concern for literary credentials. Fraser offered the experience of colour and the perspectives of proximity, distance and of lateral and vertical perceptions. Shapes, structure and forms, textures and tones convey shifting definitions within the range of light and shadow which, collectively, present the scene as one of studied, structured, landscape of harmony and order. In the conventions of the picturesque, Fraser, here, guides the observer in constructing and appreciating the experience.

Maxwell Fraser gave insight into GWR practice by way of an article published in the company magazine in March 1930 entitled, 'The Production of Holiday Haunts'.[50] It included the following statement concerning the company's policy on the composition and style of photographic material and emphasises that, within the overall context of increasing modernity and challenging perspectives, which also included the literature, the GWR was by no means as progressive or experimental as the

Illustrative introductions to the distinct sections comprising Holiday Haunts through the 1930s. Author's collection

Two sharply contrasting images indicative of the thematic and stylistic range of the GWR. The cover for the company's 1932 publication, 'The Best Location'. This book celebrated the GWR's commitment to industrial growth, emphasising the progressive modern character of its services, attuned to contemporary demand. With its particular appeal to North American interests, this was a far more exuberant presentation than, for example, the earlier work, 'Commerce and the Great Western Railway' 1924. Courtesy G Baker

From Caveman to Roman in Britain. A dramatic spectacle in vivid form. The front cover for the company's survey of the wealth of archaeological and very early historical sites to be found within its territory. The book, by Edward Burrows, FRGS, included a map and full details of the nearest town and railway station for all the numerous (and often obscure) locations listed. Author's collection.

Holiday Haunts 1929. This was the first cover in colour, the bathing belle being indicative of a gradual, if inevitable need to reflect a much less formal approach in overall presentation and style. Thereafter, under the direction of Maxwell Fraser, the handbook assumed a more open, 'popular' ethos, evident in all aspects of its production. Courtesy G Baker

Holiday Haunts 1937. The cover for this Coronation edition incorporated the dual imagery of patriotism and joy of the seaside – two definite national themes. Author's collection.

SOUTH WALES
AND MONMOUTHSHIRE
INCLUDING
RADNORSHIRE · CARDIGANSHIRE
PEMBROKESHIRE·BRECKNOCKSHIRE
GLAMORGANSHIRE·CARMARTHENSHIRE

NORTH WALES
INCLUDING
CAERNARVONSHIRE·DENBIGHSHIRE
FLINTSHIRE · MERIONETHSHIRE
MONTGOMERYSHIRE

Illustrative introductions to the distinct sections that comprised Holiday Haunts through the 1930s. 'Holiday Haunts' 1935. Author's collection.

Tenby, as promoted jointly by the GWR and the local community, was the resort 'For Sunshine and Unrivalled Golden Sands'. It was this representation as 'the family resort ... historical and beautiful' that predominated in the immediate post-war period, as evident in the final 1947 edition of 'Holiday Haunts' under the GWR. The poster is typical in character and style of that time. Courtesy, Dalkeith Publishing Co.

Facing page: *Front cover of 'Winter Resorts' 1935* Author's collection

Southern Railway, or the London and North Eastern company in their openly democratic perspectives. (See Chapter Seven).

> The chief view observed in obtaining new photographs is that each view must indicate the character of the scenery of the individual 'Holiday Haunt', and be free from the allurement of holiday seasons. If some resorts are peopled with gay bathing parties in the height of summer the picture leaves this to the imagination, or to a mention in the text – a wise rule when many of the glorious summer holiday haunts served by the GWR are scarcely less famous as winter resorts.[51]

This distinction between the Winter and Summer seasons was an important marketing feature in both the GWR literature and that of the Southern Railway. The GWR slogan, 'Winter in the West' from Maxwell Fraser's 'Winter Resorts', 1935,[52] was a marketing strategy formulated around the ideas of exclusive location, health-giving, restorative climate and the sensation of difference, as indicated earlier in the concept of 'departure', whilst, in respect of service and amenities, there was the reassurance of familiarity. 'Winter Resorts' stressed that passports and customs inconveniences were removed; that there were no barriers to understanding and communication from foreign languages; that English meals were readily available – "It is notorious that English people are so set in their "mad" ways that, instead of adapting themselves to foreign ideas, they frequently demand all the amenities of home life wherever they happen to be" ... [and that] "with the supreme attraction of equability of climate ... English resorts can anticipate the needs of English people far more readily and successfully than any Continental resort can do."[53] The 'Winter' representation was clearly intended to underline the GWR's exclusive, hierarchical credentials in terms of protocol and expectation, as Fraser's reference to Winter and Summer protocols and imagery reflects.

Looking further to comparisons in stylistic, thematic focus between the company's photographic policy and its literary work, the latter can be seen to be largely consistent with that of the studied landscape photography; of the distanced spectator relating to an historical or aesthetic spectacle or encounter wherein the only figures to be seen are usually thematic stereotypes, as in much of the poster work – fishermen, farmworkers, boatmen – defined by their work and, therefore, differentiated culturally. Maxwell Fraser's depiction of Newton Ferrers and Noss Mayo, in South Devon[54] provides a good example of this, as comparable thematically with the company's photograph of the same location in 'Glorious Devon'[55]

Maxwell Fraser also wrote 'Southern Ireland', 1932, which was a replacement for A.M. Broadley's earlier work, 'Southern Ireland, Its Lakes and Landscapes', 1904. In its style and thematic focus Fraser's book was much more accessible generally than that from Broadley. Contemporaneous and closely comparable with H.V. Morton's, 'In Search Of Ireland', 1930, [57] Fraser's work acknowledged the changed political and cultural circumstances in Anglo-Irish relations through explicit statement and the nuances of theme and style. "Since the creation of the Irish Free State, Southern Ireland has been invested with the irresistible charm of a foreign country".[58]

WINTER RESORTS
GWR
PICKING

Morton also emphasised that visitors should experience Ireland as a foreign country. Co-operation between Ireland's and Britain's railways, in the formation of the 'Travel Association of the Railways of Great Britain and Ireland', 1929, [59] encouraged working links between the two states, a practice which the GWR had developed with the Great Southern and Western of Ireland Railway three decades earlier.

Fraser also prepared the joint Great Western Railway and Southern Railway publication, 'England And Why' [60] for the Travel Association. Dating from the 1930 season onward it was directed at the North American tourist market, at a time when Britain, in common with the United States, was undergoing extreme economic hardship. A 'Come To Britain' promotion had been launched in 1927 and, perhaps identifying a patriotic duty, in the early thirties, the GWR promoted 'Holidays at Home' and the 'Buy British Holidays', 1931 [61] for example. In an expression of active citizenship it was asserted:

> It is a reproach that so many English people travel abroad without having first visited any of the English beauty spots ... every English man and woman should realise the glory of our land.[62]

The focus of 'England And Why', indeed, all the North-American orientated literature, was that of England and Wales as a treasure-house of historical, cultural and aesthetic experience. Visitors' interest was directed to representations of historic development, of authority, continuity and architectural and aesthetic excellence. These were combined thematically and in literary terms in three prestige commissions from the mid-twenties: the trilogy, 'Cathedrals', 'Abbeys' and 'Castles'.[63] These books exemplified the company's historical, political and cultural affiliations, whilst also proving extremely successful commercially. 'Cathedrals', published in 1924, in hardback and soft cover editions was written by G.E. Beer, in close consultation with the individual Sees themselves and carried a letter, by way of a Foreword, from the Archbishop of Canterbury at Lambeth Palace to Viscount Churchill, Chairman of the GWR 'Abbeys', published in 1925, was written by Dr. M.R. James, Provost of Eton College, whilst 'Castles', dating from 1926, was the work of Sir Charles Oman Chichele, Professor of Modern History and M.P. for Oxford University.

Another dimension of the GWR's participation in, and appreciation of, landscape and tradition came in the form of the 'Rambles'[64] series written by Hugh E. Page. As Secretary of the North Finchley Rambling Club, Page undertook all the routes covered in his series and, within this genre, did for the GWR what S.P.B. Mais offered for the Southern Railway's hikers. All four railway companies produced this literature, including London Transport, Underground and Omnibus services. The GWR titles comprised: 'Rambles in the Chiltern Country, 1931, ... in Shakespeare Land and the Cotswolds, 1933, ... in South Devon, 1933, Rambles and Walking Tours in Somerset, 1935, Rambles Around the Cambrian Coast, 1936, Rambles in the Wye Valley', 1938 and 'Walks around St. Ives, Cornwall', 1946. A re-worked version for South Devon also appeared in 1938. Contemporaneous with the Youth Hostels Association 1930 and the Ramblers Association of 1935, the GWR (see also Chapter Eight for the Southern Railway's contribution) was well in line with contemporary perspectives on the value of outdoor pursuits. The 'Rambles' series reflected the pronounced character of citizenship and community by specific and detailed directions as to protocol, both practical and aesthetic.[65]

The GWR Magazine, initiated in 1888 and running through to nationalisation in 1948, expressed the comprehensive, collective imagery of the company in a family-orientated focus and format. All dimensions of company business were included – commercial, industrial, social, historical and recreational interests were reported together with issues ranging from administrative items to developments in individual or group welfare projects. In the 1934 edition, for example, the October entries[66] included a detailed essay on archaeological excavations at Maiden Castle, Dorchester, followed by an article on welding technology and the maintenance of the permanent way which, in turn, preceded a survey on the Henrican castles of Pendennis and St. Mawes on Cornwall's south coast. Likewise, the 1938 editions[67] included essays on the origins of historic place-names, details of new ventilated freight wagons for the transit of fruit and vegetables, a report on new industries in South Wales, notes on the hotel gardens at the company's hotels and correspondence on its convalescent homes.

As part of the standardised format – official statements of revenue and train-working and reports from each department (annually), the 'interest' articles, the careers structure and staff changes and the broader category of staff welfare and enterprise – the magazine also incorporated full-plate photographs of company projects, of staff-orientated interests and, significantly, large plates of rural landscapes entitled 'Through Great Western Countryside', one for each monthly edition. Within this collective format the rural theme was thus emphasised. Structurally, and thematically, the GWR Magazine exemplified the company's rural-urban, past-present representation, reconciling continuity with progress.

The impact of the GWR literature might well be seen in terms of the popularity of the work, as reflected in sales returns and public reception generally. Broadley's early works, pre-World War One, were exceptionally popular and were the best selling editions of the company's overall list. 'The Cornish Riviera', and 'Devon. The Shire of the Sea Kings', each completed six editions between 1904 and 1926. The 1904 editions of 'The Cornish Riviera' exhausted its print run of 250,000 within the year. By June 1914 the book had run to four editions – 1904, 1905, 1908, 1914. Recording this success, the Preface to the 1914 editions observed:

> Nearly ten years have passed away since the publication of 'The Cornish Riviera Express.' ... The second and third editions enjoyed the same popularity and are now entirely exhausted.[68]

The new editions of 'The Cornish Riviera' and 'Glorious Devon' both by S.P.B. Mais sold their complete print run of 20,000 editions each, from publication in August 1928 to January 1929. With regard to 'Holiday Haunts', 1927 was the first year that the book exceeded 1000 pages when the GWR offered 1018 pages. The following year, 1928, saw the first edition of 200,000 copies, a significant increase on the first post-war edition in 1921, numbering 40,000 copies. This 1921 edition, however, was extremely popular with the initial 20,000 copies being sold in one month, thus requiring a repeated print run of a further 20,000. From 1928 to 1931 production was maintained at approximately the 200,000 figure but fell thereafter as victim to the Depression and to outside competition, 1938 marking the best performance, latterly, with 172,000 copies at 976 pages. The 1934 edition was the largest, at 1054 pages.[69]

As indicated, sales returns over the range of publications indicate the commercial success of the literature, but it is much more difficult to say how this translated into effective communicating. The GWR literature engaged various commercial and cultural perspectives that are difficult to isolate and convert into detailed quantifiable impact. Commercially, tourism and particular kinds of freight traffic were profitable as returns (see Chapter Five) indicate. But it is not possible to gauge, accurately, how much impact the company's projection of particular imagery of rural-historical England or that of the Celtic Sublime had on readers.

The GWR certainly acted as though all dimensions of publicity mattered a great deal, particularly during the inter-war period, with the enhanced level of competition from road traffic being apparent. Wherever possible, it co-operated with individual

Home Resorts First !

You can enjoy a charming and delightful Holiday in

SOUTH WALES

Its Mountains and Vales, its Castles and Rivers are unsurpassed anywhere.

Health-giving Air, and pleasure-giving Scenery. Nothing to equal the fine climatic conditions.

WHY GO ABROAD !

What a wonderful choice !

SWANSEA, TENBY, BARRY, SAUNDERSFOOT, MUMBLES, GOWER COAST, PEMBROKE and NEYLAND.

Excellent accommodation and abundant sports facilities everywhere.

Atlantic Breezes blow across the lands
And all the shores are laid with Golden Sands.

Write for Information

FOR SWANSEA, MUMBLES AND GOWER COAST, TO PUBLICITY OFFICE, 4, MOUNT STREET, SWANSEA ;
BARRY, TENBY, PEMBROKE AND NEYLAND, TO TOWN CLERKS' OFFICES ;
SAUNDERSFOOT, TO MR. E. H. THOMAS, SECRETARY, IMPROVEMENTS COMMITTEE, " KENMORE," SAUNDERSFOOT ;
or
SECRETARY SOUTH WALES COAST RESORTS ASSOCIATION, W. TALOG WILLIAMS, 24, GOAT STREET, SWANSEA.

FAST TRAIN SERVICES FROM ALL PARTS.

Appeal for the Home Resorts: in this case, promoting the attractions of South Wales in the pages of 'Holiday Haunts' 1934. Author's collection

resorts, local authorities and district and county representations, as in the 'Come To Cornwall' initiative. Felix Pole personally visited local chambers of commerce with both warm words and bad tidings as the company saw fit. Newquay, for example, declared that the GWR has "taught them the meaning of advertising."[70] Substantial investment in the various resorts was acknowledged by all concerned and, in terms of marketing initiatives, the company involved itself directly in issues of public health – water supply, drainage, sewerage projects – town and street planning, hotel and boarding house amenities. Detailed accounts of such work were presented in the local newspapers, to the satisfaction of both railway and resort. Richards was unequivocal on the particular contribution of the railway companies in this process:

> I believe the railways of this country have, generally speaking, done more for many resorts than those resorts have done for themselves and undoubtedly from a railway point of view it is a very difficult subject.[71]

Presentations of increasing tourist traffic during the mid-thirties, reflected in the campaigns for earlier and later, off-season holidays, indicated the need for closely structured holiday planning. 'Holiday Haunts' in 1939 carried the article: 'Popularising Earlier Holidays'. Considering the context and impact of the legislation and quoting Ministry of Labour figures on holidays with pay, it observed:

> ... that of the 18,500,000 people employed in Great Britain, 7,750,000 will this year get paid holidays – an increase of a million over 1938, and of more than two-and-a-half millions over 1937 ... The question is not one that concerns the railway companies alone. It affects all forms of transport holiday resorts, the hotel and catering industry, the entertainment profession, and, in fact every industry or person providing for the requirements of holiday makers, right down to the beach-chair attendant and the donkey man.[72]

Good relations with the resorts were vital. As General Manager, Felix Pole was unequivocal. Under his terms of reference, the local chambers of commerce presented ideal opportunities for 'propaganda' as he defined the concept.

> I regard propaganda as the means of promoting good feeling towards the company; of making its good points known by more subtle means than that by advertising or general publicity.[73]

Citing the range of these 'subtle means' – the historically focused literature, jigsaws, newspaper articles etc – Pole continued:

> Another most valuable piece of propaganda was provided by meeting Chambers of Commerce, Chambers of Trade, Business Clubs etc ... Chambers were glad to meet the man whose name appeared at the bottom of the posters etc.[74]

This latter statement is indicative of the commercial orientation of railway and resort, and this theme is pursued here by direct reference to Cornwall, indicating the determinedly contemporary focus of GWR interests in tourism at Newquay and Penzance and the extent to which the local communities co-operated.

The general statement of progress at resorts across the company network carried in the GWR Magazine, July 1935, for example, put the emphasis upon modern attractions, marking an up–beat, popular approach.

> Reports from the resorts both large and small, show how extensive and varied are the improvements this year. There are to be more swimming pools, bandstands, sports grounds, parks, illuminations, places of amusement, dance halls, cinemas, tennis courts, bowling greens and golf courses; and the purchase by local councils of beauty spots and open spaces will ensure these being preserved for the benefit of holiday makers.[75]

It was significant that these were active amenities, clearly dedicated to large-scale popular participation and were thus distinguished from the exclusive, initiate perspectives that so often defined the rural, historical presentation. Good relations with the relevant local interests were vital here.

GWR involvement with local chambers of commerce reflected the direct influence of Paddington within the local community and, in particular, the focus and degree of company interest in determining and implementing the particular agenda. Using material from Cornish case studies it is clear that, whilst the GWR pursued a consistent policy in terms of management, focus and commercial objective, the resorts, as exemplified here by Newquay and Penzance, observed no common policy and commitment with regard to tourism. In contrast with the sharp focus and consistency characterising the GWR.'s corporate identity, Newquay and Penzance, both significant holiday termini of the GWR reflected contrasting, and in the case of Penzance, ambivalent responses in matters of marketing and commercial investment. Newquay was the more noticeably innovative resort and was, accordingly, more attuned to GWR aspirations and objectives. A study of the proceedings at the annual meetings of the respective chambers of commerce suggests that at Penzance, in particular, the Great Western looked for a considerably stronger commitment to tourism.

A comparison between the two resorts and of the consequent attitude of the GWR was offered in the reports of the Annual Meetings of the chambers of commerce at Penzance and at Newquay in 1928. The former was held in the January, the latter in mid–March. At Newquay it was revealed that, for the 1928 season, 'The Newquay Advertising Committee', formed in 1926, intended to raise from £800 to £1,000 with the GWR contributing an equivalent sum. Advertisements were to be placed in leading Northern, Midland and London based newspapers whilst the resort distributed (1927) 5,000 copies of the 'Homeland Association' handbook, with the aim of doubling this amount in 1928. Furthermore, in a co–production with the GWR the resort commissioned 2,000 "Newquay" posters and produced 20,000 leaflets.[76]

At Penzance there was a somewhat different story. Addressing the Chamber, F.R. Davis, Secretary of the GWR offered the following unequivocal statement:

> In 1927, when we launched out on a bigger advertising campaign on the West of England than we have ever done before, we ploughed a lonely furrow, I am told, and had no help from the Penzance Chamber of Commerce. That is regrettable.[77]

It was further stated that, unlike many other resorts and localities on the GWR system, Penzance had not shown any record of seasonal progress and development.

As the guest of Truro, Newquay and Redruth chambers of commerce in March 1929, the GWR General Manager, Sir Felix Pole, demonstrated an evident sense of frustration and impatience with various crucial aspects of the tourist business in Cornwall. He was critical of the obvious competition that characterised the conduct and structure of tourism. Highlighting important continental practice, he called for similar co–operative development within the county and, whilst welcoming the Come to Cornwall Association,[78] formed that year, he nevertheless lamented that it was "twenty years too late."[79] Pole was also heavily critical of the range and standard of accommodation offered within the county. As part of his general message he declared:

Facing page: *Cover for Hugh E Page's 'Rambles in Shakespeare Land and the Cotswolds' 1933. This particular area would have great cultural and aesthetic resonance for North American visitors as well as the obvious associations for homeland audiences.* Author's collection

RAMBLES IN
SHAKESPEARE LAND
AND THE COTSWOLDS
BY HUGH·E·PAGE
6D

I am aware that many Cornish boarding houses are being enlarged and improved, but it is a pity that many could not be blown up and entirely rebuilt.[80]

Pole further stressed the need of more organised, all-weather amenities and felt that generally the county relied too heavily upon its natural resources, extensive though they were. Newquay's hotels and their promotion were, however, generally the subject of GWR approval.

Advertising and local enterprise was the consistent message from the Great Western to the Cornish resorts. This was abundantly evident in the proceedings at Newquay and Penzance. The meeting of the Chamber of Commerce at Penzance in late January, 1938, where F.R. Potter, Superintendent of the GWR and Major Dewar of the Publicity Office were included amongst the distinguished guests, carried specific reference to the subject of publicity. Reporting the meeting, the local newspaper, 'The Cornishman', wrote of the GWR representatives:

They impressed most forcibly, yet in a quiet business-like manner the necessity of Penzance embarking upon an enterprising policy in regard to tourist traffic.[81]

The Superintendent reminded the Chamber that the Great Western had invested £134,000 in connection with the new terminus then under construction and added; "it was for Penzance to respond."[82] Potter went on to make a direct appeal to the local authority and to the chamber of commerce in particular, with directed designations, as in "we" and "you".

With all the potentialities of this district don't you think you might as a Chamber of Commerce arrange it and go for a little more publicity. We are only too anxious to help you and make this extreme part of Cornwall the most popular place in the country ... Over and above all I want to try to instill in your minds, the ideal of development, progress and, in so far as the GWR is able to assist, we are only too happy to do what we can.[83]

The evident repetition of willingness on the part of the GWR to give assistance and advice was, not least, borne out of the impatience felt by the company as to the lack of local initiative, given the potential in West Cornwall. The diplomatic representations here scarcely concealed the thrust of company-directed policy – the Superintendent's message being a clear reference to expectations at Paddington – to the requirement that the resorts fulfil the 'Ocean Coast' identity. At successive annual meetings the GWR's various representations had invited the chambers of commerce to consider comparative developments elsewhere, casting less than favourable light upon much of Cornwall's collective record. Bournemouth and Torquay, although obviously much larger than any Cornish resort, were held up as exemplars of modern, dynamic enterprise and it was pointed out, in 1934, that Bexhill-on-Sea, comparable in size to Penzance – but by that time far more affluent and accessible – was spending £100,000 on improvements.[84] Paddington's priorities were made clear. Major Dewar for the company's publicity department, drew attention to the Great Western's extensive campaign, then underway, to lengthen the holiday season by encouraging earlier holidays in May, June and early July, and in September, to avoid the congestion and difficulties imposed by the traditional recourse to late July and August. The introduction of the Holiday With Pay Act, 1938,[85] added to the call for a more manageable season and for the greater provision of popular entertainment by the resorts themselves. This last point featured heavily in the Superintendent's speech to the Chamber. Combining themes of entertainment and accommodation, he asserted the Great Western's perspective with the definitive 'we' and 'our' – the metropolitan standard of reference and expectation that clearly identified and differentiated centre and periphery.

There is no place I know of in the country which is more amenable to a winter resort than Penzance, but what you lack at the moment is entertainment to attract our visitors. We want to see that your hotels and accommodation are adequate for our visitors.[86]

There were clear echoes here of Felix Pole's earlier criticisms of accommodation and the vital infrastructure of public health – water supply and sanitation to a better than adequate standard.

Messrs. Potter and Dewar were also the guests of the Newquay Chamber of Commerce at the annual meeting at the Headland Hotel in mid February, 1938. They were joined by S.P.B. Mais, known in Cornwall and across the GWR system for his literary work on behalf of the company. He provided the thematic focus and thrust for the meeting in his emphasis upon the celebration of Cornwall's unique identity and, implication, its significant commercial potential. Set in creative contrast with England and Englishness, Cornwall exemplified the experience of 'difference at your doorstep' – a characterisation which the Great Western had pursued in its literature and in its poster-work since 1904. The normative character and style of Mais' address to the local community was indicative of the GWR's corporate, centralist perspective, little short of a directive.

There is an intense desire on the part of the public to do something quite different – You must trade on this business of your being half foreign to England. Let this strangeness once you are on the Western side of the Tamar have its place. It is this very strangeness that you want at the present moment to cater for and allow the English mind to prey upon, not only the coast but the inland part of Cornwall which is so worthwhile exploiting.[87]

In acknowledging the guiding influence and, therein, the dominant role of the Great Western Railway in the development of Newquay, the local Chamber also recorded that the GWR had "taught them the value of advertising."[88] Without doubt, Newquay became the Great Western's most important resort in Cornwall and, as the evidence from the chambers of commerce reveal, of all the Cornish resorts, it was most closely attuned to the Great Western's cultural and commercial concept of the 'Ocean Coast'. The Annual Dinner of Newquay Chamber of Commerce, February 1934, confirmed this with the statement from G.E. Orton. Superintendent GWR, declaring "Newquay has proved itself the most progressive resort in Cornwall."[89] With a new guide book, 'Newquay on the Cornish Coast', and a promotional film, 'Newquay', the Superintendent proposed the toast: "Greater Newquay."[90] Newquay was the GWR's only Cornish resort to commit itself totally to a tourist-based economy (as was the case with Bude, for the Southern Railway) and, therein, reflected the essential thrust of the GWR's assessment on the county that the prosperity of the resorts was the effective prosperity progress of Cornwall generally. This was a fundamental expression of the dominance of the metropolitan centre and its influence in terms of shaping and structuring commercial and cultural identity. With their tourist economies and distinctive 'Ocean Coast' and 'Atlantic Coast' identities, Newquay and Bude were the two districts county-wide to both return the lowest unemployment rates. County returns for 1934[91] revealed: Newquay 10.7 and Bude 8.6 per cent, together with the highest percentage increases in population: Newquay, 8.2 and Bude, 9.2 per cent.[92] Returns for 1948 suggest this trend was sustained.[93] By contrast, the traditional mining communities, as in the Gunnislake and Redruth districts, for example, reflected unemployment levels in 1934 of 64.6 and 40.2 per cent respectively[94] It was also significant that resistance or reluctance to embrace a more committed tourist identity and economy at Penzance was based on the view that the town had wider terms of reference, commercially. It was a busy port, a thriving market town, a centre for horticulture and had large-scale interests in the fishing industry. Falmouth, with its docks, and Looe, with its fishing and agriculture interests, provided further examples of alternative and frequently rival economies locally.

The GWR's involvement with the chambers of commerce revealed not only the detailed differences of emphasis that often existed between the company and the local authorities, it further highlighted the basic distinction between the company's policy of presenting Cornwall as an overall experience – a unified, collective identity – and that of the individual resorts that, largely, looked to their own particular circumstances and perceived interests as indicated above. It is in this context that we note Pole's repeated emphasis on the need for co–operative effort. His focus – primarily commercial and administrative – was, nevertheless, directly reflected in the literary presentation. Ultimately, and always in the context of rendering it as a special place with a unique identity, the Great Western literature of the thirties presented Cornwall as an open book, the sense of its being all things to all people. 'Ocean Coast' and ancient Celtic perspectives were uppermost, but Mais in the Preface to 'The Cornish Riviera' also emphasised what he considered was "Cornwall's diversity of riches". Thus we read:

> The motto of the Duchy is "One and All", and it may be interpreted in this way, that the visitor who opens his eyes to the wooded loveliness of the Fowey Valley and closes them to the deserted broken down chimneys of old tin mines and the mountainous white pyramids of china clay refuse that litter the hillsides, has no chance whatever of getting to know real Cornwall. It is one and indivisible. You may go to the Duchy with the idea of playing gold and end by exploring tin mines. You may go there with the idea that you are in for a normal English holiday and find yourself in an atmosphere of warlocks and pixies, miracle-working saints and woe-making witches – You may go there only intent on tennis and find yourself at the end of a fortnight a devotee of holy wells and Celtic crosses. It is well to go to Cornwall with an open mind.[95]

This was, effectively, the collective characterisation of Cornwall; the Great Western Railway's carefully constructed and, likewise, carefully regulated Cornish cultural identity. A close GWR identification with the West of England generally, reached back well into the nineteenth century. Its presence effectively bridged the 'great divide' of 1914 and World War One whilst the railway grouping in 1923 had minimal disruptive impact on the GWR generally. This endowed it with a considerable sense of historic continuity and identification with its communities that was not so apparent with the other companies, who lacked such an established, coherent identity. This was evident in the structure, style and focus of the company's commissioned history: 'The History of the Great Western Railway.' Vol I 1927; Vol II, 1931, by E.T. Macdermot.[96] Inspired by Felix Pole to emphasise the GWR's historical credentials and its progressive development since 1935, MacDermot's work clearly celebrated the company's special distinction of retaining its historic structure and identity and, indeed, enhancing it by the Railways Act of 1921. This gave the GWR's commissioned history an added resonance in terms of this genre, the obligatory company history being an essential element in the overall representation of railway companies, large and small.

Left: *An illustrative introduction to one of the seven distinct sections that comprised Holiday Haunts through the 1930s. 'Holiday Haunts' 1935.* Author's collection.

Overleaf: *Wookey Hole Caves. The 1934 brochure for Wookey Hole Caves, Somerset. This included details of nearby Cheddar and of the modern facilities – restaurants, swimming pool, floodlighting – that complimented both this awesome limestone landscape and the rich, rural countryside beyond.* Cornish Studies Library

'Winter In The West' 1929 edition. The GWR made much of the West of England as a worthy alternative to the Mediterranean for winter holidays or residence. The homeland was acclaimed in terms of its competitive climate, its proximity and familiarity, and, not least, the financial and procedural advantages. Cornish Studies Library

Newquay. The frontispiece for 'Holiday Haunts' 1939. Newquay was, and remains, Cornwall's premier seaside resort and also featured as frontispiece for the earlier 1936 handbook, a clear indication of its significance. Surfing and the beach was the theme in both representations. Author's collection

WOOKEY HOLE CAVES
GWR

WINTER
IN THE WEST
S.P.B. MAIS

NEWQUAY, CORNWALL.

BRITAIN'S FINEST SURF RIDING RESORT.

For beautifully illustrated Guide Book, apply G. TAYLOR, Council Offices, Newquay, Cornwall.

REFERENCES – CHAPTER ONE

1: L.T.C. Rolt. Isambard Kingdom Brunel. Longmans Green, London 1957. Pelican Books London. 1970 P249.

2: E.T. MacDermot. Revised C.R. Clinker. History of the Great Western Railway Vol. 2 GWR 1927. (3 Volumes Ian Allan London 1964) P208. See also John Norris, Gerry Beale, John Lewis. Edwardian Enterprise GWR Wild Swan Publications Didcot, 1987.

3: A.M. Broadley. The Cornish Riviera GWR 1904.

4: R.M. Broadley Historic Sites and Scenes of England. GWR 1904

5: John Norris. Gerry Beale. John Lewis. Edwardian Enterprise GWR Wild Swan Publications Ltd. 1987.

6: Public Record Office Rail. 267:370 Minutes of Meeting. Lord Churchill GWR and Sir Charles Scotter LSWR 21 Oct. 1909.

7: Roger Burdett-Wilson. Go Great Western. A History of GWR Publicity. David and Charles, Newton Abbot, 1970. See particularly Chapters Four and Six. Also Stephen Constantine. Bringing the Empire Alive, in Imperialism And Popular Culture, ed. John M. Mackenzie. Manchester University Press. Manchester. 1986. Constantine's work on the promotory strategies of the Empire Marketing Board correlates with GWR experience and practice.

8: W.G. Chapman Cheltenham Flyer. GWR 1934 P8.

9: GWR Through The Window. Paddington to Penzance 1924; 'To Birkenhead, 1925; 'To Killarney, 1926.

10: Through The Window. Paddington To Killarney. See particularly P7.

11: Through The Window. Paddington to Penzance. P7.

12: A.C. Lock. Railway Advertising. Is it on the right lines? GWR (London) Lecture and Debating Society, GWR No. 227, January 1929 P3.

13: A.M. Broadley. The Cornish Riviera. GWR 1904

14: A.M. Broadley. Devon. The Shire Of The Sea Kings. GWR 1904

15: Beverley Cole and Richard Durack. Railway Posters, 1923-1947. National Railway Museum. York, 1992.

16: G.E. Orton. Railway Publicity. Great Western Railway (London) Lecture and Debating Society Session 1934-35 No. 284 18 October 1934. P11

17: Ibid Title Page

18: GWR Magazine, September 1934. Pp 417-419

19: Ibid P2

20: Ibid P2

21: Ibid P3

22: Ibid P5

23: Ibid P11

24: GWR Magazine, September 1934. P419. See also Roger Burdett Wilson, Go Great Western. P32

25: D. Richards. 'Advertising - with Special Reference to Railway Publicity. Great Western Railway (London) Lecture and Debating Society. GWR No. 179, February 1925.

26: Ibid P6. Richards developed this theme for railways, generally, contending that they did not "tell the public either lucidly or fully enough about the services they have to offer. The public often is in entire ignorance of many things a railway can do." P4.

27: Ibid P16

28: Ibid P16

29: GWR Magazine. Official Staff Changes. September 1934. P417

30: D. Richards. Advertising.... Railway Publicity, P16

31: Ibid P16

32: C.S. Lock and A.C. Pickford. 'Railway Advertising. Is it on the right lines?" Great Western Railway (London) Lecture and Debating Society. GWR No. 227. January 1929.

33: Ibid P3

34: Ibid P3

35: Ibid P5. The Travel Association estimated the total number of visitors to Britain in 1938 as 720,429. By comparison, the figures for 1932 were 475,088. The Travel Association 1929-1969, London 1970. P11.

36: GWR Handbook for Travellers from Overseas. The Traveller In England. Where To Go: What To See. January 1926.

37: Ibid P1

38: Ibid P7

39: Ibid P7

40: Ibid P9

41: Ibid P9

42: Ibid P10

43: Ibid P10

44: Ibid P10

45: Ibid P10

46: GWR Sunny Cornwall. England's Mediterranean Region. c 1924

47: See, for example, J.A.R. Pimlott, The Englishman's Holiday: A Social History. Faber and Faber, London. 1947. J.K. Walton, The English Seaside Resort: A Social History. 1750-1914 Leicester University Press. 1983. James Walvin, Beside the Seaside, Allen Lane, 1978. J.K. Walton and J. Walvin (eds), Leisure in Britain, 1780-1939, Manchester University Press, 1983. Stephen V. Ward, Selling Places: The marketing and promotion of towns and cities, 1850-2000, E. and F.N. Spon, Routledge, London 1998. David Matless. Landscape and Englishness. Reaktion Books, London 1998. John Urry. The Tourist Gaze. Leisure and Travel in Contemporary Societies. Sage, London, 1990.

48: S.P.B. Mais. My Finest Holiday - Southern Railway 1927 Walks in North Devon. S.R. 1928 Hike for Health. S.R. c 1930 Southern Rambles for Londoners 1931 Walking at Weekends. S.R. 1936 Lets Get Out Here. S.R. 1937

49: S.P.B. Mais. The Cornish Riviera; Glorious Devon. GWR 1928 Maxwell Fraser. Somerset, GWR 1934

50: Maxwell Fraser, The Production of Holiday Haunts. GWR Magazine, March 1930. P101.

51: Ibid P101

52: Maxwell Fraser. Winter Resorts. GWR 1934 ed

53: Ibid PPs 4-6

54: Holiday Haunts 1934 P338

55: S.P.B. Mais. Glorious Devon, GWR 1928 P78

56: GWR 'Holiday Haunts' 1937 P866

57: Maxwell Fraser Southern Ireland GWR 1932 H.V. Morton. In Search of Ireland, Methuen, London. 1930.

58: Fraser. Southern Ireland. P5.

59: P.R.O. Rail 1080: 583 min 166. This also reveals the detailed differences in style and focus between the four British companies. There was a specific recognition of the difficulties involved in sinking individualities and agreeing points of interest, emphasis and presentation when called upon to work jointly, as in the integrated approach to the American market.

60: Maxwell Fraser. England And Why, Great Western and Southern Railways 1932. ed.

61: GWR Magazine. Buy British Holidays. August. 1931. P342

62: Ibid P342

63: These three publications were distinct amongst the GWR literary works in being thorough academic productions with their own distinctive format and style, although 'Cathedrals', 1924, owed sections of its text to the earlier company production, 'Wonderful Wessex', A.M. Broadley, 1908. This trilogy, considered as prestige publications, carried no company advertisements.

64: See Wilson. Go Great Western, for thematic link with GWR 'Hikers' Specials and Mystery Trains P99

65: See Hugh E. Page. Rambles in Shakespeare Land and the Cotswolds, GWR 1933. P11. Rambles Around The Cambrian Coast, GWR 1936. P8.

66: GWR Magazine October 1934.

67: GWR Magazine May, July, August 1938.

68: Roger Burdett Wilson. Go Great Western. P98

69: Ibid. Chapter Four and Five: Sale Publications; Holiday Haunts.

70: G.E. Orton (GWR) Address: Annual Dinner, Newquay Chamber of Commerce. 'Newquay Express' 17 February 1938 P2.

71: D. Richards. Advertising. Special Ref. Railway Publicity P8.

72: GWR Holiday Haunts 1939 P246.

73: Sir Felix Pole "His Book" Private Circulation 1954. Town And Country Press 1968 P81.

74: Ibid P86.

75: GWR Magazine July 1934 P349.

76: Newquay Advertising Committee/Chamber of Commerce. Report: "The Newquay Express" January 19 1928 P7.

77: F.R. Davis Annual Dinner Chamber of Commerce. Penzance. Report: 'The Cornishman' Monday 12 March 1928 P7.

78: Felix Pole Annual Dinner Chamber of Commerce. Newquay. Report: The Newquay Express 14 March 1929 P7. The 'Come To Cornwall Association' was the county-wide publicity initiative developed by the various town and district authorities to promote tourism. Whilst, as Pole urged, it looked to the larger county reference for tourism, it nevertheless was at best only loosely integrated with each town essentially looking to its own interests. Competition, not the co-operation envisaged by the GWR, was evident in the format and style of this publication. See also GWR Magazine, 1925. P179.

79: Ibid P7.

80: Ibid P7.

81: Annual Dinner Chamber of Commerce Penzance. Report: 'The Cornishman' 26 January 1938 P7.

82: F.R. Potter Annual Dinner C of C January 1938 P7.

83: Ibid P7.

84: Ibid P7.

85: Ibid P7.

86: Ibid P7. See also GWR Magazine 1939 P246.

87: S.P.B. Mais Annual Dinner Chamber of Commerce Newquay. 'The Newquay Express', 17 February 1938 P2.

88: Ibid P2.

89: G.E. Orton Annual Dinner Chamber of Commerce, Newquay. 'The Newquay Express' 22 February 1934 P6.

90: Ibid P6.

91: Cornwall County Council. Planning Office Maps No. 5-10. H.W.J. Heck. County Planning Officer 1949.

92: Ibid C.C.C.

93: Ibid C.C.C.

94: Ibid C.C.C.

95: S.P.B. Mais Cornish Riviera 1934 ed P3.

96: E.T. MacDermot. The History of the Great Western Railway. GWR Vol I, 1927; Vol II, 1931.

SKETCH MAP
OF THE
OCEAN COAST

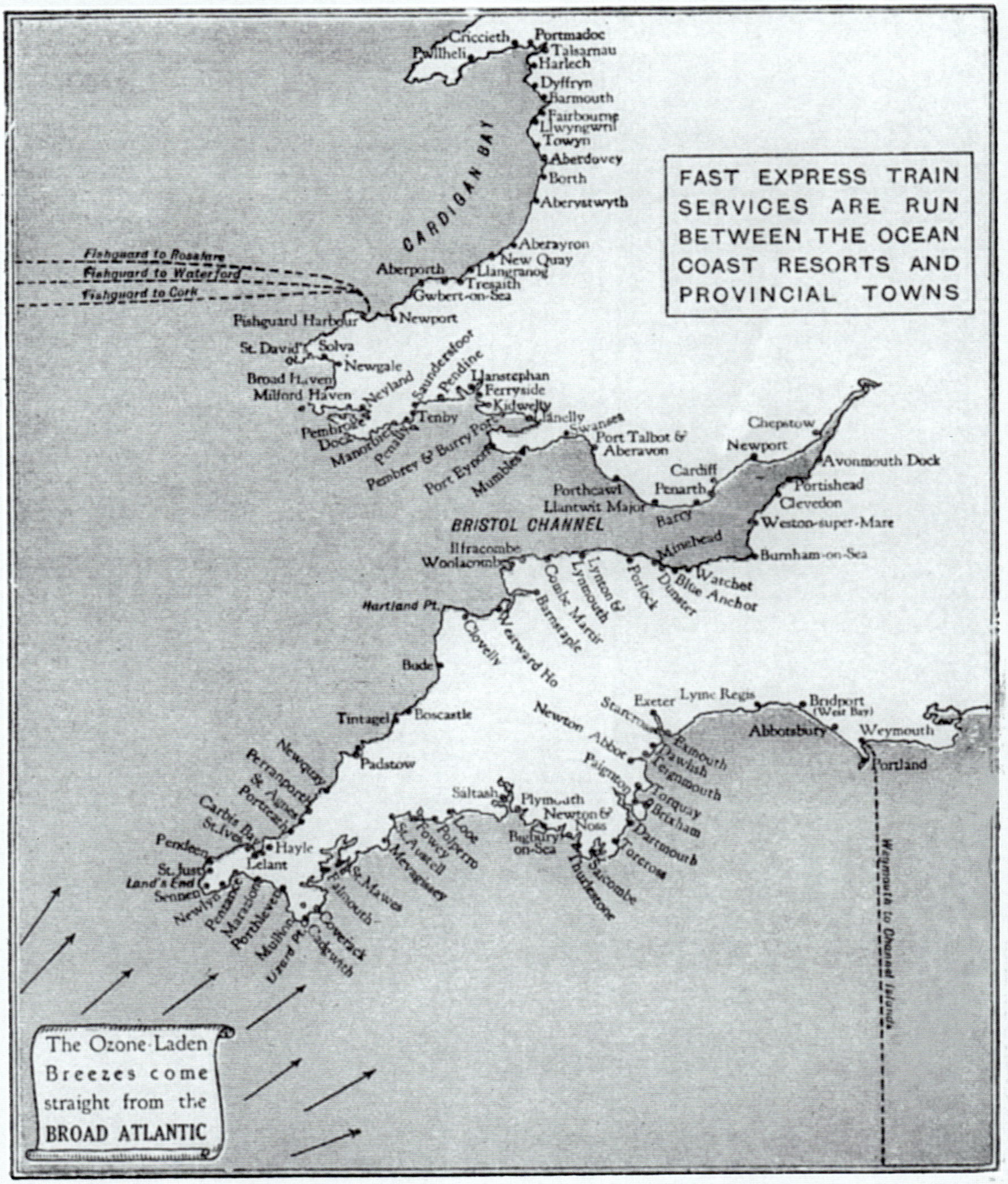

Map of the 'Ocean Coast' from the 1924 GWR publication of the same name. Author's collection

CHAPTER TWO

THE OCEAN COAST

'Ocean Coast' and 'Holiday Line' imagery was a firmly established dimension of G.W.R. identity by the mid-thirties. This was clearly affirmed by the company's choice of theme and location for its celebrated Centenary poster – '100 Years of Progress, 1835-1935' – depicting a west-bound express passenger train running along the shore-line at the variously named Horse or Shell Cove, near Dawlish in South Devon. It was a carefully composed work combining dramatic and contrasting features of land and seascape that characterised the imagery and stylistic focus of the GWR's seaside representation. Numerous 'official' GWR. photographs of this and nearby seaside locations further emphasised the 'Holiday Line' imagery as, indeed, did innumerable other photographers and illustrators at work along this favoured coastal section of the main line to the West. Together with this line between Dawlish Warren and Teignmouth, itself approached from each end by long and dramatic estuary perspectives – the Exe and the Teign – the Great Western also included several additional coastal line sections to further enhance its desired seaside character and associations. These comprised extensive and extremely dramatic sections of the Cambrian Coast, the western end of the Taunton-Minehead line, South Devon's Goodrington Sands and the final approach to the waterside terminus at Kingswear (with its GWR ferry to Dartmouth), Mount's Bay in West Cornwall where, dominated by the spectacle of St. Michael's Mount, the final two miles of the West of England main-line from Paddington to Penzance followed the shoreline to the Great Western's most westerly terminus. Finally, and perhaps most spectacular of all such locations, the branch line from the junction at St. Erth to St. Ives, again in West Cornwall, exemplified the entire spectrum of Ocean Coast perspectives, from the exhilarating, dramatic spectacle of cliffside, ocean and extensively sandy beaches to the seclusion of quiet reaches of the Hayle estuary and the historical and aesthetic experience of St. Ives as that of the traditional Cornish fishing port. In furthering its collective Ocean Coast identity, an illuminated signboard "Ocean Coast" was erected at Paddington, fulfilling the dual purpose of promoting the resorts and brightening the station.

The seaside perspective of the GWR had two basic dimensions: that of the fashionable and exclusively styled watering place, perfectly exemplified by Torquay and, by contrast, the more openly democratic family-based resorts as in Paignton and Porthcawl, where there was a premium upon organised entertainments, amusement parks and promenades in close relationship to the pleasures of the beach – sandcastles, sunshine and sea. This latter category could well be sub-divided to distinguish the larger scale, popularist recreational resorts, Weston-Super-Mare, Barry Island or Weymouth, for example, from the small, more traditional and heritage-influenced locations linking fishing and general seaport activities into a wider tourist-based perspective.

'Care-Free Democracies'

In identifying the popular family resorts, those of the "care-free democracy"[1] as the company put it, Paignton, Porthcawl, Weymouth and Weston-Super Mare were the leading contenders. Whilst focusing upon Paignton and South Devon, it is useful for comparative reference to record Great Western perspectives on these other listed resorts. Weston will be included in the later case study on Somerset.

Weymouth was undoubtedly a family resort. The company brochure of 1934 entitled: 'Bring Your Children to Weymouth, Queen of the Lovely Dorset Coast' was perfectly explicit. "Children love Weymouth. There is no 'stiff and starchiness' to dry up their spirits"[2] 'Holiday Haunts' noted "any new invention for keeping holiday makers happy and amused will speedily find its way to the town."[3]

Porthcawl, variously regarded as "The Gem of the Severn Sea," "The Brighton of Wales," or "The Blackpool of Wales,"[4] devoted itself to tourism and the unrestricted pursuit of diverse recreation. The codified reference in 'Holiday Haunts', 1929 declared of the resort: "It has fashioned its resources to modern ideas,"[5] but in less diffident style, the town brochure of the late thirties, entitled, 'Coney Beach Britain's Coney Island,' offered endless scope for modern amusement. Described as "Bang up to the minute,"[6] the amusement park comprised some thirty or so special attractions ranging from pleasurable interest to thrilling abandon.

'Holiday Haunts' 1939, recorded "Porthcawl's sole industry is catering for visitors and the indoor and outdoor entertainments and amusements so generously provided are now open on Sundays as well as weekdays."[7] 'Holiday Haunts' also noted considerable investment in promenade amenities, the Grand Pavilion, gardens, sports pavilion and children's playground. To supplement the prevailing family imagery of the resort, the GWR also stressed that the sand dunes at Porthcawl were of special interest. Making a familiar reference to European equivalents, 'Holiday Haunts' observed: "the sand dunes pile up at some points to over 200 feet and are only rivalled in the whole of Europe by those of Kurische Nehruna in East Prussia."[8] There were, conspicuously, no Celtic properties of otherness, mystery and the landscape of the sublime attributed to the resort. Porthcawl was also the destination for the GWR's largest special excursion. The company magazine (Aug 1937, p391) gave details of the Dudley Cooperative Society's visit to the town, comprising seven thousand members conveyed in twelve buffet-car trains running over four different routes.

Unlike comparable resorts of the South Coast promoted by the Southern Railway, Paignton did not receive any extended coverage in the pre-war 'Holiday Haunts.' But through the inter-war era, like Weston-Super-Mare, it had firmly established itself as one of the GWR's foremost family resorts, clearly distinct from Torquay in its overall character and appeal. One of the company's best publications on Paignton between the World Wars was the coloured brochure of 1937, 'Paignton. Glorious South Devon'. It was forthright in the expression of gratuitous enjoyment and of service.

> Paignton is tireless in studying the needs of its visitors and residents and endeavouring to anticipate their every want... Holiday makers delight in its many natural attractions and in its continual round of amusements, and especially its constant care for the happiness and safety of the children for, although Paignton has a long history, it takes more pride in its progressiveness than in the events of the past. It has developed into a family resort, meeting the family holiday needs so successfully that its visitors gain the impression that the local authority must consist of exceptionally amiable and understanding family men."[9]

The front cover of the brochure, with its curly-haired child in bright red beachwear playing on the sand with a beach ball, has become a potent image of seaside England.

Above: *Weymouth in the early thirties. The palm trees and rockery together with the single contemplative figure on the promenade contrasts, yet complements, the busy, crowded beach scene beyond. This composition of distinct foreground and contrasting backdrop conveyed the sense of variety and range of landscapes and moods to be experienced at the GWR resorts.* Author's collection

Right: *Porthcawl, one of the liveliest and most intensely promoted resorts along the South Wales coast. This poster, from 1937, was very similar to that of the town's holiday brochure, differing only in particular details, otherwise easily overlooked. The poster celebrates Porthcawl's vibrant character as a progressive, bustling and, inevitably, sunny resort.* Courtesy, Dalkeith Publishing Co.

Post-War coverage was enthusiastic and detailed, consolidating the family format. 'Holiday Haunts' for 1947, the last edition under Great Western ownership, stressed the attractions on offer, much of it relating to the municipal enterprise of the mid thirties with the development of former marshland at Goodrington.[10] Building on the reputation for its excellent beaches and bathing facilities, Goodrington Park and related developments – gardens, boating lakes, promenade, cafe, car park (a railway halt was opened in 1928 and substantially developed in the post-war years) – were completed in May 1936 at a cost of £54,000. It was ceremonially opened by Sir Robert Horne, Chairman of the Great Western Railway on the 23rd of that month.[11] 'Holiday Haunts,' 1947 reported on Paignton, enumerating its many family attractions and underlining the broad, popular appeal of the resort. Two holiday camps were also advertised in 'Holiday Haunts,' further reinforcing the image.

> It is run on modern lines with fine hotels on the sea front, spacious promenades laid out with lawns and flower beds and long stretches of sand on which there are rows of bathing huts and tents. Preston foreshore continues the main Paignton sands and Preston Green, a pleasure ground of about 10 acres, affords ample space for playing games. A short walk past the harbour beach leads to the splendid Goodrington Sands. Just prior to the war £54,000 was spent on improvements at Goodrington, which included new cliff gardens, promenades, provision of additional sites for seaside cabins and huts and up-to-date bathing stations, putting greens, a large boating lake, model yacht ponds, a Peter Pan playground, attractive cafes and tea gardens and beautifully laid out flower and rose gardens and shrubberies.[12]

Paignton also offered a zoo with the added attractions of rare tropical plants and flowers and the inevitable 'toy railway' for children. The LMS also advertised extensively on behalf of the resort, stressing the numerous through trains from the Midlands and the North and emphasising its prestigious "Devonian" service in its holiday manual. 'Holiday by LMS', Torbay being a favoured destination for tourists from the Midlands and North Country.[13]

Teignmouth provided a useful example of what could be achieved by the smaller coastal resorts of South Devon when the local corporation invested directly in the resort. The active decision of resorts such as Teignmouth and Paignton to invest heavily in the provision of tourist amenities marked a further distinction between the character and approach of the Devon resorts and those of neighbouring Cornwall. The latter depended very largely upon the natural attractions of the district and the provision of broad based entertainment other than that at Newquay was far less apparent. This situation was a specific and familiar point of contention between the GWR's Publicity Department and local authorities in Cornwall.

Whilst it criticised the perceived lack of popular entertainments within the Cornish tourist industry, the GWR Magazine, in August 1938, carried a detailed report on the progressive nature of Teignmouth.[14] Together with the installation of a new scheme for mains drainage and new water mains to ensure basic public health, the corporation focused upon attractive tourist amenities. Non-dazzle paving slabs were laid on the promenade, these being in cliff-red and buff to harmonise with the natural landscape. The promenade was supplemented visually by the provision of grassed plots, shrubberies, rockeries and sunken gardens that were floodlit at night. Tennis courts, bowling greens, a pavilion and a model yacht pond were provided to the rear of the promenade. Here, too, were floodlit rockeries and flower beds. Teignmouth was declared to be "particularly suitable for the family man and, with its mild climate, it is especially suitable for permanent residence or for those returning from overseas."[15] It was estimated that the town had invested £100,000 over a five year period in developing tourism. Thus Teignmouth reflected all the style and amenities that characterised the smaller English seaside resort. In not looking to cultivate an exclusive identity, Teignmouth flourished as a moderately sized family resort which, after the style of the Southern Railway's South Coast perspective, pursued the democratic characterisation that defined so much of the myth of inter-war seaside England.

The seaside identity was given full expression at Weston-Super-Mare, the largest of Somerset's resorts, but was also well represented at Minehead, Burnham-on-Sea, Clevedon and Portishead, each one catering extensively for family holidays. Clevedon was described in the 1937 edition of 'Holiday Haunts' as 'The Brain-Worker's Paradise': 'The Ideal Resort for the City Worker seeking Peaceful and Refreshing Holidays combined with Healthy Recreation.'[16] The urban character of the seaside mythology was made very clear here, but Clevedon, after the style of a miniature Torquay or Bournemouth, was presented as a resort of "picturesque irregularity" of hills, bay and seafront, a place where "woods invade the very heart of the town."[17] Literary associations – Tennyson, Thackery and Coleridge – guaranteed its cultural credentials. 'Holiday Haunts', 1936 edition, also evoked the essential mythology of the English seaside in a seemingly routine description of the beach at Burnham-on-Sea, "The Kiddies' Paradise", resonant of the seaside myth in its very simplicity and heavily nostalgic today.

> The seven mile sweep of golden sands and the big paddling pool are the playground of merry children who busily dig and paddle or gleefully indulge in the supreme joy of a donkey ride.[18]

This was clearly the literary counterpart of the numerous poster and photographic prints of children at play – definitive iconography, common to all four railway companies – celebrating the spontaneous delights of the beach. The front-cover of the GWR's 'Holiday Haunts', 1939 and that of the Southern Railway's 'Hints for Holidays', also 1939, were direct expressions of this seaside perspective.

Teignmouth: seafront and pier during the late thirties. The GWR Magazine carried very favourable reports as to the progressive character of the resort at that time. Author's collection

Above: *The floral clock at Weston, 1935. This was one of the many features acclaimed by the company in its extensive promotion of the resort. The Winter Gardens – opened in July 1927 by the Deputy Chairman of the GWR – was hailed as a major development, enhancing the town's status considerably.* Author's collection

Left: *A panoramic view of Weston-Super-Mare showing the seafront and piers. The foliaged foreground, big sky and the aeroplane all contribute to the sense of stylish, almost chic modernity.* Author's collection

Opposite: *Minehead swimming pool, opened, officially, by the Chairman of the GWR, Sir Robert Horne, in May 1936.* Author's collection

'Holiday Haunts' stressed the family image of all Somerset's resorts, especially that at Weston-Super-Mare. The 1937 edition, for example – with its topical front-cover seaside/Coronation imagery – portrayed Weston as having "the cheerful air of a town that is popular and glories in the fact."[19] Maxwell Fraser's 'Somerset' echoed this:

> Gay, friendly Weston Super Mare welcoming all its visitors and proud to be known as the largest holiday resort between Lancashire and Land's End. Instead of angling after exclusiveness, it bends all its energies towards making itself more attractive to holiday makers and tourists, pursuing the policy indicated in its Civic motto of 'Ever Forward', and ceaselessly endeavouring to anticipate the demands of its guests.[20]

Progressive and democratic in character and style, Weston was praised by the Great Western for its particularly creative response to tourism. 'Holiday Haunts' acknowledged:

> ... the wizardry of the Weston Town Council who are exceedingly progressive and have courageously undertaken schemes for beautifying the town which have already more than justified the extreme expense incurred.[21]

The spacious and graceful promenade was a nineteenth century investment being constructed between 1883 and 1887 and, thereafter, much extended and developed.[22] Likewise, there was an abundance of park and garden facilities, two piers – the Grand and Birnbeck Pier, the latter being served by Bristol Channel steamer services to South Wales and the Somerset and North Devon holiday resorts. There was also a fun-fair on the Birnbeck Pier offering the experience of "a water-chute, a switch-back railway, swings and other delirious delights."[23] July 1927 saw the formal opening of Weston's famous Pavilion and Cafe with its Italian Gardens, much praised by the GWR. Sir Ernest Palmer, Bart, Deputy Chairman of the GWR officiated; Sir Felix Pole, General Manager, GWR was also present, underlining the company's close relationship with the resort.[24] The GWR article, in recording the opening of the Winter Garden, drew attention to Weston's ambition to develop further as a leading winter resort: it also included reference to the particular imperative for all concerned with tourism to provide for their visitors and market their resorts effectively. It was noted that "in the year 1925 as many as six million people left England for continental resorts, of whom they might assume 5 million were British and that they spent abroad at least £50,000,000"[25] The need to attract these people was identified as an immediate necessity: "the nation had awakened to the fact that there was a tourist business to be secured and that there was a balance of trade in this as in other commercial transactions."[26] The 1937 season saw the provision of Weston's newly completed and lavishly equipped open-air swimming pool, catering for 1,400 swimmers and 5,000 spectators.

Maxwell Fraser reinforced the prevailing sense of a dedicated pleasure resort in 'Somerset', again stressing the family image with the accent on fun and unrestricted enjoyment.

> Weston's provision for the amusement of its visitors is on a lavish scale. The Marine Lake has boats of various types with a popular feature in the specially constructed harbour for children's paddling boats. A paddling pool has also been built ... Bathing huts and enclosures and a splendid diving raft are also provided. There is a model yacht pond; and a day nursery where parents can leave their children to play under the care of a trained nurse.[27]

Weston was also the venue for the first of the GWR's "Kiddies Express" trains. Whit Monday, 16th May 1932 saw the departure of the very first of these services from Paddington. 1,500 children were the guests of the resort, with free entertainments provided at the beach. Weston again co-operated with the GWR in May 1946 to organise and fund the "Kiddies Express" – the first day excursion from Paddington to the seaside in the post-war era. Hailed as "the Brighton of Bristol"[28], Weston was identified as the West Country's equivalent of the London-Brighton, city-seaside relationship on the South Coast. Drawing upon large-scale tourist traffic from Bristol, the Midlands and from Paddington itself, together with both rail and sea links with South Wales, Weston secured its identity and status as a major-league resort.

Further west, Minehead was promoted as "The Garden Paradise of the West ... Where glorious Exmoor meets the Sea"[29] Minehead station was situated virtually on the seafront, underlining the Great Western's 'Holiday Line' imagery. The Great Western Magazine, in 1934 and 1936, recorded significant improvements in tourist provision. The Council purchased twelve acres of Pine Woods on the town's notable landmark on North Hill and in 1935 new gardens were opened on the lower slopes of the hill and on the seafront as part of a Jubilee commemoration. In the following year, Sir Robert Horne, Chairman of the GWR, opened Minehead's new open-air swimming pool, also on the seafront. Considered an important modern amenity for the town, the GWR Magazine gave details promoting this modern, progressive image, incorporating a restaurant, buffet bar and floodlighting, in July 1936.

Cornwall featured heavily in Ocean Coast perspectives:

> The Ocean Coast climate is most perfectly exemplified in Cornwall because that county is almost entirely surrounded by sea. Unless it comes straight down the one neck of land, every wind must be a sea wind, tempered by the watery expanse over which it has passed.[30]

Three examples of the 'Ocean Coast' ethos as experienced from the train itself. The St Erth-St Ives branch line of 40 miles must surely rank as the most evocative expression of Ocean Coast imagery in any railway-based context. Seen here is the 'down' Cornish Riviera Express heading across the Lelant sand dunes on its 1 in 60 climb towards Carbis Bay. This was a 'through' train on Summer Saturdays, the ten-coach working being doubled-headed over the branch. 30 August 1958. Peter Gray

Above: *A definitely Great Western, Ocean Coast composition. A mid-afternoon service to St Ives leaves Carbis Bay on 30 July 1960.* Peter Gray
Below: *The return service with 4500 class 2-6-2T No.4571 rounds the headland from St Ives and approaches Carbis Bay. 30 July 1960.* Peter Gray

If Cornwall best represented the company's coastal seaside imagery generally, then Newquay was considered as unique amongst the Great Western's Cornish resorts. It was not only the largest within the county, it was the only one where economy and identity was linked totally to tourism. 'Holiday Haunts' asserted "... with its facilities for sports and amusements, Newquay hardly needs the attraction of history to enhance its already enormous popularity."[31] Its numerous beaches, caves and cliffs exemplified the desired 'Atlantic' ethos. 'Winter Resorts for the Great Western', 1934, stressed that Newquay had "that air of carefree disregard of more stringent conventions which makes a holiday in Cornwall such a joyous affair",[32] whilst Mais in 'The Cornish Riviera', 1928, had underlined the resort's prevailing family identity.

> Day after day in hot weather whole families troup down on to these vast beaches immediately after breakfast laden with bats, balls and luncheon baskets and papers and towels and stay there until the sun has set over the bay. These may lay no claim to know Cornwall, but they may certainly lay claim to getting the best out of Newquay.[33]

In line with its popular, recreational image, totally identified with the sea, Newquay was also celebrated as "one of England's chief centres for surf bathing."[34]

Ocean Coast perspectives were pursued at St. Ives itself and for the GWR's Tregenna Castle Hotel at the resort. Mais wrote of the town in 'The Cornish Riviera': "It is doubtful whether there is a more popular seaside resort in England. There is an impression of life, colour, movement everywhere."[35] From the palmed surroundings of St. Erth, the junction with the main line, through the waterside station at Lelant and the cliff-side location of Carbis Bay, to the terminus, immediately above Porthminster Beach, no other railway journey on or beyond the Great Western system, was said to offer such varied and dramatic perspectives of coastline, seascape or seaside itself. In the absence of an official GWR account of the branch line journey, 'The Homeland Handbook: St. Ives, Carbis Bay and Lelant',[36] offered its version, illustrating the text with official Great Western photographs.

> This branch line from St. Erth to St. Ives is such as to make the traveller rejoice at the glimpse it affords of the pleasant places among which his days are to be spent. But to get this view in all its beauty, choose a corner seat on the right of the carriage facing the engine.[37]

Carbis Bay was the epitome of the 'Ocean Coast' perspective, the small coastal location dedicated to residential identity and seaside activity. 'Holiday Haunts' noted the increasing numbers of cliffside residences, "built with an appreciation of their setting"[38] and the general contemporary nature of the community – All Saints Church was consecrated in 1929 – all of this reflecting the character and spirit of 'Ocean Coast' ideals.

The numerous references to residential status carried in 'Holiday Haunts', particularly those relating to Cornish and Devonian locations, were developed into a fully focused theme in the GWR's publication, 'The Ocean Coast', 1924.[39] This book, in many ways a coastal version of 'Metroland',[40] or the GWR's 'Rural London', put heavy emphasis upon the residential perspective. Ocean Coast imagery was a blend of the ancient or traditional, with modern styles. It was a direct reflection of the urban/rural accommodation prominent in the Great Western literature by the thirties.

Coastal communities – Carbis Bay, Marazion, St. Agnes, Perranporth, Carlyon Bay, Looe, Whitesand Bay, as examples, by no means all – from locations all round the Cornish coast, serve to illustrate from this one county alone, the decisive thrust of this concept. The essential message had two vital dimensions. Firstly, the extremely positive quality of healthy environment.

> To live where the sun and soft air are, imparts a new flavour and relish to the whole of life. We begin again to see life clear and see it whole ... Hand in hand with this comes a physical change every bit as wonderful. Nerves are soothed and steadied, tissues cleared and revitalised by sun and wind. Soon you begin to get that sound sleep each night that you thought belonged to youth alone. The whole of life becomes as sweet as a hazel nut.[41]

The second dimension emphasised availability: that this quality of life required no sacrifice at all. In this reassurance the company identified all the salient features of modernity, progress and technology that characterised the 'return to nature' in its rural and coastal configurations. Convenience was a key-note:

> It must be insisted that there is nothing you have to give up to obtain these benefits. There is no need to sacrifice the hard won spoils of the ages, no need to go back to the simple – but convenient – life, to obtain the manifold blessings of an ocean climate. On the ocean coast you can live in a town with wide, well-paved streets, where the shops, the restaurants and theatres are as modern as any inland. There are seaside concert halls where the greatest musicians of the day perform.[42]

Continuing the theme of modern convenience, the literature stressed interaction:

> Today the tiniest hamlet on the Cornish coast is so linked up with the great world ... by railway and bus, by post and newspaper, by telephone and wireless, that you can live there without sacrificing any of the social enjoyment, the culture, or the intelligent interest in the affairs of the world that you rightly set such store by.[43]

In final reference to overwhelmingly comfortable urban perspective defining the 'Ocean Coast', the book offered a scenario of the ideal existence; variously, that of lotusland or Metroland-By-Sea.

> You can enjoy it all in the soft warm air that gently stirs the palm trees in your garden. You sit and watch the changing face of the waters and listen to the calling of the sea birds. Dusk falls but you still sit on in your garden – for it is warm on the ocean coast. The view fades, you turn a switch and over the wireless comes a classic concert, an opera perhaps, as clearly as if you were sitting in the hall where it is being played, with its advantage – you are enjoying the delicious Atlantic air. Later, the news of all the world is heard. You switch off and, leaving the star-studded canopy of heaven, seek your bed, to sleep the sound sleep of an Ocean Coaster.[44]

This conspicuously suburban perspective, identifiable with the Southern Railway's synthesis of urban and rural dimensions, was significant for GWR image building in that it marked a progressive development of the company's concept of Englishness to incorporate urban-orientated imagery, powerfully asserted through its seaside interests. In pursuit of heightened Ocean Coast publicity an illuminated sign 'The Ocean Coast' was installed at Paddington in 1925 to fulfil the triple function of advertising, of brightening the station surroundings and, therein, registering modern company credentials. The popularist style and presentation of the rival Southern Railway did not go unnoticed in GWR circles. The 1934/35 session of The GWR (London) Lecturing and Debating Society included a specific criticism of company presentations in the debate: "Railway Publicity", 18 October 1934.[45] Responding to G.E. Orton, the Commercial Assistant to the Superintendent of the Line, G.R. Penny called for more lively, dynamic, humorous presentation. He specifically targetted the travel literature.

> Take travel literature. Mr. Orton has said that we have produced three new books and I have no wish to criticise these. They are excellent. ['The Cornish

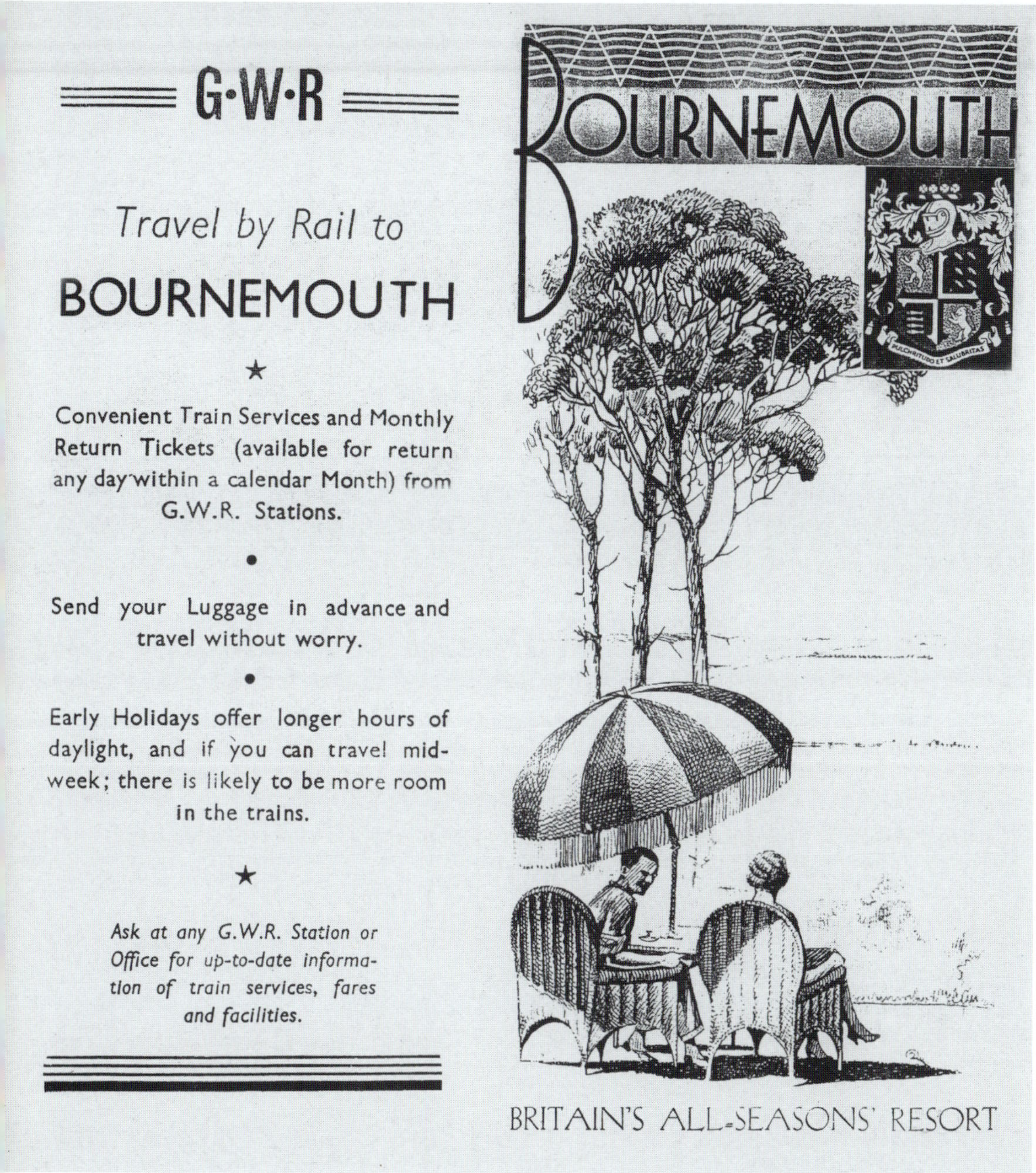

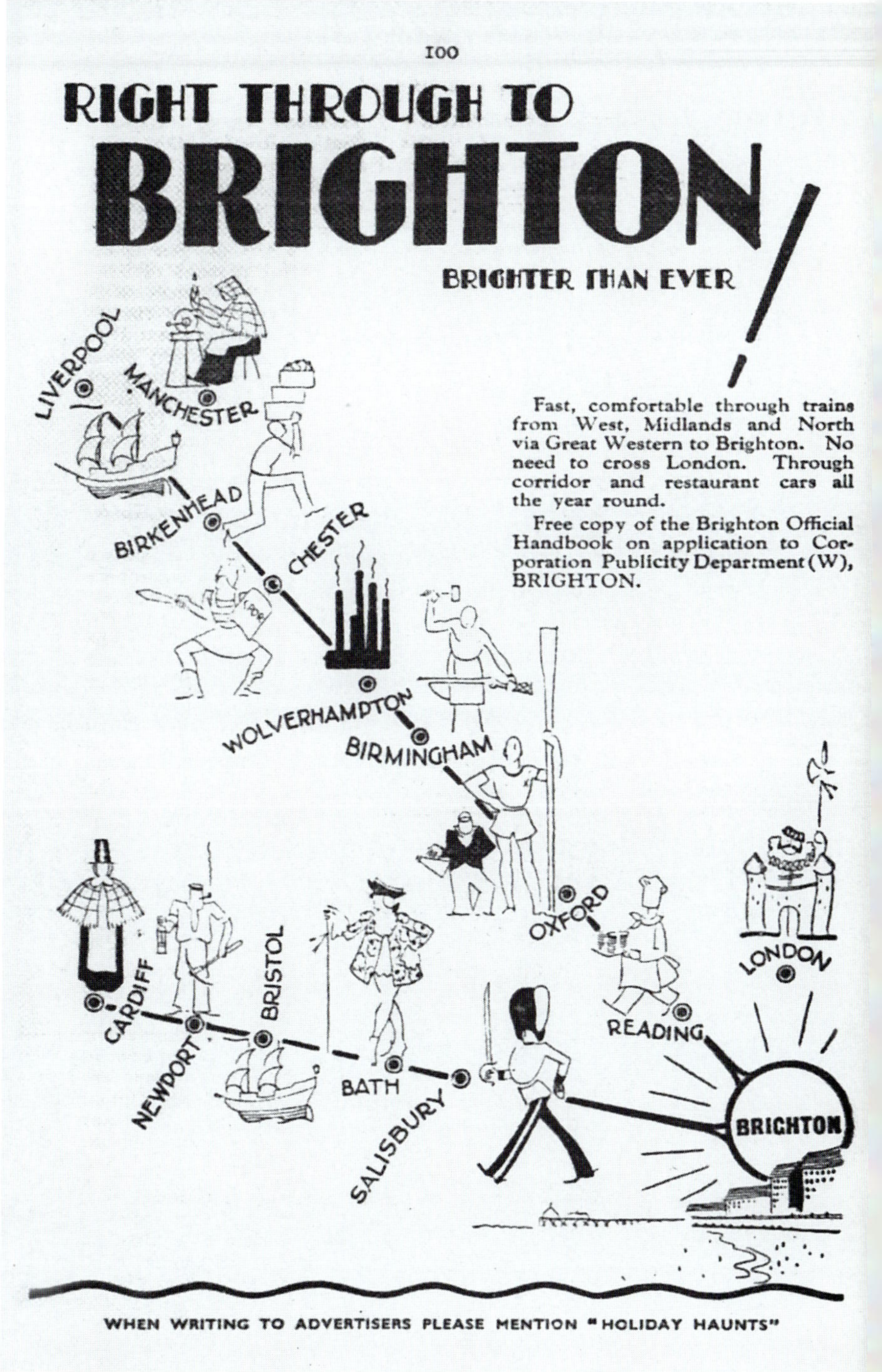

Left: *GWR brochure on Bournemouth and the surrounding district.* Author's collection

Right: *Advertisement for through services over the GWR to Brighton. The commercial and cultural associations identifying the many locations listed en-route emphasised the company's message of wide-ranging interests within its network. 'Holiday Haunts' 1938.* Author's collection

> Riviera': 'Glorious Devon' – Mais and Somerset', Maxwell Fraser]. There are, however, others which are not so good and which are, to my mind, stodgy. I look around at the travel literature published by other railway companies and find books being written by such men as Leigh-Bennett and Dell Leigh. Somehow their styles are more attractive, more friendly than ours. I do not know if it would be possible to get a little more of that friendliness into our own literature.[46]

The 'friendly', accessible representation advocated here carried considerable commercial import which, by the thirties and in the context of evident competition, cautioned the GWR to temper, somewhat, its hitherto more exclusively defined cultural imagery. The Southern Railway's handbook, 'Hints For Holidays', reflected the contrasts in character and style with the GWR's 'Holiday Haunts'.

The Southern's presentation of Portsmouth and Southsea, for example, was in every sense explicit. 'Hints for Holidays' through the thirties was eloquent as to Southsea's undoubted attributes as a popular holiday destination, dedicated to progressive recreational perspectives and to their unmistakeably contemporary character. 'Hints for Holidays', 1934, left no room for misrepresentation. Announcing Southsea's attractions through its would-be "Southsea News Hints", the contrived newspaper led with the headlines: "Deliberate Act of Sun", and "Mrs. Grundy Dies."[47] The latter with its sub-heading, "A Happy Release", reflected the popular clamour for greater freedom of expression and the pursuit of gratuitous pleasure and the release from former restraints imposed through now outmoded convention and protocol. The essential focus was that of variety; of choice, spontaneity and progressive development.

> Mrs. Grundy died at Southsea last year. On all the tennis courts, bowling greens and golf courses you can now play all day, Sunday. Free bathing is allowed. Free parking along the front and you can fly at the new aerodrome on Sundays.[48]

The newly opened miniature railway, the canoe lake and the children's swimming pool were emphasised as an important element in Southsea's claim to be the 'Kiddies Resort.'[49] Southsea's "Rock Gardens", landscaped and floodlit in a variety of colours and effects, together with the general sea-front illuminations, offered further opportunity for holiday enjoyment, extensive lighting being a particular expression of modernity and challenging aesthetic perspectives.

The holiday and general recreational ethos was powerfully reinforced, indeed, symbolically so, by the conversion of former military sites to leisure complexes. Lumps Fort to the east of South Parade Pier was purchased by the Corporation in 1931 and thereafter was landscaped to a garden setting with tennis courts and putting greens. On the site of former defences in the northern, Hilsea district of Portsmouth, the city provided a large new lido. 'Hints for Holidays' provided the details and the prevailing contemporary character.

> Hilsea Lido is all that a modern and up-to-date open-air swimming pool should be ... spacious sun bathing accommodation, a compound for physical training, floodlighting by night, a large car park, loud-speakers, a children's paddling pool and cafes for bathers and spectators complete with amenities.[50]

An extended survey of the South Coast resorts is not the intention here: the focus is that of comparative representations as in the case of Brighton, as indicative of the distinctive character and styles projected by the Southern and the Great Western Railways. As indicated, the essential differentiation came with the GWR's evident reluctance to stress all aspects of popular, commercial culture, and with its close identification with pursuits conforming to a more traditionally-perceived, exclusive status. Across the GWR network itself, as with Paignton, or Weston-Super-Mare, the company's largest commercialised family resorts offered, at best, muted and generalised reference to fun-fairs and amusement parks. (In Devon and North Cornwall, however, the Southern Railway, likewise, pursued similar policies. Bude, for example, was the antithesis of Brighton.) Direct comparison and contrast was available on the South Coast given that the GWR served the likes of Hastings, Eastbourne, Brighton, Portsmouth, etc. with its numerous cross-country services. 'Holiday Haunts' carried detailed reference to these resorts and for present purposes the comparative approaches with regard to Brighton and Eastbourne are considered.

Southern Railway literature on Brighton was inevitably more extensive and detailed than that offered by the GWR but there were other distinguishing features in their respective styles and presentations. 'Hints for Holidays' reflected the dynamic, progressive imagery of a resort well attuned to contemporary perspectives.

> Every year Brighton becomes more popular and with the constant improvements in the way of five new amusement buildings, widened boulevards, gardens, boating pools, etc., it can be truly said that the town is not merely meeting the requirements of the passing moment, but the demands of the future.[51]

The LMS guide, 'Holidays by LMS', likewise noted "the extraordinary diversity of attractions ... its all embracing entertainments,"[52] and, in pursuit of the open, democratic perspective, also emphasised "the abundant accommodation for all types."[53]

Great Western literature acknowledged that Brighton had its "many imitators (who) in spite of their gallant efforts, remain but a shadow of the joyous Sussex resort with its multifarious amusements."[54] The latter were detailed in an extensive entry for 'Holiday Haunts' which surpassed those devoted to its own resorts of Paignton and Weston-Super Mare. Amongst the references to 'brilliantly illuminated streets, gay restaurants and cabarets' etc., were also expressions such as, "the town keeps its guests as happily amused by night as by day," whilst the cinemas, dance-halls and arcades "ensure that every passing whim can be gratified."[55] "Happily amused" and "passing whims" suggests a not completely unqualified endorsement of such lavish provision.

The Great Western's preferred perspective, in line with its presentation of its own resorts, was that of Brighton as an exclusive location of unique character in Britain, clearly differentiated from its many would-be rivals and closely identified with continental attributes.

> Brighton, like London, has achieved the Continental air so naturally that visitors find it almost impossible to believe that they have not been transported across the Channel. The Boulevard habit, which no other resort in Britain has succeeded in introducing, is part of the very life of the town where the most conventional take their morning coffee in the open air as a matter of course, chatting gaily and basking in the sun.[56]

Eastbourne was given an equally exclusive image but one of a somewhat different emphasis and style. Here, it was not a continental identity that predominated; it was one of essential Englishness, "a delightful example of what a large town can be when built under careful direction."[57] The town's two miles of sea front, built on three levels and distinguished by its floral displays, its Municipal Orchestra, 'the largest of its kind in the country' and its reputation as a 'scholastic centre', for example, gave the resort a decidedly select ethos. 'Holiday Haunts' stressed this:

> Unlike most Sussex resorts, Eastbourne has neither a Continental atmosphere nor a complete carefree democracy. The town is essentially dignified and *English*

in its atmosphere, a place which is largely residential, where the majority of visitors take houses for long periods indulging in the sports which are such a feature of the town ... A distinctive feature of the front is that there are no shops, one of the many pleasant developments which demonstrates that this resort, although progressive, has no desire for a cheap popularity.[58]

Pursuing the reference to sports, 'Holiday Haunts' also stated that there were probably "more horse-riders to be found in Eastbourne than in any other coastal resort in the Kingdom."[59] It was also significant that 'Holiday Haunts' stressed the word "English" in this passage by printing it in italics.

Southern Railway presentations of Eastbourne also emphasised its dignified, elegant character, but 'Hints for Holidays' focused upon a strong sense of aesthetic distinction and put less explicit emphasis on the social and cultural exclusivity that defined the Great Western's perspective. The 1939 edition of the Southern Railway's guide described Eastbourne as "an example of perfect town planning"[60] and, having clearly established the outstanding aesthetic credentials, it underlined the modern "up-to-date" beach and general recreational amenities and, in one telling sentence, revealed:

In its gayest hours the town never loses its sense of dignity, and consequently it is exceedingly popular with all types of holiday makers.[61]

The Channel Islands, presented in 'Hints for Holidays' as 'The Riviera of Great Britain', perpetuated the 'garden' imagery albeit enhanced by the pervading Anglo-French characterisation. But the overall ethos was that of variety and choice, incorporating Jersey's shopping facilities, its lavish leisure amenities, promenade illuminations and 'abundance of amusements', for example, with that of the aesthetics of landscape and seashore. GWR coverage stressed the island's particular historical traditions, emphasising also the archaeological inheritance. It further stated that amenities generally were "as modern and luxurious as their customs are ancient."[62]

The detailed and unqualified recognition given to the major south coast resorts reflected the company's intended identification with them. Through services from the North-West, North-East, the Midlands and South Wales were extensively promoted in 'Holiday Haunts' to underline the company's wide-ranging 'holiday' credentials. Further west, however, the GWR celebrated its sole 'ownership', as it were, of an outstanding and exclusively defined resort of national reputation.

Torquay was the centrepiece of the South Devon district identified by the company as 'The English Riviera'. Torbay generally, and Torquay in particular, was characterised, almost invariably depicted, in terms of Mediterranean imagery, and specifically, that of the Italian 'Campanian' coast and the Bay of Naples. As a location of both outstanding, classically-inspired and picturesque beauty combined with a litany of distinguished personages, past and present, the GWR had a clearly established tradition of superlatives to draw upon for its own promotional work.

GWR literature identified Lord Nelson, Napoleon – as a captive – Queen Victoria, the Duchess of Sutherland and Princess Louise, likewise Tennyson and Charles Kingsley as most distinguished visitors. An early Ward-Lock guide of 1897 wrote of the town as 'The Italy of England', endowing it with classical properties and perspectives, which were eagerly reinforced by the GWR:

The first view of the town is usually obtained from the road leading from the station. Turning the corner that leads into the marine drive that skirts the waters of Torbay, the scene cannot fail to win admiration and 'lovely' is the adjective that is suggested by the first glimpse of this terraced town, ensconsed, like Rome, on seven hills and embowered in trees and flowers that would do credit to the Pincian Gardens. Tier above tier rise mansions and villas each in its own grounds and built in excellent taste so that the eye wanders over the scene without being arrested by any jerry-builders folly and takes in at a glance the whole panoramic view.[63]

The 1904 edition of 'Seaside Watering Places' described Torquay as the rightful recipient of both "Nature and Art, prodigal in their gifts."[64] Imagery was invariably feminine as in the following extract from the earlier 'Tourist Guide to South Devon.' 1878.

Torquay is regarded as the queen of watering places ... Seen from some well chosen eminence under a glowing sky, Torquay is more like a domain in fairy land than any portion of this work-a-day world. Truth to tell, there is a good deal of the lotus-eaters about many of its inhabitants.[65]

The Ward-Lock Guide for 1897 similarly referred to Torquay as:

A lovely queen of some sunny southern land who has been transported from her native environment and set down in a far-off land.[66]

Exclusive imagery prevailed, the essential ethos of the resort being further clarified in the GWR's "Devon, Shire of Sea Kings," 1904.

Minstrel entertainments and other kinds of beach shows find no favour in the eyes of those who are responsible for the social success of Torquay. On the other hand, yachtsmen, golfers, cricketers and oarsmen find themselves in a place where provision has been made for every kind of sport. Hunting is available and anglers can choose between lake, river and sea.[67]

Mais drew upon definitively feminine characterisation in 'Glorious Devon'. 1928, emphasising successive revelatory perspectives that ordered and structured the individual's perception and appreciation.

Torquay unveils her beauties very gradually. It is not from the railway which is tucked away unobtrusively that her particular glories are to be seen. Built like Bath and Rome on seven hills, her full majesty is not to be realised unless perhaps from the sea or the height of her new reservoir. Each separate arc of beauty is self contained and individual. Here is no hard glittering ruler of a grand promenade, going endlessly, tirelessly on until it emerges into the grander no less straight and tiring promenade of the next resort. Instead you find yourself in the cleft of a vast bay where you may see without being seen. The high rocks stretching down to the front are hidden in a forest of wonderful exotic palms and flowers which seem to flourish nowhere but here.[68]

From the explicit reference here to "her beauties", Mais presented what was clearly a perspective of carefully organised, but privileged, aesthetic revelation. The subtle unveiling, the sense of shared intimacy in an exclusive personal encounter, the contrast of sensuous curves – "each separate arc of beauty" – with "hard glittering ruler lines" and, elsewhere, the imagery of "exotic palms and flowers" and the romantic association with the seven hills of Rome, evoked the unique ethos of this "Queen of Watering Places".[69] The entire presentation of Torquay as set out here exemplified the collective cultural spectrum of fashionable imagery and stylistic expression. 'Holiday Haunts', 1936 declared: "There is probably no town in the world - certainly not in England - which has such an amazing variety of coastal scenery." There are no less than eight glorious bays within the limits of the town itself and these are not merely completely different in contour, but also in colouring and type ... "[70]

In Torbay the very atmosphere of the Mediterranean is found. Colour, light and life are everywhere. In the long Rock Walk, brilliant exotic flowers and sub-tropical trees flourish with a rare luxuriance ... the star-lit summer nights scented by the fragrance of masses of flowers, have an almost unbelievable witchery. With palm trees lining its roadway and its all-pervading air of carefree joyousness, Torbay more nearly resembles one of the famous Mediterranean resorts than any other English town.[71]

Torquay's positive image was further enhanced in its status as a winter resort and, in this guise, the Great Western determined upon firm continental parallels offering an atmosphere of highly privileged, exclusive society. 'Winter Resorts on the GWR', 1925 edition, provided the detail:

In addition to being one of the best pleasure resorts in Europe, Torquay has rapidly come into the forefront as the Premier Marine Spa. The Medical, Electrical, Turkish, Tepid and Walt Water Swimming Baths are replete with all the latest British and Continental methods of Spa Treatments ...[7]

As ever in the strictly hierarchical society served by the GWR, the clientele were assured of the highest standards of service, commensurate with social distinctions:

The Baths' Staffs of Masseurs and Masseures are highly trained and patients for whom any form of Treatment has been prescribed can rely on having all their requirements fully met... The Winter visitor need never have a dull moment. All the entertainment houses are open and the Hotel Proprietors are never weary in catering for the absolute comfort and enjoyment of their guests.[73]

The fact that post-war British Railways' editions of 'Holiday Haunts', as recent as 1959, continued to stress the provision of medicinal baths – "Aix and Vichy douches, Navheim vapour,"[74] and other such treatments – testified to the ingrained, substantive character of Torquay as the Great Western's supreme expression of the fashionable, exclusive resort.

Aberystwyth, the largest resort on the western coast of Wales, was described in promotional work as "The place in the Sun ... where the Mountains come down to the Sea.[75] Presented by the GWR as a stylish, somewhat chic, location, the town offered several features essential to the fashionable resort. Its setting of mountains and sea was emphasised, confirming natural grandeur.

Cardigan Bay, with its vast sweep of amber sand and its limpid blue waters, is entrancingly lovely, and the great mountain ranges backing the town, chameleon- like in their response to the ever-changing play of light and shade, rise and fall until lost in the blue haze of distance.[76]

The town was also recognised, historically:

Aberystwyth is invested with the dignity which only the consciousness of an historic past can give a town. Although Aberystwyth is modern and progressive, it cherishes the slight relics of its once-powerful castle, and is justly proud of the part it has played in the affairs of the nation.[77]

Moreover, its scholastic identity conferred special status:

Aberystwyth is also one of the chief centres of learning in the Principality. The University College of Wales was founded there in 1872 and the National Library of Wales received official recognition in 1912. Both these institutions attract scholars from all parts of the world.[78]

The 1939 edition of 'Holiday Haunts' announced recent investment at the resort in line with the town's modern, yet distinguished, identity. These comprised; "a new Pavilion and Palm Court on the Marine Terrace, a new bandstand, shelters on the South Marine Parade and an extension of the National Library."[79] Floodlighting and illuminations were also listed as a further enhancement of the town's holiday image. In its recognition of Aberystwyth's distinctive character, the GWR declared the town to hold "supremacy among Welsh seaside resorts,"[80] a recognition that had been substantiated in the company's rebuilding programme for the terminus, completed in 1926.

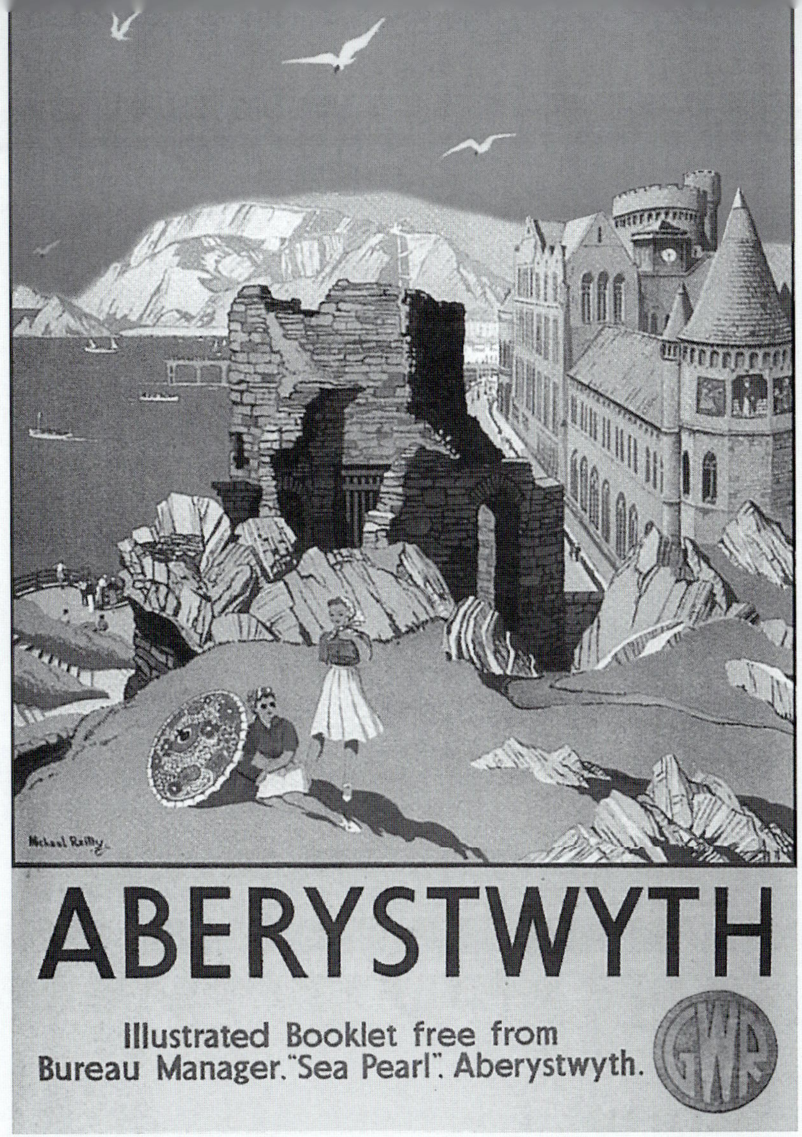

Above, left: *'Holiday Haunts', 1936, identified Aberystwyth as variously, "The Biarritz of Wales" and "The Brighton of Wales" ...'Aberystwyth itself is invested with the dignity which only the consciousness of an historic past can give a town". The poster evidently reflects this perspective.* Courtesy, Dalkeith Publishing Co Ltd.

Above, right: *The extensive shoreline and Paignton Green are the main features in this late 1920s poster. Note also the pier towards the far end of the beach and the sense of perspective in height and distance provided by the cliffscape in the foreground.* Courtesy, Dalkeith Publishing Co Ltd.

Facing page: *Advertisement for Guernsey from the 1935 edition of Holiday Haunts.* Author's collection

REFERENCES – CHAPTER TWO

1: GWR Holiday Haunts, 1934. P100.

2: GWR Brochure. Weymouth, 1934, unpaginated.

3: GWR Holiday Haunts, 1936. P650.

4: Local Authority Brochure, 'Porthcawl'. c1936 unpaginated.

5: GWR Holiday Haunts, 1929 P575.

6: Local Authority Brochure. Circa 1936. The brochure included the statement: "The BBC have recognised its unique attractions and its popular appeal by their broadcasts from Coney Beach to Great Britain and the British Empire."

7: Holiday Haunts 1939 P821.

8: Ibid P821.

9: GWR Brochure. Paignton. Glorious Devon. 1937.

10: GWR Holiday Haunts, 1947, P251.

11: GWR Magazine, July 1936 P317.

12: GWR Holiday Haunts, 1947 P251.

13: LMS 'Holidays By LMS' 1938 P682.

14: GWR Magazine, August 1938 P318.

15: Ibid P318.

16: Holiday Haunts, 1937, P618.

17: Ibid P583.

18: Ibid 1936 edition, P577.

19: Ibid 1937. P594.

20: Maxwell Fraser. Somerset. P113.

21: Holiday Haunts, 1937, P594.

22: Ward-Lock Guide, Weston-Super-Mare, 1924. P13.

23: Ibid P18.

24: GWR Magazine, August, 1927. P311.

25: Ibid P314.

26: Ibid P314.

27: Maxwell Fraser, Somerset. P114.

28: Ward-Lock Guide, Weston-Super-Mare, 1934. P4.

29: Holiday Haunts, 1937, P622.

30: GWR The Ocean Coast (1924), 1927 ed P7.

31: Holiday Haunts, 1937 P173.

32: GWR Winter Resorts, 1934, P19.

33: S.P.B. Mais. The Cornish Riviera, 1928, P116.

34: Holiday Haunts, 1937 P173.

35: S.P.B. Mais. The Cornish Riviera, GWR 1934 ed P116.

36: The Homeland Association Homeland Handbook: St. Ives, Vol. 78.

37: Ibid P5.

38: Holiday Haunts, 1934 P156.

39: GWR The Ocean Coast, 1924.

40: Metropolitan Railway 'Metro-Land'. Annual editions 1915-1932. The 1924:25 editions are particularly interesting for their coverage of the British Empire Exhibition.

41: GWR The Ocean Coast. P4.

42: Ibid P4:5.

43: Ibid P5.

44: Ibid P5.

45: GWR GWR (London) Lecture and Debating Society Session 1934-35, No. 284, "Railway Publicity".

46: Ibid P214.

47: Hints For Holidays 1934. P351.

48: Ibid P351.

49: Ibid P351.

50: SR Hints For Holidays 1939 P348.

51: SR Hints For Holidays 1934 P461.

52: LMS Holidays By LMS 1938 P805.

53: Ibid P805.

54: GWR Holiday Haunts 1937 P101.

55: Ibid P102.

56: Ibid P102.

57: Ibid P101.

58: Ibid P102.

59: Ibid P102.

60: Hints For Holidays 1939 P541.

61: Ibid P541.

62: Hints For Holidays, 1939 P882. Holiday aunts, 1936. P6654.

63: Ward-Lock and Co. Guide To South Devon. Torquay. Paignton. Dartmouth 1897 P20.

64: Seaside Watering Places 1904. Upton Gill London 1904-05 Season. P139.

65: R.N. Worth Tourist's Guide To South Devon 1878. P63.

66: Ward-Lock South Devon P21.

67: A.M. Broadley Devon. The Shire Of The Sea Kings GWR (1904) 1912 ed P46.

68: S.P.B. Mais Glorious Devon GWR (1928) 1934 ed.

69: Ibid P35.

70: GWR HOliday Haunts 1936. P345.

71: Ibid P344.

72: GWR Winter Resorts On The GWR 1925 P50.

73: Ibid P50.

74: British Railways, Holiday Haunts, Western Region, 1959. P78.

75: GWR Holiday Haunts, 1936 P826.

76: GWR Holiday Haunts, 1934 P854.

77: Ibid P854.

78: Ibid P854.

79: Holiday Haunts, 1939. P806.

80: Ibid P806.

CHAPTER THREE

SELLING TO AMERICA

The homeland of Shakespeare has ever been, and always must be, regarded in the light of a place of pilgrimage by every member of the great Anglo-Saxon race and it is, moreover, a sacred spot, the key to the gates of which is firmly held by the Great Western Railway'.
'Shakespeare Land'. GWR. 1924

I had long been convinced that this country could and should attract many visitors from America and elsewhere and, being a keen advocate of a good understanding with America, I was an enthusiastic supporter of Sir Frances Towle when he started what was known as the Come to Britain movement.
Felix Pole, General Manager, GWR 1924-29

The GWR took a leading role in marketing Britain internationally. In its self-designation, formulated in the American-orientated literature, as 'The National Holiday Line', 'The Holiday Line of the British Empire', 'The English Speaking Peoples' and 'The Line of the American Pilgrim', the company, in line with the British Travel Association generally, identified the USA as the primary overseas market. GWR interests, cognisant of the commercial potential of tourism and of the limitations of Britain's domestic economy, advocated government involvement through the Travel Association to enhance international tourism, calling repeatedly for increased funding in advertising and direct fiscal reform, not least in the form of the repeal of the visa charge of ten dollars per person on American visitors to Britain. Elsewhere in Europe visas were either not required or issued on a nominal sum of up to two dollars maximum. The American market represented a far more valuable source of tourist revenue than that of the Empire as the thrust of the joint schemes under the 'Associated Companies' indicated. The Minutes of Meetings of Advertising (Publicity) Representatives – Railway Clearing House across the entire inter-war era reflected the overall primacy of trans-Atlantic considerations and, on occasion, registered them in almost open preference to clearly defined imperial interests.

Perspectives of 'Crown Imperial' and 'Greater Britain' were central to tourist marketing schemes, indicating, in the climate of early thirties depression, the necessity of economic expediency. This was indicated in the somewhat desperate rallying cry of HRH The Prince of Wales, Patron of the Travel Association of Great Britain and Ireland, in January 1932: "This is the moment when we want to impress upon the world that our country is still alive; that it means to go forward again"[1]. It was also echoed in Felix Pole's plea in accord with the Travel Association for vital Government assistance to promote overseas markets and again, later, in 1946, in a blunt admission from the Minister for Overseas Trade – "We so badly want their dollars."[2] Both the GWR and the Travel Association issued what was, in terms of its imagery and theme, an almost identical statement recognising the relative importance of tourism for the British economy by the mid thirties. In October 1935 the GWR recorded the total income from tourism for 1934 to be £25,573,000, "a figure that compares very favourably with the revenue of £28,846,000 and £31,854,000 from woollen and coal exports respectively"[3]. The Travel Association's official history notes that visitors to the United Kingdom by 1938 numbered 720,429, from 475,088 in 1932. It concluded that, with an

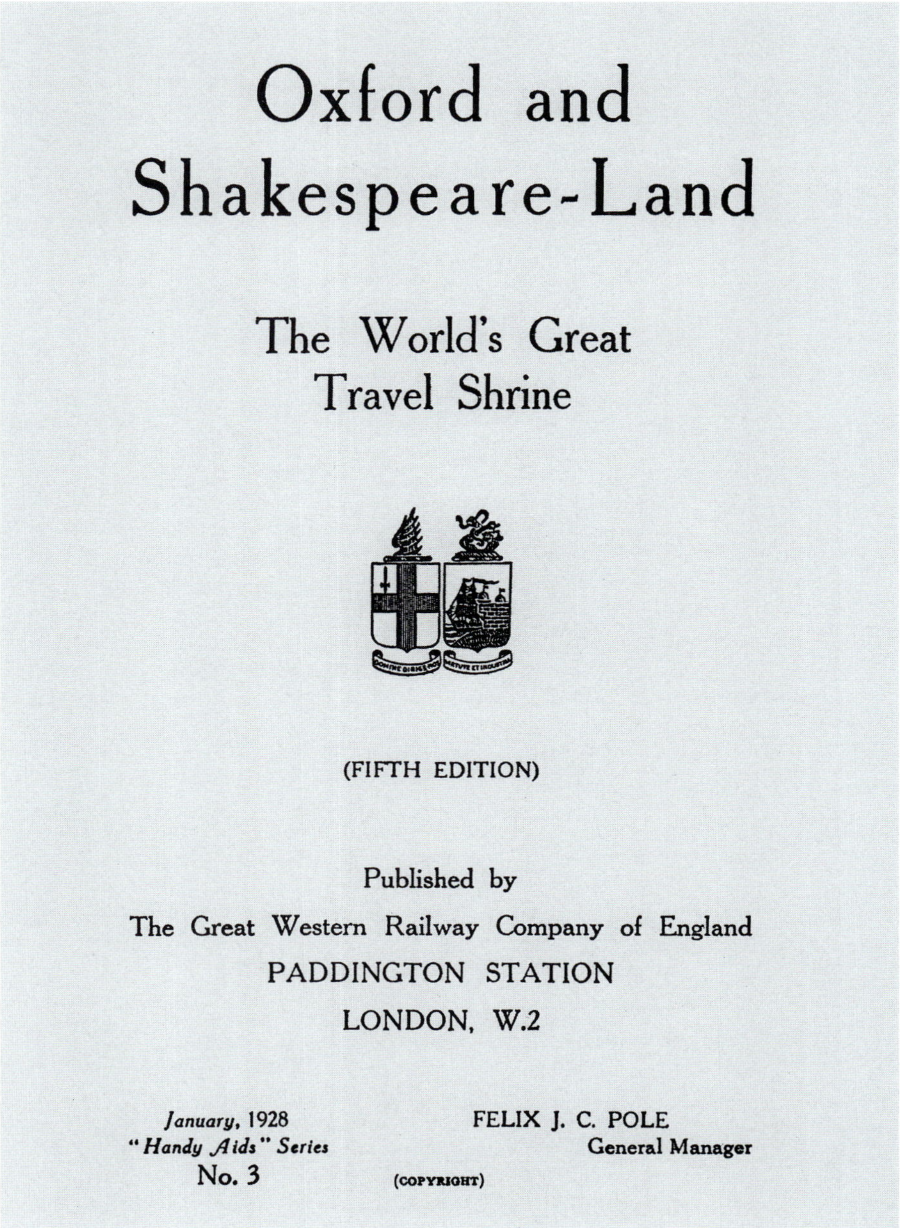
Oxford and
Shakespeare-Land

The World's Great
Travel Shrine

(FIFTH EDITION)

Published by
The Great Western Railway Company of England
PADDINGTON STATION
LONDON, W.2

January, 1928
"Handy Aids" Series
No. 3

FELIX J. C. POLE
General Manager

(COPYRIGHT)

Title page for 'Oxford and Shakespeare-Land' 1928.

A DAY IN SHAKESPEARE'S COUNTRY

INCLUSIVE RAIL AND ROAD DAY TRIP

in the

Shakespeare Country

BY GREAT WESTERN OR LONDON MIDLAND & SCOTTISH RAILWAYS

Every weekday (not Sundays) from May 3rd to September 30th inclusive (Bank Holidays, May 29th and August 7th excepted) CHEAP DAY TOURS are run from London as follows :—

By **G. W. R.**

LONDON (PADDINGTON)	dep.	9c10 a.m.
LEAMINGTON SPA	arr.	10.43 a.m.

By **L M S**

LONDON (EUSTON)	dep.	9a 5 a.m.
" (Sats. only)*	dep.	9a 0 a.m.
COVENTRY "	arr.	10.57 a.m.

a—Restaurant Car Express
c—Slip Carriage
**—Applies only from July 8th*

Thence the tour is by Midland "Red" Road Motor Coach over a route of 50 miles to Kenilworth (Historic Castle) Guy's Cliffe (interval here for sight-seeing), Warwick (interval for lunch and visit to Castle), Barford and Charlecote Park (The Arden Country), Stratford-on-Avon (visit Shakespeare's Birthplace and Holy Trinity Church), Shottery (Anne Hathaway's Cottage), Leamington (noted Spa). Here G.W.R. passengers rejoin their train. L M S passengers proceed via Stoneleigh Park to Coventry.

RETURN JOURNEY

By **G. W. R.**

LEAMINGTON SPA	dep.	6.30 p.m.
LONDON (PADDINGTON)	arr.	8. 5 p.m.

By **L M S**

COVENTRY	dep.	6.43 p.m.
LONDON (EUSTON)	arr.	8.20 p.m.
" (Sats. only)*	arr.	8.40 p.m.

Dining Car Expresses
**—Applies only from July 8th*

INCLUSIVE FARES FOR THE SHAKESPEARE-COUNTRY DAY TRIP

FIRST CLASS, **34s. 9d.** (Children under 14, **23s. 0d.**)
THIRD CLASS, **27s. 0d.** (Children under 14, **18s. 9d.**)

FARES INCLUDE :

Rail and Road transportation as above ; Services of Conductor through the Shakespeare Country ; Lunch at Warwick ; All Gratuities ; Admission Charges to : Kenilworth Castle, Warwick Castle, Shakespeare's Birthplace, Anne Hathaway's Cottage, Holy Trinity Church.

Fares for the Combined Rail and Road Motor Tour (exclusive of Extras) :
FIRST CLASS, **24s. 0d.** THIRD CLASS, **16s. 6d.**
Children under 14 half price

Passengers holding through tickets from London to Liverpool (or vice versa) may avail themselves of these Motor Trips providing there is room on the cars, and also if room is available any passengers may make the trips by booking locally. Fares : from Leamington Spa Station **5s. 0d.** ; from Coventry Station **5s. 6d.**

NOTE.—The dates, fares and train times shewn in this folder are subject to alteration. Passengers should verify when taking their tickets.

Above: An Associated British and Irish Railways brochure, 1937. 'The Shakespeare Country'. This was also produced as a joint GWR/LMS project and in a French language format. Author's collection

Left: Details of Road-Rail Day excursions included in 'The Shakespeare Country' brochure

income, 1938, of £28,981,000, this was a figure that "compared with the revenue accruing from the nation's exports, at that time, of wool or of coal"[4]

Literary perspectives during the inter-war years, and increasingly so during the thirties, reflected the intensification of cultural-commercial themes defining the Anglo-American relationship. Partial parallels might also be offered with the increasingly common reference to 'family' imagery in terms of Empire where geo-political considerations became particularly important during the thirties. The 'Come To Britain' campaign dating from 1926 and the Travel Association of Great Britain and Ireland, 1929, closely involved with the Railway Clearing House in its efforts to co-ordinate the railway companies into joint or preferred centralised initiatives and, again, the participation of the International Hotels Association, reflected both the promotional efforts and the projected character and style of the British experience. The GWR Magazine carried a detailed article on the Travel Association in November 1931, presenting Britain's cultural heritage as a vibrant, living experience, making direct appeal to a past-present interaction in the style of a cultural encounter. But, within the substance of this appeal, the sense of commercially driven urgency was apparent as, indeed, was the implicit recognition of competition elsewhere and, consequently, the need to offer active events, as in the reference to "these islands as far than dead territory."[5]

> Moreover, it is not 'dead' territory that we offer our visitors. These islands pulsate with life and activity. Castles, if no longer inhabited, are backgrounds for pageants recalling the thrilling scenes of their histories; cathedrals hold their services interspersed with music festivals; county towns have their fairs and historic galas; rivers and seaside places have their regattas and industrial tours have their exhibitions. Everywhere there are events as well as places of interest.[6]

The Travel Association here, in evoking the idea of living heritage, was however careful to maintain the traditionalist agenda definitive of both British formulation and American expectations, culturally. This much was apparent in the joint company arrangements for the American Tourist Agents' Tour of October 1929.[7] With an itinerary comprising Oxford, Leamington, York, Edinburgh, Melrose, The English Lakeland, Chester and Bath, thence Bournemouth, via the Somerset and Dorset route – a classic railway of rural England – the central theme of historical tradition and of common cultural identity was uppermost. Further inducements agreed between the companies included various gratuities as in the provision of first class travel, meals, wines and cigars en-route, also the inclusion of a number of extra guided tours. Whilst this was considered expedient, commercially, if not generous on the part of the hosts, it was, however, recognised practice in continental terms.

Together with newspaper coverage and the supply of promotional films, the joint advertising strategy included a series of talks on Britain, broadcast from some 500 wireless stations across North America whilst, earlier, in April 1931, the Travel Association opened an office in Paris. Commercial enterprise was deemed a vital factor, but for all such efforts, publicity generally was considered small-scale by American and Continental standards as confirmed in the following statements by the American Ambassador to Great Britain and the General Manager of The Travel Association of Great Britain and Ireland respectively. Offering the wider, international context, the Ambassador observed:

> Possessing one of the loveliest bits of the whole world, you are not very willing to admit the fact and you are most unwilling to proclaim it from the housetops. People go to those lands whose attractions have been most persuasively and directly brought to their notice. Hence the hurried rush of American visitors in three or four days through England if they come at all and their weeks elsewhere.[8]

Likewise, L.A.L. de Meredith for the Travel Association on the vital issue of publicity:

> Confess it to your shame, you must admit that the term (publicity) is new to you. That is the trouble. On the continent it is not unfamiliar to anyone. In America it is equally well known. But within our shores we have yet to realise its significance and its possibilities.[9]

For its part, the Railway Clearing House, in January 1926, had proposed a detailed, joint approach to the promotion of Britain and Ireland in America, arguing the comprehensive coverage of that country could only be achieved collectively; that a corporate central office in New York was required and that the four companies should agree to 'sink existing individualities.'[10] But two years later this, and a GWR proposal that the Big Four companies should establish railway offices on board trans-Atlantic liners for the advanced distribution of promotional literature, itineraries and railway tickets en route, was formally rejected. Administrative difficulties, liaison and differing priorities as in perceived individual styles, reference and imagery, were given against the collective initiative.[11]

Whilst it was clearly committed to the joint approach to publicity, delivered through the Railway Clearing House and the Tourist Association, the GWR was always the most prolific of the four companies in addressing and developing the American tourist market. One such strategy was that of the pilgrimage.

The GWR's concept of pilgrimage – broad, in the sense that there were differentiated categories both of interests and encounter – was an extremely successful synthesis of cultural and commercial interests. At every stage in the promotion of cultural heritage, the company stressed the provision of the highest standards of service. This was by no means confined to material comfort alone, although this was a vital factor. As with the perceived agenda of the Travel Association generally, the Great Western made every effort to present a detailed literary guide that addressed all dimensions of received protocol, determining not only what was to be seen or experienced but also the perspective – aesthetic, literary or historical, for example – that contextualised the location, the experience or event. The company literature invariably presented the maximum American-orientated perspective wherein English history was contextualised within an American agenda. Englishness served to define an American identity celebratory of the increasingly dominant Anglo-Saxon republic. Content, historically, was therefore crucial to the projected identity – effectively, the celebration of the Anglo-Saxon period and, thereafter, the thematically formative sixteenth and seventeenth century narrative – and was delivered in an uncompromising context of progressive development that, in turn, accorded directly to American ideals of the 'Manifest Destiny'.

In many respects the GWR literature presented the English landscape as one of numerous shrines to early American founders, the language and imagery of commemoration being to the forefront. Thus, 'Rural London' and its depiction of the Chalfont Country (1924 edition).

> Although the average Londoner has shown a greater interest in recent years in the Chalfont Country, its historic sites have for many years held high rank in the majority of intelligent American travellers as places of interest – to the shrine of Thomas Gray at Stoke Poges and thence past Jordans, the last resting-place of William Penn, Founder and Proprietor of Pennsylvania ...[12]

This reference is significant for its differentiation; the juxtaposition of "average Londoners" and "intelligent

Americans", likewise, the "recent" interest of the former and the established presence of the latter. Not surprisingly, the sub-text of the American pilgrim as being more sensitive and aware than the native population in terms of England's historic and aesthetic heritage is apparent throughout the Great Western's literature.

As a landscape of commemoration, Jordans demanded the appropriate representation, as reflected in the definitive imagery and literary style apparent here. 'Places of Pilgrimage' quoted from the report by the Pennsylvania Society of the Penn Commemoration in 1911.

> The little brick building has no external aspect of ecclesiastical character; nor has the burial ground beside it any of the dismal monumentation that is so generally distinctive of such places. It is a small green field, bordered by lofty trees, standing as silent sentinels in solemn crowded rows watching day and night the hallowed ground within.[13]

'Rural London' characterised Jordans as "embossed in forest trees and overrun with jasmine", whilst the surrounding countryside was that of:

> luxuriant woods, expansive commons, limpid streams and fruitful cornfield, where ancient churches, timbered houses and village greens form, as it were, a living link between the twentieth century and the old-world days of "Great Elizabeth."[14]

In the received imagery of dissent and of commemoration, this depiction of Jordans corresponded to the Great Western's overall presentation of England to America. 'Rural London' was defined, thematically and stylistically according to the determinants of historical-cultural legacy, rural identification and accessibility.

To complete the reference to pilgrimage and shrine we can refer to two very different styles and representations.

Whitchurch Canonicorum, a small West Dorsetshire village, was featured in all the American-orientated literature. It was:

> beyond doubt the only place in the whole world which can claim the distinction of giving shelter to the remains of a British Saint (St. Gwen; the Breton St. Blanche) as well as to those of a great American coloniser.[15]

The latter was Sir George Somers, coloniser of Virginia, in the reign of James I. The teleological context, the given lineal consistency, sealed in effect by latter day Americans visiting the site, enhanced the sense of providence and destiny, definitive of the Anglo-Saxon inheritance.

Plymouth, as a final and sharply contrasting example, had special significance, not only historically but also in terms of past-present interaction. All the appropriate Great Western literature, particularly 'Glorious Devon', 1928, celebrated the city's identity. It was the supreme example of the gateway to the New World.

> Plymouth Sound has the capacity to awaken more memories than any other place in the world ... It was from here that Martin Frobisher set out to explore Labrador, and Drake to sail around the world. It was from here that Raleigh set out for Virginia and the first Puritans in 1607 sailed to find a new land. The stone still stands, and Americans flock to it, which marks the departure of 101 pilgrims on their sixty days voyage into the unknown to found the New England.[16]

Mais emphasised the significance of place and event with his repetition of the phrase, "It was from here." The 'Mayflower'

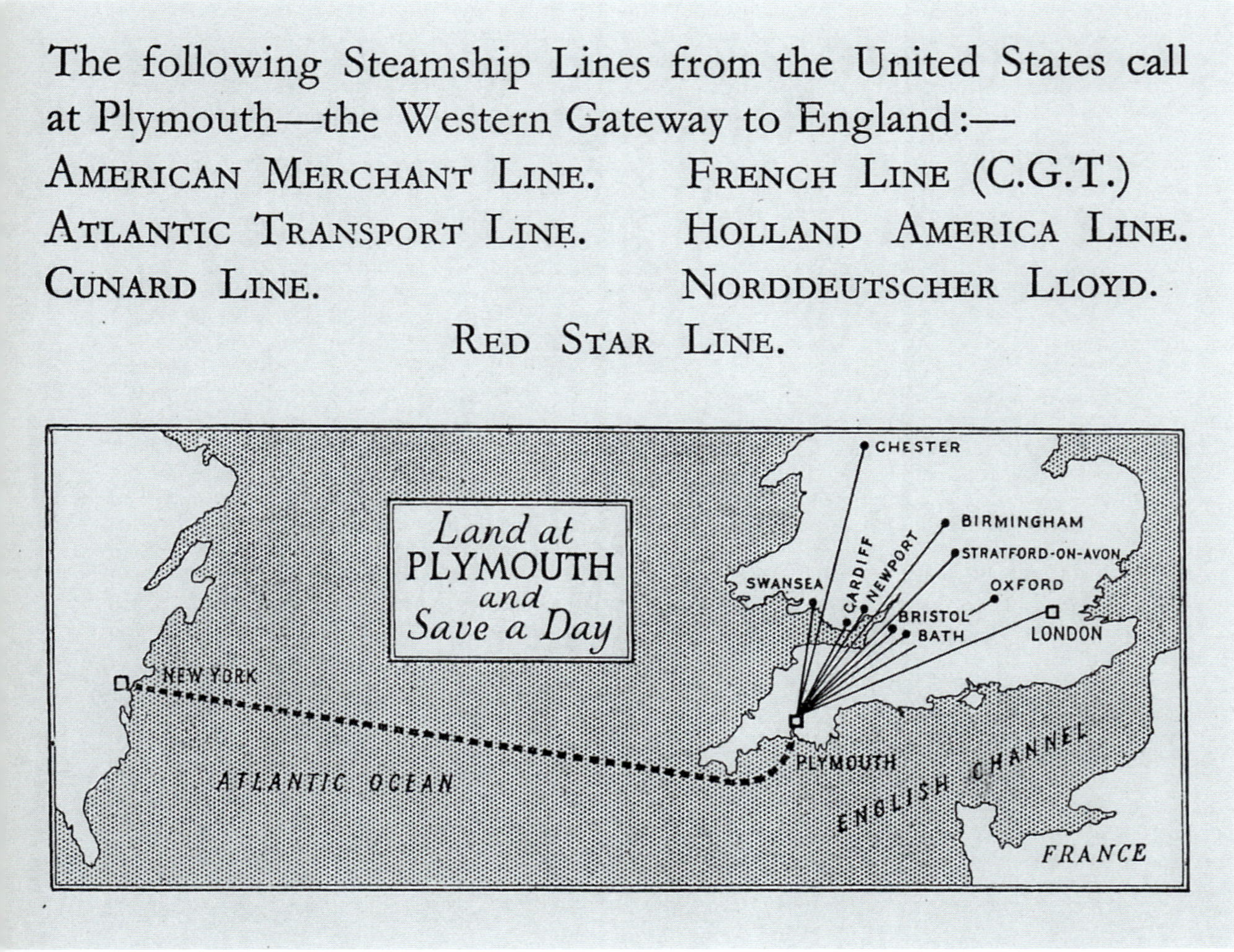

An appeal to North American visitors to 'Land at Plymouth', as included in the 1927 Centennial Presentation for the Baltimore and Ohio Railroad.

stone and steps underlined the shared Anglo-Saxon heritage of Britain and America. 'Devon. The Lovely Land of the Mayflower', 1924, proclaimed:

> Much of the history of the Anglo-Saxon race on both sides of the Atlantic is summed up in the inscription inserted in the sea wall at Plymouth.[17]

Being a vital feature in its Anglo-American appeal, the GWR proudly proclaimed modern Plymouth as the "Gateway into England from the Atlantic Ocean."[18] As the first port of call for many of the prestigious trans-Atlantic shipping companies in the inter-war era, Plymouth was the railhead for vast numbers of American tourists eager to get to London in order to embark upon their various pilgrimages: to effectively assert or reclaim their cultural identity, not least on the grounds of their international standing, politically and economically. This was a process intensified substantially in the context of World War Two – the New World coming to the assistance of the Old – and was thus a highly charged and complex cultural configuration of decisive importance, historically and commercially. A vital factor in the GWR's overall strategy was, of course, its focus upon service within the collective context of pilgrimage to the 'Old Country'.

'Historic Sites and Scenes of England' 1924 edition, the GWR's first and largest work for the American market, read as a cultural litany, with Paddington as the gateway to a priceless heritage; in fact, to an England effectively presented after the manner of a comprehensive itinerary. The full reference is appropriate here so as to convey the desired effect – the total commitment to service and the wealth of cultural experience offered: two definitive characteristics of Great Western Railway identity. London as the metropolitan centre was also clearly defined.

> It is from Paddington that the traveller must start for Royal Windsor or Oxford, or Bath, or that delightful expedition into Shakespeare's country which is destined hereafter to become one of the most cherished and agreeable memories of this never-to-be-forgotten English tour. The very names of Windsor, Oxford, Stratford Upon Avon and Bath suffice to conjure up visions of those glories and traditions of which the American and the Englishman are today equally proud. If our visitor has a fancy for the folk-lore to remote antiquity, he can investigate Arthurian Legend in situ, either on the cliffs of Cornwall, in South Wales, or amidst the rocks of Scilly or in Avalonian Glastonbury itself. The student of ecclesiastical history or Medieval architecture will be able to compress a visit to many of the famous Cathedrals of England into a fortnight or even less. Possibly the traveller is specially interested in the battlefields of history. If this is so, he will be grateful for the information that in many instances the Great Western Railway passed in close proximity to notable British, Roman and Saxon earthworks ... to such celebrated scenes of Medieval contest as Shrewsbury and Evesham and to spots which witnessed the fierce fights and sieges of the Civil War, such as Worcester, Gloucester, Newbury, Oxford and elsewhere.[19]

'Shakespeare Land' and "the green heart of England" was, together with the appeal of London, the most popular of all the GWR locations, as evident in the range of literary works devoted to it in both independent company publications and in the joint initiatives distributed through the Four Companies and the Tourist Association in the thirties. It was also an early choice as the subject for the "radio broadcasts" across the USA and Canada.[20] 'Shakespeare Land' was in every sense directed at the North American market. Stratford is quoted here again, not in repetition, but to show, in this instance, the range of quality of service offered – the process being very much part of the overall cultural product. Having asserted the unique cultural legacy of Stratford and its greatest son, Fraser then continued:

> The Great Western Railway of England have arranged combined rail and road tours from London Paddington Station to the Stratford Upon Avon district, via Leamington Spa, to enable tourists with but little time at their disposal to see all the chief places of interest in Shakespeare's Country in one day ... The whole tour only takes ten hours ... Motor coaches await the tour passengers at Leamington Spa Station and the journey is continued by road, passing through the wide tree-lined streets of this delightful Spa. Though completely modern, Leamington stands on the site of a Saxon village which must have been visited frequently by Shakespeare in his rambles through the countryside.[21]

This was England from the express train and luxury motor coach, with an emphasis upon close organisation and efficiency, ease of access and the highest standards of service. Fraser assured her readers that departure from Paddington guaranteed them the fastest and nearest access to rural England. Moreover, as with the 'Through the Window' series, the glories of the pastoral English landscape offered added enjoyment, but in one telling paragraph, Fraser set out an interesting, if unintentional contrast, in her evocative rendering of the rural/historical heritage celebrating apparent continuity, she wrote of the view from the train:

> Every mile of the way between Paddington and Leamington Spa there are fertile pasturelands and low-lying, wooded hills ... a graciously lovely landscape, typical of the scenes which Shakespeare loved, traversed by Roman and British roadways which were ancient in his day, and giving glimpses of time-worn churches, no less familiar to his eyes than the names of the old-world towns and villages through which the train rushes were to his ears.[22]

In this deliberate marketing strategy of the journey, noted in Chapter One as 'prestige advertising' Fraser registered no note of irony in the juxtaposition of ancient roadways, time worn churches and the impact and speed of the train itself within such a setting. The express was, by definition, the epitome of modern engineering achievement. This perspective applied equally to the Great Western's concept of the 'Land Cruise' employing first class train travel, luxury motor coaches and the best of hotels, en-route, in the determined quest for rural, historic England. It was the recurrent theme of the interaction of historic community and modern, progressive service, thus London, Oxford and Stratford were obvious destinations for members of the International Hotel Alliance, visiting England from New York in April 1926. 'The Great Western Railway of England: Souvenir'[23] recorded the event with commemorative copies being presented to the visitors. As in all such prestigious initiatives, dedicated to progressive cosmopolitan reference, two special trains met the S.S. France on its arrival at Plymouth thereby confirming luxury travel throughout, from New York to London. The GWR's own hotels, likewise, conformed to American expectations and general perceptions of England in their intended combination of the traditional and modern as at Tregenna Castle Hotel, St. Ives.

> [Tregenna] unites all the old-world charm of the higher class English mansion with modern improvements which tend to make hotel life comfortable and attractive.[24]

The Hotel's literature was instructive in its conspicuous celebration of the professional ideal as detailed, for example, in Harold Perkin's 'The Rise Of Professional Society,' 1989. In all cases, imagery and association reflected the characteristic representations of affluence, hierarchy and authority, thus drawing heavily upon historical and received rural-aesthetic constructions. Thus, The Manor House Hotel, Moreton-

GREAT WESTERN RAILWAY

Attractive Rail and Motor Coach

DAY TOURS *from* LONDON

embracing

1 STOKE POGES, BURNHAM BEECHES, BEACONSFIELD, THE CHALFONTS AND ETON AND WINDSOR.

2 LEAMINGTON SPA, KENILWORTH, GUY'S CLIFFE, WARWICK, AND THE SHAKESPEARE COUNTRY.

On Weekdays during the Summer Months

TICKETS for these Tours and full particulars as to Train Service, Etc., obtainable at

PADDINGTON STATION Booking Office. G.W.R. American Bureau, 7 & 8 Charing Cross. Pickfords, Ltd., 206 High Holborn. American Express Co., Inc., 6 Haymarket. Thos. Cook & Son, Ltd., Berkeley Street, London, W.1. Frames Tours, Ltd., 92 Southampton Row, London.

HISTORIC SITES AND SCENES OF ENGLAND.

THE DEPARTURE OF THE PILGRIM FATHERS.
(The "Mayflower" sailed from Plymouth on September 6th, 1620.)

ISSUED BY THE
GREAT WESTERN RAILWAY COMPANY
OF ENGLAND.

PADDINGTON STATION,
LONDON, W.
August, 1910.

JAMES C. INGLIS,
General Manager.

Your Travel Problems Solved

Apply IN ENGLAND *to*

THE SUPERINTENDENT OF THE LINE,
GREAT WESTERN RAILWAY,
PADDINGTON STATION,
LONDON, W.2

and

IN THE UNITED STATES OF AMERICA *to*

K. W. C. GRAND,
General Agent,
GREAT WESTERN RAILWAY OF ENGLAND,
505 FIFTH AVENUE, NEW YORK

Visitors from Overseas will be cordially welcomed at the GREAT WESTERN RAILWAY COMPANY'S
OVERSEAS TRAVEL BUREAU
7 & 8 CHARING CROSS
WHITEHALL, S.W.1

&

TOURS ARRANGED TO SUIT REQUIREMENTS

Printed in Great Britain by Kelly & Kelly Ltd., London, E.C.2

FISHGUARD BAY HOTEL

GOODWICK (Pemb.)

(Under the Management of the Great Western Railway.)

Ideally situated, overlooking the harbour and surrounding country. A delightful place to stay at en route to or from Ireland, or for a Summer or Winter holiday. Sub-tropical Gardens of great extent and beauty. Electric Lift. Central Heating. Service Telephone in every room. Croquet, Hard Tennis Court. Private accommodation for Sea Bathing. Trout Fishing in 8 miles of private and preserved water in Western Cleddau River, and Deep-Sea Fishing. 9-hole Golf Course near. Billiards. 12 Lock-up Garages.

Winter terms (Oct. 1st to May 31st, excluding Christmas, Easter and Whitsun), 4½ guineas per week including all meals, accommodation, baths and early morning tea.

Book to Fishguard Harbour Station. Hotel Porter meets trains and conveys luggage free of charge.

Illustrated Brochure obtainable from Hotel Manager, or Mr. G. J. Walker, Great Western Royal Hotel, Paddington Station, London, W.2.

Telegrams: "BAY HOTEL, GOODWICK." 'Phone: FISHGUARD 234.

Above, left: *Notice for American Visitors included in 'Oxford and Shakespeare Land'.*
Above, right: *Advertisement for Fishguard Bay Hotel included in 1935 edition of Holiday Haunts.* Author's collection

Facing page, top: *Title page of 'Historic Sites And Scenes' 1910 ed. The first edition dated from 1904 and was directed at North American audiences.*
Facing page, bottom: *Notice of combined Road-Rail Tours – 'Oxford and Shakespeare Land'.* Author's collection

hampstead, Devon, with all the attendant perceptions of seeing and being seen: of conspicuous success.

> "Completed in 1907, to replication, enlarged in 1935, is a Jacobean replica in stone, with stone mullions, oak window frames and stone-tiled roof, built on broad South and West terraces ... In every direction are beautiful views across pleasure grounds and rock gardens falling to a lake and to the River Bovey which flows through the property, winding through woods and meadow lands. In the distance are vistas of the incomparable moors. Easdon Tor is within two miles of the house."[25]

Fishguard Bay Hotel was likewise celebrated for its luxuriant, exotic gardens resonant of imperial and international character generally. The carefully landscaped gardens were host to plants and trees from all parts of the world as the company was clearly anxious to emphasise.[26]

In both its work with the British Travel Association and in terms of the specific company-based literature, the GWR mounted a powerful campaign to promote Britain internationally. The interactive nature of its commercial and cultural objectives has been emphasised, but in particular reference to the latter, the GWR was by far the most detailed and committed of the four great companies in promoting and celebrating the role of historical development; the cultural impact of landscapes, personalities and events. London was always of paramount importance in GWR considerations.

London

The GWR's presentation of London focused upon the Capital as the hub of race, nation and empire. Company publicity identified the city as the central expression of the national narrative integrating themes of past and present, country and city, people and place. Historical and cultural perspectives thus defined the company's approach. Its concern was, therefore, primarily with the 'official', received symbols of English cultural heritage as in Westminster Abbey, St. Paul's Cathedral, Westminster, Whitehall and other such institutions, landmarks and their associated personalities. 'Holiday Haunts' was unequivocal in its celebration of London's role in the context of 'Greater Britain'.

> Full of beauty, life, colour and interest with the ever enthralling ebb and flow of humanity against its vast background of history and legend, London is more than the hub of the greatest Empire that has ever been: it is the concentrated essence of the centuries and an epitome of British history – the most fascinating holiday centre in the world.[27]

Westminster Abbey exemplified the pronounced historically-rooted, ethnically-defined presentation offered by the GWR. This was evident in the company's specially commissioned work,

'Cathedrals', 1924, the first in the themed trilogy completed with the publication of 'Abbeys' in 1925 and 'Castles' in 1926. 'Cathedrals' underlined the sense of tradition and continuity, characteristic of the GWR's literary perspective generally. Westminster Abbey was singular in its expression of national identity.

> It is the most unique and priceless treasure of our race – a great heritage from our Anglo-Saxon progenitors. It is the most widely celebrated church in the British Empire, occupying at the same time a position without parallel amongst the ecclesiastical edifices of the world. Here, before the High Altar, all the sovereigns, excepting Edward V, have been crowned, from Harold, the last of the Saxon monarchs and William the Conqueror, to our august sovereign, King George V.[28]

Moreover, to stress the essential imperial theme, the account made direct reference to the Scottish Stone of Scone, the ancient seat of Scots investiture, as brought to London by Edward I. This effectively symbolised overall English authority.

> Here is the Coronation Chair with the Scone stone, or Stone of Destiny on which Celtic Kings were crowned. In that chair every British sovereign since Edward I has been crowned...[29]

Together with past monarchs, Westminster Abbey was also acclaimed as the resting place of "the illustrious dead [whose tombs] are an epitome of our Empire."[40] Statesmen, philanthropists, military men, poets, men of letters and "Empire" builders were listed. Paramount position, however, was accorded to "The Unknown Warrior."

> In the centre of the Nave is undoubtedly the greatest of all tributes – that to the Unknown Warrior – the memorial of our reverence for the great and glorious British dead who sacrificed all for the honour of Country and Empire in the Great War. No more fitting resting place, no more honoured spot, could have been chosen for the Nation's tribute to its sons and daughters than this.[30]

The manifold resonance and collective experiences of World War One were thus thematically integrated into the national narrative in the past – present, nationally – internationally perceived dialogue, definitive of GWR concern.

The imperially-inspired theme was sustained in the company's reference to St. Paul's Cathedral.

> St. Pauls may rightly claim to be the Imperial Cathedral of the British nation ... throughout the ages it is to St. Pauls that men's minds have turned instinctively in any great time of crisis or rejoicing in the life of the Nation. It is the official Church of Empire ... a spiritual centre firmly fixed in the hub of the Universe ...[31]

GWR poster work underlined the company's close identification with London's 'official' character, the perspective of Crown Imperial and sceptre and sword. The Palace of Westminster, the Tower of London, St. Pauls Cathedral and militarily inspired depictions as in the Horse Guards were prominent, as were Whitehall, Buckingham Palace, Tower Bridge, Westminster and 'Big Ben', "the Empire's Timepiece",[32] for example, in official photographs.

Two thematically related dimensions clearly definitive of the GWR's literary work on London, were those of the capital's definitive historical and rurally-based identifications. Beyond London's major set-piece landscapes, the historical perspective was integral to the capital's identity. 'Holiday Haunts' was explicit.

> [London's] history is so plainly written for all to see that the mere noting of street and place-names yields to the passer-by an infinity of interest ... St. Clement-the-Dane testifies that the Danes once had a small town on the site ... Savoy Hill, Essex Street, Norfolk Street, and the innumerable little roadways running down to the Embankment commemorate the various sites of the great riverside palaces of bygone nobles. Ludgate Hill preserves the name of a half-legendary British King. Newgate Street recalls the infamous prison which once stood nearby. ... Blackfriars and Whitefriars are reminiscent of long-vanished monasteries.[33]

London's original rural identification was also celebrated in similar fashion.

> ... the greatest city in the world breathes the very spirit of a country village in the majority of its most important place-names! Hatton Garden, Covent Garden and Short's Garden on the outskirts of the City proper. Curiously named "Poultry" and the essentially countrified "Lanes" in the heart of the City area: Love Lane, Ivy Lane, Water Lane, Maiden Lane and endless other rustic fancies like charming Apple Tree Yard, St. James; Cherry Garden Street, Bermondsey; Shepherdess Walk, Hoxton; Lavender Grove and Forest Road, Hackney; and the pastoral-sounding Lincoln's Inn Fields, Bunhill Fields, Chalk Farm, Primrose Hill and Gospel Oak.[34]

Elsewhere, 'Holiday Haunts' also cited "The Strand", reminiscent of the days when that great thoroughfare was the grass-grown bank of the River Thames. Likewise, "Haymarket" recalls the not so distant days when that broad street was thronged with hay-wains.[35] This heavily historical and rural perspective was central to the GWR's self-image; in its conspicuous promotion of an overall integrated identity that could relate deepest rural England to the world's largest city and, indeed, to the properties of Empire.

One of the clearest indications of this theme of integration was that of the company's representation of the River Thames. In 'The Glories of the Thames', GWR 1923, the company proclaimed: "From its very source to its mouth, the Thames is inextricably linked with British history"[36] Similar sentiments applied in a feature in a later work of August, 1937. "Holiday Charms of the Thames" declared: "Some rivers in particular have a place in men's affections and this is true of none more than the Thames. An England without the Thames is unthinkable."[37]

The river featured prominently in GWR poster work on London, most powerfully, as the great highway of commerce and trade linking the capital with overseas locations in a dynamically charged national and international configuration. River excursions and an extensive range of rail-river combined tours intensified the experience of the Thames. "Holiday Charms", 1937, identified the combined excursion:- rail to Marlow, steamer to Windsor and thence rail to Paddington, as the most popular of these options. With Windsor as the main objective, the company noted that approximately 200,000 visitors took one or other of these trips in the 1936 season.

Looking beyond London, historic Oxford, Chester and Salisbury, for example, were identified as sites of deep Anglo-American resonances, whilst further westward, the Wye Valley was always incorporated in American-led itineraries.

Facing page, bottom: *Photographic page on London, from Holiday Haunts. Main photograph – a dramatic portrait of Big Ben, proclaimed in typical GWR terms as 'The Empire's Timepiece'.* Author's collection

Facing page, top: *Advertisement: Chester, celebrating its historical and scenic attractions whilst also emphasising its many modern facilities. 'North Wales. The British Tyrol,' 1906, claimed that the history of Chester was 'inseparably bound up with the history of our nation and race' and that many thousands of American visitors came there each year.* Author's collection

ST. MARTIN-IN-THE-FIELDS, TRAFALGAR SQUARE

THE EMPIRE'S TIMEPIECE

Chester

Still sheltered by its Walls, the only complete circuit in England, the riverside City of Chester offers to the visitor attractions, both ancient and modern, in unsurpassed variety.

Built by the Romans and rebuilt and extended by the Saxons, the Walls have largely accounted for the preservation of Chester's world-famous " Rows," Cathedral, monastic buildings, old churches and mediæval houses.

The unique " Rows," known to have existed in 1303, now contribute not a little to the City's fame as a shopping centre. That Chester is not content to live in the past alone is also evidenced by its excellent hotels, cafés, car parks and transport services, and there is an almost unlimited choice of entertainment, sport and recreation.

Chester's ready accessibility by road and rail also makes it an ideal centre from which to explore the beautiful countryside of Cheshire and North Wales.

Send a p.c. to the Publicity Officer, Dept. 3, Chester, for beautifully Illustrated Official Guide.

The Wye Valley

The GWR played a central role in the appreciation of the Wye Valley. 'Historic Sites and Scenes of England' included the following assurance for its readers: "For the traveller who has little time at his disposal there is no better way of seeing the beauty of the sylvan Wye than from the carriage of a Great Western train."[38] Similarly, 'The Wye Valley', Vol II, proclaimed "The Great Western Railway holds the keys to the Wye Valley, as it does that of almost all famous holiday-haunts of the West."[39] whilst 'The Wye Valley'. Vol I, noted that, "the Cambrian railroad [GWR, following the Railway's Act, 1921] is on more consistently intimate terms with the river than the road."[40]

Both volumes of 'The Wye Valley' focused upon the sense of spectacle and aesthetic distinction but it is also evident that the literary style celebrated the sensation of movement as reflected in the references to successive, challenging angles of vision and the extensive recourse to active verbs - "climbing, rushing, falling, running," – in the interactive presentation of the train within the landscape. Thus, the thematic focus of journeying and of progressive discovery was not simply stated but was engaged through active participation, after the manner of R.G. Bradley's "poetry of rapid motion through rural England"[41]

This overall perspective on the Wye Valley inevitably sharpened the commercial potential of the line, not least, in terms of the North American market, given the stylised focus of aesthetic, historical encounter. As always, the GWR stressed the easy access to the Wye Valley and the various, convenient starting points. It offered three particular gateways, each one linked to Paddington, to underline this convenience and to promote cultural and collective identity. Llanidloes marked the northern approach, with Hereford and Ross-on-Wye offering access to the lower reaches. Through trains from Paddington served each of these three 'gateways' whilst Moat Lane Junction, for Llanidloes, also catered for valuable trade from Liverpool, Manchester and the North generally. This survey concentrates on 'The Wye Valley,' Vol II.

The second volume covered the better known and easily accessible lower districts along the river, from Hereford to Chepstow, where it met the Severn. This entire stretch of the River Wye was presented in the literary context of the picturesque and the sublime, given the numerous opportunities en-route, to celebrate the dramatic combinations of landscape, historical interest and challenging aesthetic perspectives.

Hereford was the key location in every sense. It was presented in terms of its distinguished historical identity which was paramount, but the overall cultural context was significantly enhanced through the specific interaction of the historical imagery – the iconography of cathedral, castle and city, – with the rich, rural landscape that characterised the wider social and political identity. Together, they evoked Englishness, as in the resonant cultural imagery of "the English cathedral city that has stood for more than a thousand years on the banks of the Wye. [in a landscape] largely made up of tree-clad hills, and meadows dotted with pollard oaks."[42] The GWR was forthright in asserting historical identity, as in 'Holiday Haunts'.

> Hereford was one of the great towns of Saxon England and was the capital of the Mercian Kings, who founded the cathedral, which in its present form, is chiefly from the eleventh century. Apart from the fine Norman work, Hereford Cathedral is rich in treasures and curiosities. The Mappa Mundi, a great wall map dating from 1300, is unique and the chained library contains over 2000 rare and beautiful books.[43]

Attention was also drawn to the Cathedral School, endowed in 1382; The Bishop's Palace, the castle, "built by Harold in 1055 . . . completely demolished by Cromwell's soldiers," and "some beautiful half-timbered houses to link the town with its long and troubled past."[44] The emphasis in this literary celebration was clearly that of a distinguished cultural heritage celebrated in a clearly formulated past-present spectrum.

In maintaining the stylistic presentation of 'the journey', however, 'The Wye Valley' created the spatial dimension and the sensation of onward progress by defining the landscape between Hereford and Ross-on-Wye thematically, as the 'prelude' to ever-more impressive experience.

> The portion of the Wye Valley that lies between Hereford and Ross must be regarded as a prelude to that supremely impressive scenery which is to be found on either side of "the bounteous river" between Ross and its junction with the great tidal stream, "the Severn Sea." You no sooner quit the capital of Pomonia than you find yourself amongst verdant meadows and fruitful orchards, traversing some of the richest pasture land in all England.[45]

The sensation of movement, surprise, discovery and, significantly, expectation is evident here. It was also significant that this landscape "between Hereford and Ross" represented the fitting 'prelude', hence the thematic, preparatory imagery of prosperity, abundance and stability as conveyed in the celebration of verdant meadows, fruitful orchards and 'richest pasture'.

The Great Western designated Ross-on-Wye "The Gate of the Wye".[46] The imagery of gateways again offered with the sensation of movement; that of entry and exit, of moving from one area to another with all the attendant associations of demarcation, differentiation and hierarchical categorisation that constituted the ongoing sub-text. 'The Wye Valley', Vol II, offered an unequivocal statement of the superlative landscape of the Wye from Ross to Chepstow on almost every page. Having offered a short, historically-defined reference to Ross, the GWR went on to intensify its 'gateway' imagery. Goodrich Castle was celebrated as an aesthetic experience every bit the equal of its historical impact: the one, in effect, informing the other. Both dimensions were celebrated in the GWR's acclamation that the site represented, "The Inner Gate of the Wye".[47] Thus, 'The Wye Valley'.

> The castle as well as the neighbouring church, seem to guard as sentinels the deep gorge at the entrance of which they stand ... the stream almost surrounds three sides of the ancient fortress which reminds one forcibly of the far-famed castles of the Rhineland.[48]

Favourable comparisons of English landscape and architecture with European sites, evident here, enhanced the GWR's English cultural agenda of historical and aesthetic congruence. 'The Wye Valley' also identified Goodrich Castle as 'A Saxon Stronghold'.[49] Looking to perceived cultural credentials, ethnic identification was proclaimed. "Experts pronounce the windows of the river-front to be as Saxon as they can be."[50] The GWR's own commissioned expert, however, thought otherwise. Charles Oman in 'Castles', GWR 1926, declared the keep, the oldest part of the castle, to date from the time of Henry I and was, therefore, clearly Norman.[51]

Facing page, left: *Ross-on-Wye, clearly identified here as 'The Gateway of the Wye Valley'. The town was also the subject of several company-based photographs, given its distinctive location. Maxwell Fraser in 'Winter Resorts' described Ross-on-Wye as 'a pleasant, prosperous old town ... increasingly popular for winter holidays and residence', as depicted here in this early post-war work.* Courtesy Dalkeith Publishing Co.

Facing page, right: *The Wye Valley from the summit at Symonds Yat. This view shows the close proximity of railway and river as emphasised in GWR literature.* Author's collection

Facing page, below: *Symonds Yat station. 'Rambles in the Wye Valley' informed visitors that a path to the summit left the station platform seen here in the foreground.* Author's collection

ROSS-ON-WYE
THE GATEWAY OF THE WYE
GWR
Information and Accommodation List from
The Secretary, Chamber of Commerce, Ross-on-Wye

View from
Picnic Wood.
Symonds Yat.

Having entered the 'Inner Gate', the Great Western's survey then focused on what it considered a definitive location for the entire Wye Valley: the experience of Symonds Yat. Great Western literature in respect of Symonds Yat left no room for misrepresentation. It was a statement of total identity and celebration. 'The Wye Valley' included two particularly significant observations: one, proclaiming the pre-eminent status of Symond's Yat in the hierarchy of aesthetic experience, and the other, recognising the role of the railway in directly contributing to creative perspective.

> Symonds Yat may very well claim to be the most picturesque spot in all England, and the gem of the inland scenery of the National Holiday Line ... You are now in the very heart of the Wye Valley.[52]

From the perspective of the valley floor it was argued that "full justice to the wonderful views can only be obtained from the railway."[53] A.G. Bradley's 'Rivers and Streams of England', 1909, was enlisted by the GWR for 'The Wye Valley', Vol II.

> The railway with the help of tunnelling has broken through all barriers, and for a long distance gives the passenger an admirable passing view one cliff or the other..[54]

The GWR's 'Rambles in the Wye Valley'[55] also informed visitors that the path to the summit at Yat Rock began from the northern end of the station platform. Maxwell Fraser's contribution for 'Holiday Haunts' offered sublime proportions, setting the location into relationship with the surrounding landscape, near and far; from the panoramic heights to the intimacy of riverside detail. It was a powerfully-charged, emotional encounter with landscape, laden with the imagery of harmony and received resonances of an inheritance of fragile form, but vitally of ownership.

> People come from all over the world to see Symonds Yat ... Great orchards, shady woods and fantastically shaped rocks alternate with lush flower-decked pasture lands, tiny cottages of old-world beauty and ancient, lichen-clad churches, backed by the shapely wall of the Welsh Mountains, intensely blue with the magical haze of distance to form the setting for the peerless River, which, as though reluctant to leave such matchless loveliness, sweeps around in a magnificent bend almost forming itself into a circle. Whether seen from the summit of Symonds Yat Rock, or from the waterside, it is a view to remember with joy as long as life lasts[56]

Moving on to Monmouth the Great Western again celebrated the town's history and, in particular, historical and literary figures of recognised cultural resonance. It was the perspective of 'England Triumphant,' a definitively Great Western characterisation. 'The Wye Valley' set the larger rural context; 'Holiday Haunts' provided the historic literary heritage. Thus, 'The Wye Valley' declared of Monmouth:

> It lies embowered among gentle hills, diversified by wood, corn and pasture and rises from the river with considerable stateliness in the form of an ampitheatre.[57]

'Holiday Haunts' built upon this with the historical dimension.

> From the time a Norman castle replaced the ancient Saxon fortress a constant succession of glittering personalities and notable events has ever woven into the splendid fabric of the city's history. In this tiny walled and moated medieval town, Geoffrey of Monmouth was born to enrich the literature of the world by his fabulous histories.[58]

A litany of English cultural achievement followed in 'Holiday Haunts' with the literary legacy of the 'hero' as bequeathed by Geoffrey, Shakespeare, Sir Thomas Malory and Tennyson, but the survey culminated in the celebration of Monmouth's most famous son, King Henry V. Great Western literature proclaimed him, "the most brilliant warrior in the history of our land, the one English king who never knew defeat."[59] Nelson was also linked with the town and, like the Town Gateway and Bridge, commemorating Henry V, so also, Monmouth was host to what 'Holiday Haunts' described as "the finest collection [of Nelsonian relics] of its kind in the world."[60] Collectively, the Great Western's presentation of Monmouth marked the sustained celebration of Englishness integrating rural imagery with the historical and literary record into dramatic experiential encounter by close reference to personage, place and event – an overall expression of cultural authority.

Southward from Monmouth, the Great Western literature focused upon Tintern, setting the location into an overall context of the larger Wye Valley and, beyond that, to an international dimension. The focus was primarily cultural, drawing on a powerful aesthetic and historical perspective as it had been generally throughout the course of the Valley. But Tintern was perceived to be distinct, in as far as 'The Wye Valley' called it, "the great architectural treasure, not only of the Wye Valley, but of the whole of the Welsh Marches. There is nothing quite like Tintern in all England ..."[61] In wider-ranging reference, 'The Wye Valley' continued:

> Can one wonder at the spell which glorious Tintern has exercised over countless generations of travellers and poets? It must help very materially to make the Wye Valley a travel shrine to every member of the Anglo-Saxon race all over the world.[62]

'Holiday Haunts' sustained, indeed, intensified the magical element in the depiction of Tintern and, in doing so, underlined the sense of privileged awareness; informed perception. It was primarily an emotive, aesthetic perspective of encounter within the discourse of citizenship.

> Tintern has such a sublime beauty that it is forever a thing apart in the memory of all who have been there.[63]

Celebrating "the supreme fact of its overwhelming beauty."[64] 'Holiday Haunts' went for heightened sensitivity, akin to the fragility definitive of Symonds Yat. The exclusive, initiate perspective, defining and differentiating "people with spiritual vision", was explicit.

> But if Tintern is fair in the sunshine, there are no words to express its strange and magic beauty in the silvery rays of the moon and during the Harvest Moon period, this ethereal charm culminates in a tradition which draws people from all over the world. The great, Honey-coloured moon then shines through a particular window with weird effect and people with spiritual vision can see the shades of monks who once lived in the Abbey, stealing through the radiant light.[65]

Below Tintern, the River Wye became tidal and the last great landmark was the town of Chepstow. The castle was acclaimed for its superlative situation and, likewise, the efforts of the community "to retain the atmosphere of the Middle Ages."[66] Having offered the panoramic perspective over the course of the railway journey southward through the Wye Valley, 'Holiday Haunts' included one further notable example. This concerned the Wyndcliffe, 800 feet above the river at Chepstow. In the structured presentation of this dramatic landscape, as defined by the vantage point of the observer and their relationship to it, the GWR provided a further expression of thematic integration; that of harmonious relationship between landscape and people.

> From the summit of the cliff, the varied beauties of the counties of Gloucester, Somerset, Wilts, Devon,

Facing page: *Tintern Abbey – and the Wye Valley generally – was the subject of LMS and GWR publicity initiatives. Both companies exploited the rich resources of history and landscape in shared territory from Chester and Shrewsbury southward to Bristol, Bath and Weston-Super-Mare.* Courtesy, Dalkeith Publishing Co Ltd.

Glamorgan, Hereford, Monmouth, Brecon and Worcester can be seen spread out like a vast and exquisitely coloured contour map and threaded by the silvery lines of the Wye, the Usk and the mighty Severn.[67]

The GWR's literature on the Wye Valley was in many respects an innovative exercise in literary representation within the context of railway-based publications in Britain. It exemplified the panoramic vision. It also included sustained representations of picturesque perspectives organised around a range of challenging angles of vision – a perceptual process which, like the principle of panoramic vision, shared the pursuit of dramatic, novel spectacle in landscape. This conceptual structure – of distance and proximity, and of high-line and low level projection delivered in the progress of the train – presented a heightened appreciation of landscape and, in the cultural agenda of the GWR, sealed the relationship between historical process, its setting and its evaluation. Tintern Abbey, or Goodrich Castle, within the carefully composed rural-historical environment that similarly contextualised the likes of Hereford and Monmouth, all served to reflect the GWR's appreciation of the need to deliver distinctive, dynamic literary perspectives of both open and subliminal cultural and political resonance. Thus, 'The Wye Valley', in exemplifying these qualities, can be said to directly challenge any suggestion that GWR literature was stylistically and thematically unadventurous, instinctively conservative in policy and practice and, in terms of its wider reference, no more than that of guide-book status.

REFERENCES – CHAPTER THREE

1: G.W.R. Magazine, January, 1932. P8.

2: Lord Hacking. Quoted, Felix Pole, His Book, P205. Douglas Hacking, M.P., Secretary of the Department of Overseas Trade became Chairman of the Association's Executive Committee in February 1929, holding this office until 1950.

3: GWR Magazine, October, 1935, P560.

4: British Tourist Authority. The British Travel Association, 1929-1969, London, 1970. P11.

5: GWR Magazine November, 1931. P469.

6: Ibid P469.

7: P.R.O. Rail 1080: 585. 12-9-29.

8: GWR Magazine June, 1927. P218.

9: GWR Magazine November, 1931. P469.

10: P.R.O. Rail 1080-583 5-1-26.

11: P.R.O. Rail 1080-584 15-5-28.

12: GWR Rural London, 1924 ed. P16. See also Anthony D. Smith. The Ethnic Origins of Nationals. Blackwell, Oxford, 1986. Chapter Eight: Legends and Landscapes.

13: GWR Places Of Pilgrimage For American Travellers, 1925 ed. P7.

14: GWR Rural London, 1924. P6.

15: GWR Places of Pilgrimage, 1924. P34.

16: S.P.B. Mais. Glorious Devon. GWR 1934 ed. P73.

17: GWR 'Devon. The Lovely Land of the Mayflower', GWR 1924. P2. "Much of the history of the Anglo-Saxon race on both sides of the Atlantic is summed up in the inscription inserted in the sea wall at Plymouth." The plaque to the Pilgrim Fathers was dedicated in 1891 – at a time when Anglo-American sentiments of inheritance and destiny were fulsome.

18: GWR Great Western Railway Docks, 1937. P76.

19: GWR Historic Sites and Scenes, 1910 ed. P14.

20: P.R.O. Rail: 1080-587 Minutes 1211 and 1234. British Tourist Authority. The British Travel Association 1929-1969. London. 1970. P5.

21: Maxwell Fraser, Shakespeare Land, GWR: Associated Companies, 1933. P1.

22: Ibid P1.

23: Great Western Railway of England Souvenir. Log of Special Trains conveying American Members of the International Hotel Alliance from Plymouth to Paddington. April 9, 1926.

24: GWR Hotels And Catering Services 1937. P6. The Hotels literature was instructive in its conspicuous celebration of the professional ideal as detailed, for example, in Harold Perkin's 'The Rise Of Professional Society', Routledge, London. 1989. In all cases, imagery and association reflected the characteristic representations of affluence, hierarchy and authority and, therein, drew heavily upon historical and received rural-aesthetic constructions. Thus, The Manor House Hotel, Moretonhampstead, Devon with all the attendant perceptions of seeing and being seen. "Completed in 1907, to replication, enlarged in 1935, is a Jacobean replica in stone, with stone mullions, oak window frames and stone-tiled roof, built on broad South and West terraces... In every direction are beautiful views across pleasure grounds and rock gardens falling to a lake and to the River Bovey which flows through the property winding through woods and meadow lands. In the distance are vistas of the incomparable moors. Easdon Tor is within two miles of the house." ibid P41. Fishguard Bay Hotel was celebrated for its luxuriant, exotic gardens resonant of imperial and international reference generally. The carefully landscaped gardens were host to plants and trees from all parts of the world as the company was anxious to emphasise. See GWR Magazine, May, 1938, P199, and the earlier mission statement. – Souvenir of British Empire Exhibition. GWR 1924, P19.

25: Ibid P41.

26: GWR Magazine. May 1938 P199.

27: GWR Holiday Haunts 1936. P44.

28: GWR Cathedrals 1924. Pps 3-4.

29: Ibid P4.

30: Ibid P5.

31: Ibid P8.

32: Holiday Haunts 1938 P18.

33: Holiday Haunts 1936 P41.

34: Ibid P42.

35. Ibid P41.

36: GWR The Glories of The Thames 1923 P2.

37: GWR Magazine August, 1937.

38: A.M. Broadley. Historic Sites and Scenes of England, GWR, 1904, 1924 ed, P57.

39: GWR Wye Valley. Vol. Two, 1924. P5

40: GWR Wye Valley, Vol. One, 1924, P3.

41: A.G. Bradley. The Rivers and Streams Of England. A and C Black. London. 1909. The GWR drew substantially in theme and style from Bradley. See, particularly, pps 193-196 and Bradley's total identification with "the poetry of rapid motion through rural England [and] the corner-seat of a railway carriage." P194.

42: A.M. Broadley. North Wales. The British Tyrol, GWR (1904) 1924 ed. P86.

43: GWR Holiday Haunts, 1937 P950.

44: Ibid P950.

45: GWR Wye Valley, Vol. Two. P13.

46: Ibid P14.

47: Ibid P16.

48: Ibid P16.

49: Ibid P16.

50: Ibid P16. The geo-political significance of the Welsh Marches contextualised in the thrust of GWR English hegemony has resonance here.

51: Charles Osman. Castles, GWR, 1926. P149.

52: GWR Wye Valley, Vol. 2. P17.

53: Ibid P17.

54: Ibid P17.

55: Hugh E. Page. Rambles And Walking Tours In The Wye Valley, GWR 1938. Re-printed British Railways, 1951, Ramble No. 5. P40.

56: GWR Holiday Haunts,. 1936. P949.

57: GWR Wye Valley, Vol. Two. P19.

58: GWR Holiday Haunts,. 1936. P853.

59: Ibid P853.

60: Ibid P853.

61: GWR The Wye Valley, Vol. Two. P25.

62: Ibid P26.

63: GWR Holiday Haunts, 1936. P854.

64: Ibid P854.

65: Ibid P854.

66: Ibid P851.

67: Ibid P852.

CHAPTER FOUR

WESTERN WONDERLANDS

Although the GWR presented the strongest imagery of, and associations with, Englishness of all four companies in the inter-war era, it also stressed a further, very different, cultural identification. In its representation of specific regions "half foreign to England", as S P B Mais put it, the company celebrated Cornwall, Wales, Southern Ireland and, initially, Brittany, as qualitatively distinct from England; as romantically charged, mystical lands of dramatic landscapes and people. These were the ancient 'Celtic' domains, places of infinite beauty, endlessly fascinating in their would-be total contrast with English landscape and traditions. The GWR's insistence upon this clear distinction was, of course, an invaluable marketing strategy which it employed to its utmost; although the directed sense of contrast also reflected an often less than subtle, but inevitable precedence on the part of the English, or Anglo-Saxon, tradition. The 'Celtic' lands were essentially places to visit, to experience as a spectacle. However beautiful, mysterious or dramatic they might be, their role was clearly recreational in either a popular or more culturally exclusive representation. In all instances, as this chapter indicates, these locations were ultimately "holiday playgrounds" from which the traveller eventually returned and against which representations of Englishness could be delineated.

This perspective could not have been better exemplified than in the final section of A.M. Broadley's 'Southern Ireland, Its Lakes and Landscapes', July 1904. Setting the scene of the homeward journey – "the morning express bearing you swiftly eastward... ample leisure over a capital breakfast admirably served in one of the luxurious corridor coaches... the exchange of ideas, impressions and reminiscences"... the definitive context, the urban-metropolitan agenda is revealed: "One returns to England" from one of the "playgrounds of Empire".

> One *returns* to England with a profound conviction that nothing could possibly be brighter than the prospects of South and South-Western Ireland as one of the great *playgrounds* of the British Empire.[1]

The classifications were, likewise, indicative of leisured, affluent status and, therein, of authority.

> For the sportsman, be he angler, golfer, cyclist or pedestrian ... To the historian, the antiquarian and the thoughtful [in] pilgrimage To the historic sites, scenes and shrines....[2]

Wales

The GWR's presentation of Wales, beyond, that is, the heavily industrialised 'valleys' and coastal regions of South Wales, was that of a land of romantic spectacle. 'Cardigan Bay Resorts', 1925 set the style for 'Celtic'-inspired adventure; differentiating the observer and the observed.

> With all this glamour of history, song, sea, wild romantic scenery, of cromlech, castle cray and llyn, there is all that we moderns demand for either recreation or residence.[3]

'Through The Window. Paddington To Birkenhead', 1925 drew an even more explicit distinction clearly underlining English cultural authority. Subtitled, 'The Welsh Marches', this section of the book reflected the company's perspective on King Edward I and the conquest of Wales in the thirteenth century. There was also, perhaps, a certain parallel, contemporary resonance for the GWR in terms of its recent acquisition of the extensive Cambrian Railway, through the company Groupings, in the Railway Act of 1921.[4]

> The rugged landscape with its natural fortresses and vantage points, sheltering valleys and excellent possibilities for ambushing tactics, helps imagination to conjure up a vivid picture of the long and bitter struggle between a valiant, turbulent and almost unconquerable race with its home in the mountains and the greater nation advancing across the eastern lowlands to force upon its troublesome neighbour a measure of subjection which time has happily turned into a bond of union. Here is stage worthy of the drama played out upon it – but we may think of King Edward the First of England as something much better than a stage hero. He was every inch a statesman who saw through conflict to the ultimate good.[5]

Structurally, the passage was organised around contrasts – England; eastern lowlands, civilisation and progressive order; Wales, that of western wild freedom; of romantically-perceived mountain people committed to a tribal, warrior culture, ultimately doomed to extinction. The great Edwardian castles that ringed Wales which were so enthusiastically celebrated in GWR promotional literature – 'The Country of Castles' – were powerful symbols of English military, economic and cultural supremacy.

'North Wales. The British Tyrol', 1924 ed. carried two particularly apt statements. The first, from the 'Preface', was resonant of the urbanised, twentieth century society to which this literature was targeted.

> Year after year a period of rest and change becomes more and more a necessity of human existence and the need of holiday haunts and health and pleasure resorts easily accessible and inexpensive grows consequently more urgent and more universal to the busy toilers in great cities.[6]

The second extract, again from the Preface, was in fact the GWR quoting 'The National Geographic Magazine,' Washington, 1923. It presented Wales as an aesthetic and historical experience. From a somewhat patronising tone, initially, favourable comparisons were then drawn on an international scale, but, despite the litany of delights, this portrayal of Wales, like that by the GWR of Southern Ireland and Cornwall, fashioned a two-dimensional identity. It was a classic statement of landscape as recreation and spectacle.

> Within this little principality, having an area considerably smaller than New Jersey, one will find the loftiest peaks and finest mountain scenery of England and Wales; the loveliest waterfalls of the British Isles; beaches that rival those of Atlantic City, Deauville or Brighton; streams that team with trout and other fish dear to the heart of the angler; footpaths through vale and forest that cannot be surpassed in the Tyrol or the Pyranees, and the grey ruins of tessellated towers and frowning bastions each of which has its own tale to tell of romantic adventures and of daring in the Dark or the Middle Ages....[7]

Mid and North Wales was identified as having great potential for holiday traffic in the early twenties, to rival and surpass that of the West of England. Most certainly, the GWR up-dated the former Cambrian Railway and provided much improved facilities and access, as it also did in West Wales with its promotional work on 'The Country of Castles,' and its 'The Garden of Wales'

Caer Cynan Castle in Carmarthenshire. From a colour print, Holiday Haunts 1934, heading the section on South Wales and Monmouthshire. Author's collection

The famous and awesome Precipice Walk, Dolgelley, North Wales; a landscape of sublime proportions characteristic of the western wonderland. Author's collection

London By Night. Three definitive features characterise this poster: The Tower of London, the River Thames and Tower Bridge. Collectively, they embody Englishness, as celebrated by the GWR. The Tower testifies to the ongoing historical tradition: the Thames, here bathed in moonlight, represents both the romantic imagery of historical and aesthetic association, and that of the great national and international highway of trade (note the incoming ship): Tower Bridge, raised for the ship to pass, dominates the surrounding dockland as an imposing gateway and landmark.

London was celebrated as the Heart or Hub of Empire, as evident in both the literature and poster work of the GWR. This portrayal of the cavalryman is resonant of the company's commitment to the perspective of 'sword and sceptre', empire and national pride. Courtesy Dalkeith Publishing Co.

The Cornish fishing village with its imagery of the harbour, cottages and hillside, their seagulls, and, crucially, the men at work on their nets or boats, was central to the GWR's presentation of Cornwall. Simplicity, order and continuity resonated through the company's literature for the likes of Looe, Polperro, Mevagissey, Mousehole and St Ives. Courtesy Dalkeith Publishing Co.

The front cover of Maxwell Fraser's 'Southern Ireland' 1932. This was a much more accessible work in its content, presentation and style than that of A M Broadley's 'Southern Ireland, Its Lakes and Landscapes' 1904. The latter, as with Broadley's work, generally, was clearly outdated by the early thirties. Fraser's Ireland was that of a romantic wonderland, 'a country of glorious lakes and mountains ... drenched in history, rich in folk-lore'. Author's collection

– Cardiganshire and Carmarthenshire. The ex Cambrian Railway network was thoroughly Great Westernised. Taking stations alone, one might cite the transformation at Oswestry, 1929, or Aberystwyth, 1926, for example, as indicative of the resonance of the corporate identity. Authority was also enlisted. What formerly had been designated 'The Cambrian Coast,' 1922, became in the GWR work of 1925, "Cardigan Bay Resorts." an evidently more Anglicised identification. Both 'South Wales. The Country Of Castles' and 'North Wales. The British Tyrol' by the early twenties emphasised the impact of the GWR in Wales following the Railway Act of 1921. 'The British Tyrol' declared:

> The absorption of the Cambrian Railways by the Great Western Railway under the Railway Act 1921, has led to an improvement in the already excellent train services to the coastal towns of North Wales... From the experience gained since the close of the Great War it is safe to prophecy that in the near future the Dee Valley and the Country of the Marches – the British Tyrol in fact – will become one of the most popular of our great national pleasure and health giving districts.[8]

Barmouth was acclaimed by 'Holiday Haunts' for its particular character and setting. Designated as a likely "Eighth Wonder of the World" and a place of "magical beauty", the guide stated:

> Nowhere in Britain is there a town so royally situated as Barmouth... The pageantry of Barmouth Estuary from sunrise to sunset with the ebb and flow of the sparkling blue sea over its immense stretch of tawny golden sand, and the wonderful play of light and shade on the exquisitely shaped hills, headlands and mountains which stretch away inland for miles, transcends mere description. It is the inspired work of Nature.[9]

The railway journey itself, specifically the panoramic presentation on crossing Barmouth viaduct, intensified and varied this aesthetic perspective. Inland, Dolgelley was described as "a perfect holiday resort for nature lovers."

> Cader Idris is upon its very doorstep and the clear waters of the Wnion flowing under its ancient bridge show the way to the wooded gorges of Pont Newydd and Dolserau, whilst the world famous Precipice Walk, and the equally beautiful Torrent Walk command an amazing panorama of the Wnion Valley and the enchanting estuary of the Mawddach.[10]

The detail, the stylistic intensity in imagery, association and structure within this one sentence exemplifies Maxwell Fraser's accomplishments in endowing the company's promotional work with considerable literary distinction.

Looking to 'South Wales. The Country Of Castles', this work, likewise, attributed the development of the region to the improvements introduced by the GWR. The opening paragraph in this book read:

> Since the assumption by the Great Western Railway over the line formerly known as the Manchester and Milford leading from the capital of Carmarthenshire through a country of varied charm and undeniable beauty to Aberystwyth and the picturesque shores of Cardigan Bay, the 'Garden Of Wales' "is no longer a terra incognita to holiday makers from London and the Midlands, or to dwellers in Swansea, Cardiff, Newport, Monmouth, Bristol or Bath and the South West of England generally."[11]

'Holiday Haunts' emphasised the dramatic, romantic character of Carmarthenshire, describing it as "a land of mountainous solitudes and wide-spreading uplands deserted by all but the shepherds and their flocks." In the context of "the silence of these great hills and lovely rivers," the guide confirmed:

> ... so numerous are the castle ruins, glamourous with the memory of stirring fights and romantic love stories that in this one corner of Wales there are probably more fortresses than in all the other counties of the Principality put together.[12]

Castle and Abbey ruins, dramatic landscape and an intense magically-inspired tradition were also the focus of the GWR's presentation of Southern Ireland.

Southern Ireland

The Great Western's portrayal of Southern Ireland shared close similarities in terms of content and style with that of Wales, but in certain of its Irish portraits, Killarney for example, the company blended elements of the imagery of the dramatic 'difference' in Celtic identity, with that of the widely recognised, traditionally inspired pastoral imagery of rural England. Maxwell Fraser's 'Southern Ireland', GWR, 1932, presented a magical country of infinite beauty, intense historical tradition and an endless source of legend and myth relating to the ancient landscape and to the sea. Southern Ireland was:

> A country of glorious lakes and mountains and exquisite valleys drenched in history, rich in folk-lore and filled with poetic fancies... In such a land it is impossible not to believe in fairies[13]

Throughout its portrait of Southern Ireland, the GWR focused its attention upon the country's ancient history and the aesthetic and mystical properties of the landscape. Maxwell Fraser could, therefore, celebrate the important historical dimension without reference to the infinitely more controversial and intensely painful pattern of Ireland's more recent past, explicitly, that of the ongoing religious, political and economic conflicts since the Tudor period. Thus we read:

> Ireland can boast one of the oldest civilisations in the world – her culture ranks with that of Greece and Rome, in splendour and antiquity and her kings were reigning in Tara two thousand years before the birth of Christ.[14]

Similarly:

> The railway from Clonmel to Castle Connell and Killaloe runs through a smiling and gracious countryside of lush pasture lands and clear rivers, where every village is prosperous and contented and even the ruins hold no hint of sadness, seemingly only to speak of the greatness of the past, without regret for the lawless cruelty that is gone for ever. This south-western corner of Ireland has some of the richest and fertile soil in the whole country and its people do not have to contend with the extreme poverty which is so apparent in the wild, unproductive loveliness of the far west coast.[15]

As in H.V. Morton's work,[16] the romantic presentation of people and place was unmistakable, projecting both into the realms of fantasy for an ideal holiday land.

> The quiet dignity of her humblest peasants, who each and every one, have a regal bearing and innate good manners which would grace the greatest noble in the land whilst a vein of imaginative poetry and keen perception of natural forces gives them a vividness and force-fullness of speech which is an eternal riddle to those foreigners who do not realise the centuries of culture which have gone to the making of Ireland.[17]

Ireland's ancient Celtic cultural heritage was mystical, elusive and, above all, romantic.

> Everywhere in Ireland there are picturesque castles hinting at stirring deeds and high romance whilst in the monastic ruins may be read the story of innumerable Irish saints who spread the gospel far and wide. Christianising many districts of England and penetrating far into Europe, Ireland's monks were so

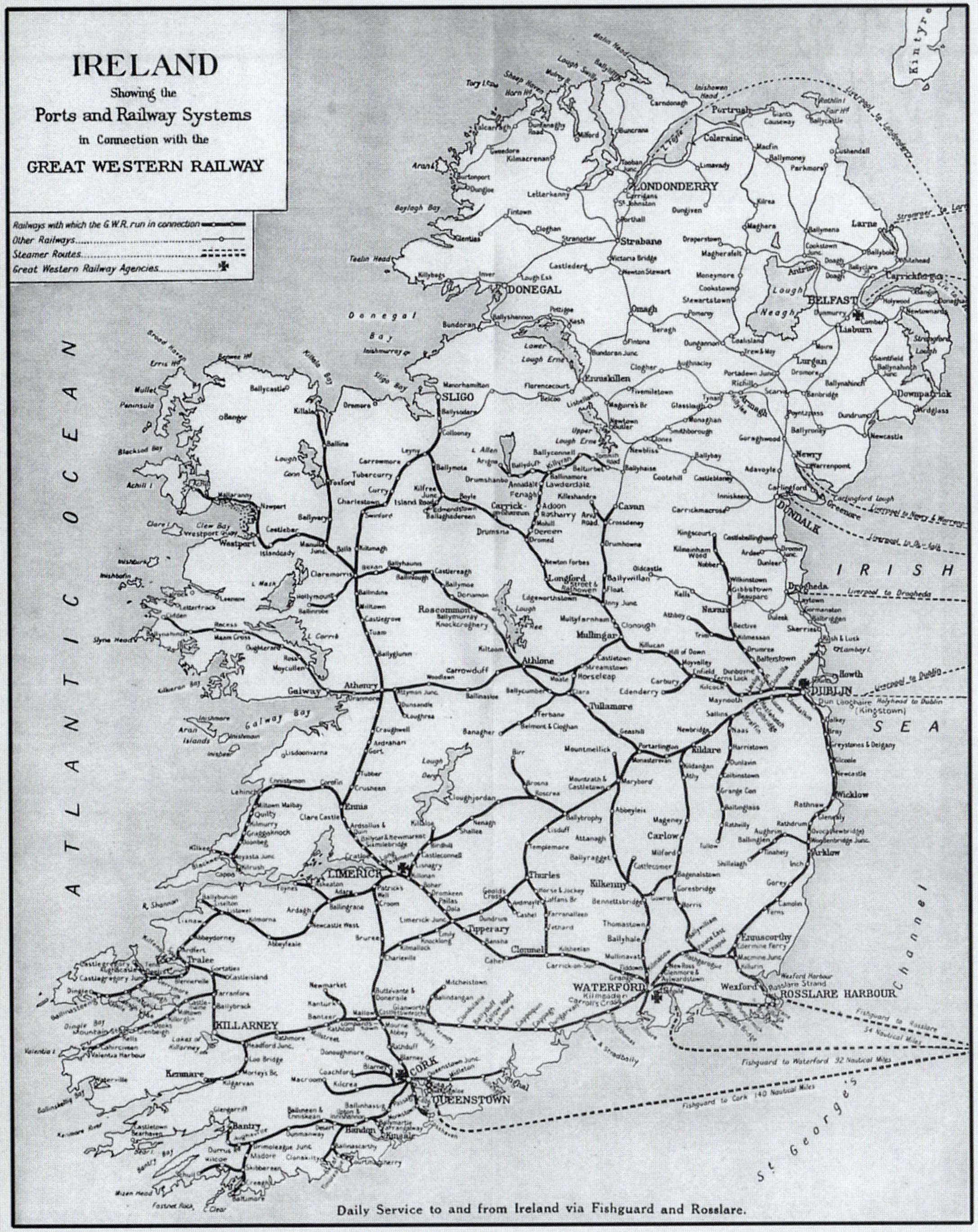

Advertisement for GWR sea routes to Ireland from Fishguard. 'Southern Ireland', 1927.

Map of Irish Railway System from 'Southern Ireland. Its Lakes and Landscapes'. Handy Aids series, May 1927. Author's collection

famed for learning in the early days of Christianity that people came from all over the known world to study in the great Irish monasteries.[18]

Together with its cultural links, Ireland also shared close similarities in terms of landscape and literary definition with both Wales and Cornwall. Southern Ireland's "Grand Atlantic Coast Route" from Killarney to Caragh Lake, Valencia, Waterville, Parknasilla and Kenmare, a distance of over eighty miles along the far South West, was a much larger version of the 'Atlantic Drive', a feature of West Cornwall extending from Land's End to St. Ives, as promoted in 'The Cornish Riviera'. The imagery and associations of both the Irish and Cornish locations were of the same order. Parknasilla was reminiscent of the character and climate of Cornwall's southern coast. Here was a "veritable jungle of colour and fragrance".

> Subtropical flowers and plants are not alien but flourish happily like natives in the warm and sunny atmosphere. Through the tangle of palms and brilliant tropical flowers, the translucent water of the bay creeps into many unexpected creeks and bays, which penetrate far into the gardens. In point of climate and subtropical vegetation, Parknasilla is the culminate triumph of Ireland's Riviera for its mean annual temperature is higher than that of Torquay or Ventnor.[19]

Southern Ireland, like Cornwall, was distinctive in that they each possessed "the irresistible charm of a foreign country",[20] whilst retaining sufficient features of recognised customs, values and, significantly, language. Maxwell Fraser described this as "the English tongue and customs with a difference."[21] Two further identifiable links between these two Celtic lands were also apparent. Southern Ireland and Cornwall, given their clear differences from English urban society, offered a great sense of release from the pressures of modern life. Chapter Two of 'Southern Ireland', stressed the sense of solace and retreat into leisure and rejuvenation that characterised its landscape and history. Closely associated with this was the direct emphasis, on the part of the GWR, in offering easy access to Ireland via its Fishguard to Rosslare crossing. This was consistent with the theme and content of 'The Ocean Coast' focusing largely upon Cornwall. The Lakes of Killarney were especially popular as a place of pilgrimage and were the subject of numerous picturesque celebrations defining the district. Fraser considered that, for most people, Killarney "has become almost a synonym for Ireland itself"[22] and that, in view of "the praise lavished on it so constantly for the last two centuries... it is no less 'compulsory' for those who visit Ireland in the present day than it was in the Victorian era when every writer of note made the pilgrimage..."[23] The earlier company literature on this district 'Southern Ireland. Its Lakes and Landscapes', 1904 and 1924, emphasised the high standards of service provided and the prominent commercial perspective of tourism, particularly in terms of the American market.

> To the average American visitor, Killarney is to Ireland what Stratford Upon Avon or Oxford are to the sister kingdom... The once rollocking old-world town of which Thackeray drew so diverting a picture, may nowadays be said to consist almost entirely of hotels and boarding houses, while the greater part of its population is made up of boatmen, guides and carvers of arbutus wood.[24]

In completing her introduction to Killarney, Maxwell Fraser offered an unmistakable rendering of the rural myth, incorporating landscape, legend and the emotional relationship of time and place; past and present. Nature and Man were in complete harmony and, significantly, inhabiting an uncompromised, pre-industrial landscape that appeared to owe nothing to the twentieth century. Amongst the silver birch, limes, chestnuts and lakes cradled by the mountains, Killarney was "more fitted to be the haunt of fairies than mortals."[25]

> Gracious ruins mellowing in the sunshine which floods the valleys with golden light point to man's activity there in past ages, but the story of Ross Castle, of Aghadoc, of Muckross Abbey and of Innissfallen is laid on pleasant lines, as though the peace of Killarney soothed even the angry passions of the fierce restless Irish warriors. Few people take the trouble to inquire into even such history as there is, preferring to rejoice in the sheer loveliness of these ruins and their enchanting setting. That is the true magic of Killarney. Its beauty is so triumphant that nothing else seems to matter. It is a beauty so incredibly, ravishingly lavish that it almost seems unreal and the beholder is consumed by a desire to gaze and gaze before some mystic spell dissolves it for ever.[26]

This was pre-eminently a landscape and experience of solace and deep peace; a mystical perspective, definitively a historical in explicit statement and in style. Totally rural and pre-industrial, there was always the clear contrast with modern, urban life. Killarney, as presented by Maxwell Fraser, was fundamentally an emotional experience and a definitive statement by the GWR of the rural myth. Retrospective and romantically melancholy, two defining features of all culturally inspired 'Celtic' locations, this work gained its impact not least by reference to positive associations and intense imagery drawn from the careful use of appealing adjectives – "gracious, mellow, golden, enchanting, lavish and mystic." The mystical dimension was definitive of all Celtic culture, recurring almost endlessly in reference to pre-industrial Ireland, Wales and Cornwall.

Cashel, reached from the railway line from Waterford to Clonmel, was an excellent example of an historic Celtic cultural shrine, after the manner of Tintagel in Cornwall, or Glastonbury in Somerset, with their close associations with Arthurian legend. It was "a place of memories and splendid ruins, set in scenery which is fittingly wild and magnificent."[27] Maxwell Fraser outlined its historical and cultural significance.

> ... Cashel became the most sanctified spot in all Ireland. Linked at first with the remote days of Munster's earliest kings, with the coming of St. Patrick in 450 it became one of the principal seats of Christianity in Ireland.[28]

Compared favourably to Tara, in Northern Ireland, Cashel offered a more stirring visual impact:

> ... for whereas Tara is a bare hilltop whose soul-stirring memories have to be conjured up in the mind of the imaginative, Cashel has magnificent buildings to arrest the eye and inspire interest in the fascinating story their grey old stones can tell.[29]

The GWR's fullest exposition of the magical Celtic Western Lands and their character and traditions, however, came in the presentation of Cornwall, as the company's long-term and extensive promotional initiative reveals.

The Cornish Riviera

Cornwall was promoted as a unique possession for the GWR initially for its mild, equable climate and medicinal properties, its convenient location and, increasingly, its perceived Celtic cultural identity. Mediterranean-inspired imagery was also important, as, collectively, the focus and thrust of company literature was with the attempt to portray the profound sense of difference, culturally and geographically, of the Cornish experience. Exotic imagery and dramatic associations were plentiful. Celebrating the "Mysterious Gift of the Gulf Stream", 'Sunny Cornwall. England's Mediterranean Region', 1924, announced: "Herodotus said Egypt was "the gift of the Nile." The equable, gentle, comfortable climate of the Cornish Riviera is the gift of the Gulf Stream".[30] Twenty years earlier, 'The Cornish Riviera' offered incentives to 'the pilgrim to Penzance' declaring that, when he or she walked in the Morrab Gardens, its wealth of sub-tropical vegetation, the envy of Nice or Monte-Carlo, they might easily think themselves to be in Algiers. Similar, exclusive imagery applied to St. Ives, where "Gulf Stream and West Indian associations"[31] were offered.

'The Scenery Attractions and Historical Associations of the Cornish Riviera', 1913, was explicit as to special identity, which engaged both Mediterranean properties and dramatic Celtic perspectives.

> The Cornish Riviera possesses all the climate advantages once considered the attribute of Madeira, Southern France and Italy, Algeria and still more distant Delta of the Nile, while the 'Delectable Duchy' generally has been more than once described as "the playground par excellence of the British Empire." The beauty and variety of its scenery are as remarkable as the richness of its historical associations, which go back to times even more remote than those in which the Pheonicians came from Carthage to Cornwall in quest of tin. Cornwall is not only celebrated for the picturesqueness of its indented coastline and rugged beauty of its rocks, cliffs and uplands, but at every turn the traveller finds himself face to face with venerable cairns and cromlechs, with ancient wells and moss-grown crosses and with churches and other buildings, the origin of which is often shrouded in mystery. It is in Cornwall only that the memorials of our Celtic ancestors can be satisfactorily explored and the recent development of railway travel carried out by the 'Holiday Line of England' enables holiday-makers to do in a few days or hours more than could formerly be accomplished in weeks or even months.[32]

Cultural and commercial interests worked in tandem here as indicated through the decisive alignment and identification of Celtic Cornwall with the Great Western's provision of the very latest engineering excellence. With its distinct cultural heritage and the exclusive service offered by 'The Cornish Riviera Express', it was impressed upon the traveller that, "With the Cornish Riviera practically at our doors, the necessity for costly and fatiguing foreign travel exists no longer".[33] This message was sustained throughout the company's work from 1904 onwards and was powerfully illustrated in poster form comparing homeland locations with well known continental venues. Particular emphasis was placed on the Cornish and English Riviera characterisations. Moreover, the "Buy British Holiday"[34] campaign, featured in early thirties editions of 'Holiday Haunts' argued that it was, given the depressed economic state of Britain, everyone's patriotic duty to holiday in the homeland. By 1934, however, the company's colour brochure 'Cornwall' relied solely upon the county's inherent attractions to draw visitors.

> It is difficult to understand why English people in their longing for complete change of atmosphere and for an assurance of warmth and equability of temperature take their holidays abroad when Cornwall can so easily gratify each of these natural inclinations. Cornish towns have discovered the secret of combining progressiveness with the intimate charms of village life.[35]

'The Official Guide To Penzance' by the corporation had earlier acknowledged the GWR's services in the opening section of the book, this edition being from 1908. The journey in itself became an integral part of the overall experience.

> The journey from the Metropolis was at one time a rather trying experience but, thanks to the enterprise of the Great Western Railway, it now occupies only a few hours and nothing that can contribute to the traveller's comfort and convenience is left undone. The Paddington to Penzance expresses, which make the longest "non-stop" runs in England, are among the fastest,

Brochure for Penzance, GWR, 1924

> smoothest running and most luxuriously appointed trains in the world. Excellent meals, at moderate charges, are served en-route and, on the night trains, accommodation for sleepers is provided.[36]

By the thirties Cornwall was promoted as offering something for everyone, a feature emphasises by S.P.B. Mais in his 'Cornish Riviera', 1928. But beyond the broadly popularist approach the GWR also distinguished between casual sight-seers and serious, dedicated visitors, the latter often being referred to as "initiates" or the "initiated." Two specific examples of this can be seen in reference to Land's End and to Kynance Cove, on the Lizard Peninsula.

'Holiday Haunts' addressed this theme in its material on Land's End:

> Thousands of people visit Land's End every year and stand upon the wave-beaten cliffs looking across the great expanse of ocean now tossing above the lost land of Lyonesse to the distant Scilly Islands. The majority of these visitors pay a flying visit to the Logan Rock and then return with the comfortable reflection that they have "done" Land's End. They have no conception of the real glory of Land's End.[37]

As with all the Great Western's writers and the range of 'Homeland Handbooks', for example, the style was that of an invitation to indulge in an encounter with special landscape and atmosphere. As Maxwell Fraser put it, choosing her words carefully to convey such emotionally charged experiences, it was; "bewitchingly lovely."[38]

Kynance Cove, much photographed by the GWR Publicity Department, the subject matter for several posters and the inspiration for many more, provided another location for the initiated. The GWR's literary celebration of Kynance Cove drew stylistically from the romantically-inspired genre of dramatic and romantic encounter with awesome Nature. Filtered through this perspective dating from the mid eighteenth century and through popularist accounts of a century later – as in Wilkie Collins' 'Rambles Beyond Railways', 1861 and his "perfect palace of rocks",[39] 'Holiday Haunts' evoked the sense of special place. Exclusivity was expressed in the imagery of "the initiated" and of "rarer loveliness". It was also reflected in the structural contrast offered between those who make the "casual visit" and those who "thoroughly explore." In effect, it was an open statement of demarcation, dramatically evoked in the context of "this peerless bay."

> Though it is impossible to pay even a casual visit to Kynance Cove without being impressed by its beauty, only the initiated, with plenty of time at their disposal, are able to find and rejoice in the rarer loveliness which rewards those who thoroughly explore the caves in this peerless bay.[40]

St. Michael's Mount fulfilled all agendas: legendary site, ancient port, monastery and fortress. It occupied a special place in GWR literature and was the subject of several posters. Mais called it "one of the Seven Wonders of England."[41] and wrote enthusiastically of it in "The Cornish Riviera", presenting it in the dramatic, romantic form of contrasting manner and mood.

> From far and near in whatever weather, at whatever time of day, St. Michael's Mount stands out as one of the Seven Wonders of England, mysterious, exquisitely beautiful, a citadel of romance on which to base the castle of dreams. I had myself, the great good fortune to see it first at midnight under a harvest moon with the lights in its high walls flashing over the sea. I have seen it emerge above a sea-mist like a magic place on the clouds. I have seen it with the storms beating great waves against its granite sides and I have seen it shimmering in the noon-day heat of a perfect midsummer day. Each time it has seemed beyond

St Michaels Mount in mellow evening mood in this late 1920s poster encapsulates the atmosphere of 'The Land of Legend and Romance'. It accorded closely with S P B Mais' representation of the Mount and its many moods as featured in "The Cornish Riviera", 1928.
Courtesy, Dalkeith Publishing Co Ltd.

compare, the most exquisite gem of all England's homes.[42]

'Beautiful Brittany', 1909, had celebrated Mont Saint-Michel along similar lines, whilst GWR poster work offered close physical comparisons between the two sites. Overall, Cornish and Breton landscapes and cultural traditions bore close resemblances, thus the iconography and thematic structure of literature, legend and art work reflected shared perspectives, best expressed in the celebrations of their antiquities, dramatic coastal cliff-scapes and the numerous fishing communities.[43]

Even the most cursory glance at GWR presentations of Cornish fishing communities – Sennen, Mousehole, St. Ives, Looe, Polperro, Mevagissey – reflects their picturesque quality. The GWR Magazine, June 1938, 'A Picturesque Cornish Fish Market', for example, describes the summer morning market in the context of a tourist spectacle.[44] Poster work was conclusively picturesque.

The company's overall presentation of Cornwall and its particularly traditional image was influenced by the art work of the late nineteenth century 'Newlyn School' of painters, best known in the canvases of its founder Stanhope-Forbes.[45] In pre-dating the GWR's earliest promotional literature on Cornwall and shaping a specific perception of the Cornish landscape and culture, the work of the Newlyn School of painters was a valuable source for ideas and imagery. Active during the later years of the last century and the early part of the twentieth, the 'Newlyn School' concerned itself with various subjects and themes popular at the time, which were to become central to the GWR's cultural construction of the county. This was particularly so with regard to poster production where the imagery of the fishing communities was widely adopted.

The Newlyn School focused upon the fishing communities, centering upon Newlyn and the rural landscape of the West Penwith, notably the Lamorna, district. Forbes' work, significantly, exhibited at the Royal Academy, celebrated the working environment and the people and culture of the fishing communities. There was also interest in Cornish folklore and mythology as popularised at the time by Robert Hunt in his anthology, 'Popular Romances of the West Country',[46] but the essential focus was the community in the local landscape. The overall impression was one of a sense of order, of continuity and harmony underlining a strong sense of identity and purpose within the community. The paintings reflected a strong representational, if romanticised, style in the depiction of simple, dignified working people, a popular theme in literature and painting at that time. Forbes wrote of Newlyn in 1900:

> ... every corner was a picture, and more important from the point of view of the figure painter, the people seemed to fall naturally into place and harmonise with the surroundings.[47]

In offering up vivid images of landscape and people, the Newlyn School caught the imagination of large numbers of people, thereby helping to shape the perception of the area as one of infinite charm and romantic appeal. Great Western promotional work in poster form and in the literature drew upon this in its portrayal of Cornwall, yet again reinforcing the sense of special place and people, vital to its 'half-foreign' theme.

The Isles of Scilly, however, offered further scope for exotic, exclusive imagery in terms of their unique setting and aesthetic qualities. But in promotional terms the GWR had, as ever, to incorporate the necessary assurance that access was easy. The emphasis was placed on high standards of service, smooth efficiency and every consideration for the travellers. Thus, this "Garden of Eden",[48] as S.P.B. Mais called it in 'Isles of the Island', 1934, was readily available. The 1908 edition of 'The Cornish Riviera' confirmed the exclusive context; the fundamentally metropolitan perspective in imagery and expectation, not least, for the journey itself.

If you are in a hurry, leave Paddington at 9 pm, enjoy a comfortable night's rest in the sleeping car and wake up in time to catch a passing glance of "Majestic Michael." Breakfast at your leisure in Penzance in a sunny room overlooking Mounts Bay; go on board and lunch luxuriantly on the S.S. Lyonesse.[49]

The Abbey Gardens on the island of Tresco, famous for their exotic plants from all parts of the world, underlined the unique climate and setting of the Islands. Mais referred to the 'Japanese banana, Australian lobsterclaw plant, Mexican yucca, Chilian paya, Burmese honeysuckle and Himalayan ginger.'[50] The overall impact of the Islands as celebrated in 'The Cornish Riviera' was "as a place taking such a hold of the imagination and the affections that it can never be lost or forgotten"[51] A final reference to the Islands, from the 1910 edition of 'Historic Sites and Scenes of England', combined themes of legend, romance and the significance of special place. Concluding the section on the Isles was a typically Celtic theme of the far West – the imagery of mystic islands and the sea and of ancient communities lost beneath the waves.

It is in the fitness of things that the great romance of the days of chivalry should end amongst its rocks, its sapphire sea and fields of narcissi, even if the echoes of the fabled bells of the churches lying buried fathoms deep below the waves do not actually reach the ear.[52]

The GWR's Celtic lands of the West, mysterious and legendary regions of ancient ruins, "stirring deeds", distinctive people, customs and awesome landscapes met all the dimensions of the company's promotional drive for "difference", foreign characterisation and "otherness". Defined in terms of an "escape", a unique adventure and spectacle, the Celtic landscapes were presented in a perspective much removed from that of the GWR's most prominent and consistently formulated characterisation – that of its direct identification with the imagery and associations of rural, historical England; its particular expression of Englishness.

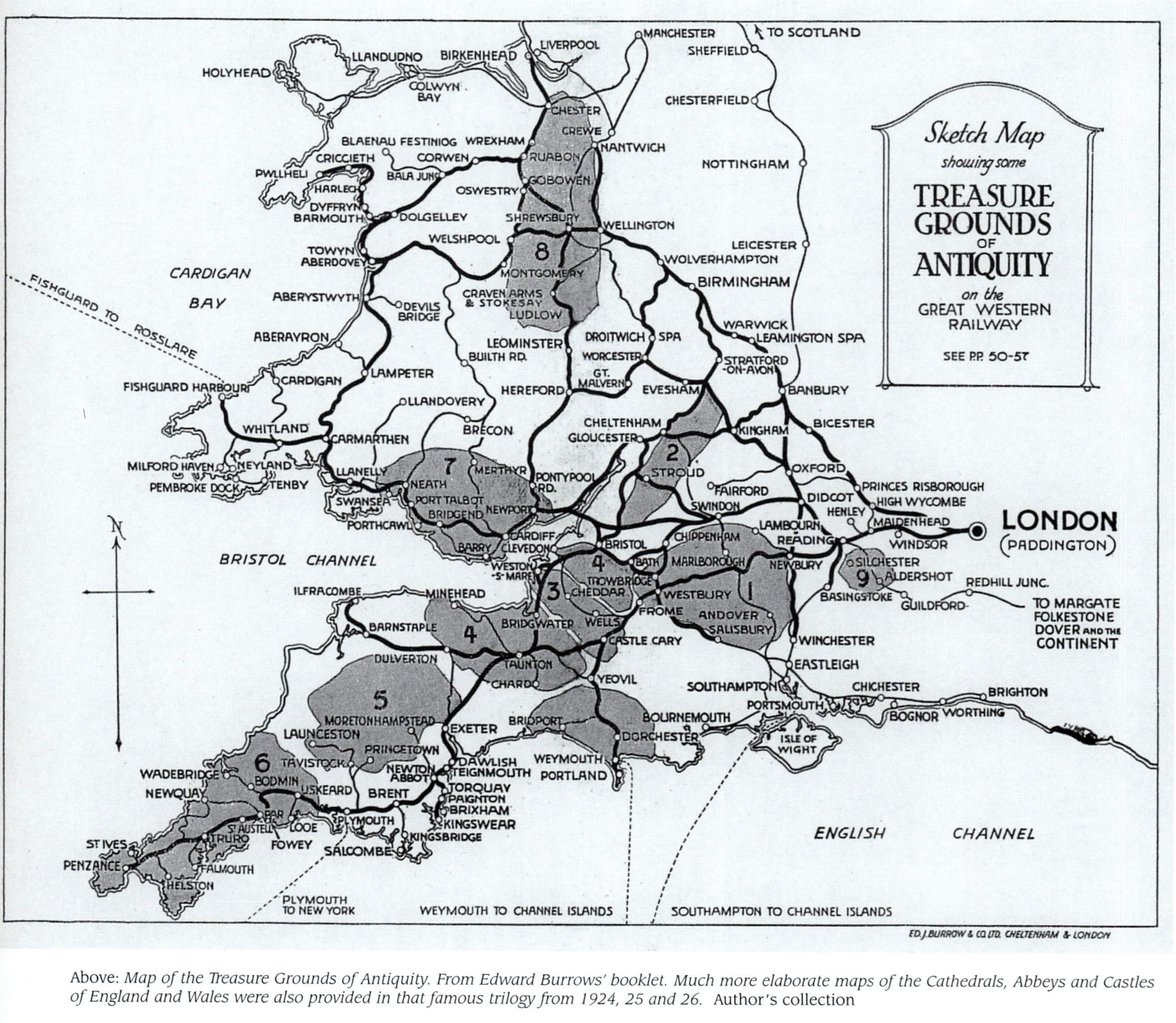

Above: *Map of the Treasure Grounds of Antiquity. From Edward Burrows' booklet. Much more elaborate maps of the Cathedrals, Abbeys and Castles of England and Wales were also provided in that famous trilogy from 1924, 25 and 26.* Author's collection

UFFINGTON TO SHRIVENHAM

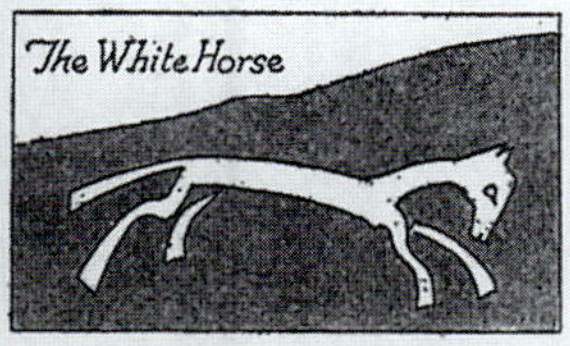

FROM UFFINGTON STATION (1), where the FARINGDON BRANCH (2) goes off to the right, we may look over the points of our famous WHITE HORSE (3)—a fine upstanding animal, guaranteed as sound in wind and limb as the day he was born. His age?—ah! that's the question! The most generally accepted tradition is that he was cut in the turf to commemorate the defeat of the Danes by Ethelred and Alfred in the battle of Aescendune, A.D. 871, but in recent times archæologists have suggested the horse is much older than that, one writer pointing out that "any trophy cut by such pious kings would probably be in the form of a Christian cross, as at Whyteleaf and Bledlow, and not the horse of their idolatrous ancestors." Whoever the designer may have been he was a man of expansive ideas and no small amount of skill.

The White Horse of Uffington is 374 feet long and spreads its active limbs (for the horse is shown in full gallop) over an acre of ground. The design is worked out in trenches about ten feet broad and from two to three feet deep. Below the horse is a deep concavity in the hillside appropriately called "The Manger," and the summit of the hill has a whole series of earth-works upon it. One of them is Uffington Castle, already mentioned, another HARDWELL CASTLE (4) rather farther west, and a third Liddington Castle still further in the same direction. The Downs abound in burial mounds, ancient trackways and other evidences of remote occupation. The railway runs almost parallel with the pre-Roman RIDGE WAY (5).

Such dramatic contrasts of ancient and modern give us a sense of the wonderful continuity of history and pre-history in England.

The hamlet a mile away on the right is FERNHAM (6), and a little farther along the village of LONGCOT (7) shows us a little church amid the clustering houses and trees. Beyond these places is a view across the Vale to where BADBURY HILL (8) with ... it (not to be confused with the ... Rings in Dorset) ... Berkshire t...

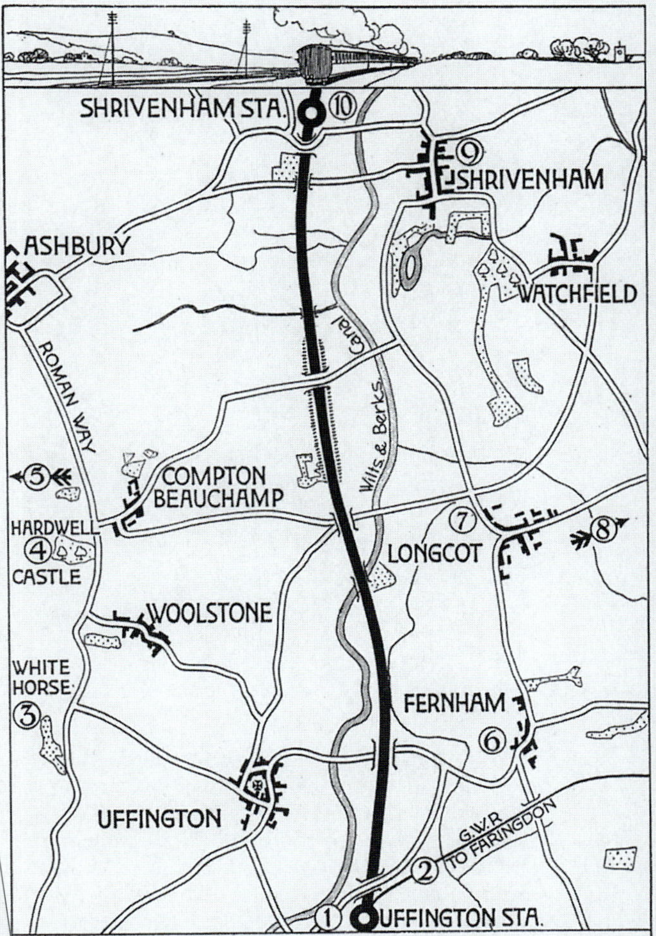

THE VALE OF WHITE HORSE

SHRIVENHAM: $71\frac{1}{2}$ miles from London, $398\frac{1}{4}$ miles to Killarney.

37

From Cave Man TO Roman in Britain

By

EDWARD J. BURROW, F.R.G.S.

PRICE SIXPENCE

Published by the Great Western Railway Company
PADDINGTON STATION, LONDON, W.2

(COPYRIGHT) FELIX J. C. POLE, General Manager

Above: *Sample pages from the 'Through the Window' series: this one from 'Paddington to Killarney' 1926. The detailed, stylised map, illustrations and informed text are all evident here.*

Left: *Title page for the company's celebration of its rich archaeological and assumed 'Celtic' credentials. 'From Cave Man to Roman in Britain' c 1924.* Author's collection

REFERENCES – CHAPTER FOUR

1: A.M. Broadley. Southern Ireland: Its Lakes And Landscapes, GWR July, 1904. P88.

2: Ibid P88.

3: GWR Cardigan Bay Resorts, 1925 P5.

4: E.T. MacDermot. History of the Great Western Railway, GWR 1931. Revised. C.R. Clinker, Ian Allan, London, 1964. PPs 243-44.

5: GWR Through The Window. Paddington To Birkenhead, 1925 P73.

6: GWR North Wales. The British Tyrol, 1924 ed P6.

7: Ibid P5.

8: Ibid P6.

9: GWR Holiday Haunts 1936 P762.

10: Ibid P763.

11: GWR South Wales. The Country of Castles, 1924 ed. P5.

12: GWR Holiday Haunts, 1936 P831.

13: Maxwell Fraser. Southern Ireland. GWR 1932. P3.

14: Ibid P4.

15: Ibid P14.

16: H.V. Morton. In Search of Ireland. Methuen, London, 1930. H.V. Morton's 'In Search of Ireland', a vastly popular work that went through thirteen editions between 1930 and 1938, presented Ireland in much the same manner and style as that of the GWR and illustrated Brown's later assessment of the projected Irish identity. Morton's Ireland was a mystical, aesthetic and historical experience that seduced the visitor into the deepest of sensuous pleasures. As with so many of the Great Western locations, Ireland was a series of dramatic and emotional encounters demanding the total surrender to experience and sensation, not the engagement of the intellect nor of analysis. It was this cultural tradition and perspective that attracted Great Western interest as the celebration of ancient culture and landscape was well in line with the company's aspirations, offering a 'safe' Irish identity that could be readily assimilated into the corporation imagery of the GWR, as in Wales and Cornwall. We therefore find common reference in all the Celtic orientated literature to familiar content and style focusing upon the dramatic qualities of landscape, to a mysterious, mystical, rural people and to a rich vein of legend and mythology. This was, in effect, the cultural identity projected by the Irish people from the 1880s onward. Terence Brown, 'Ireland. A Social and Cultural History, 1922-1985', (Fontana, London 1981) identifies the rural perspective as being definitive of the national character. From the literary tradition of the 1880s and 1890s, celebrating the heroic and mythological deeds of ancient times to the later rural writing of the 1920s, Brown notes: They celebrated a version of Irish pastoral where rural life was a condition of virtue in as much as it remained an expression of an ancient civilisation uncontaminated by commercialism and progress. In so doing they helped to confirm Irish society in a belief that rural life constituted an essential element of unchanging Irish identity.

17: Maxwell Fraser. Southern Ireland. P4.

18: Ibid P4.

19: Ibid P29.

20: Ibid P29.

21: Ibid P5.

22: Ibid P5.

23: Ibid P19.

24: Ibid P19.

25: A.M. Broadley. Southern Ireland. Its Lakes And Landscapes, GWR Handy Aids series, No. 10, May, 1927. P17.

26: Fraser. Southern Ireland, P20. See also Morton's depiction of the Connemaran seaweed gatherer, a girl, "perhaps eighteen years of age" whom he describes in terms of the archetypal child of nature, primitive but alluring, endowed with both "her massive ignorance" and "queer smothered nobility." Morton drew heavily, here, upon the received feminine gendering of Celtic identity and upon the concomitant imagery of the seashore as a place of desire and danger. Elsewhere, he speculates: "How on earth do these wild children settle down in America?" In Search Of Ireland. PPs 185-192. Also PPs 193, 197:98.

27: Ibid. P20.

28: Ibid P11.

29: Ibid P12.

30: GWR Sunny Cornwall. England's Mediterranean Region. 1924.

31: A.M. Broadley. The Cornish Riviera, G.W:R. (1904) 1908 ed P61.

32: GWR The Scenery Attractions and Historical Associations of the Cornish Riviera, 1913. P1.

33: Broadley. Cornish Riviera P5.

34: GWR Holiday Haunts 1931 P342. It is a reproach that so many English people travel abroad without having visited any of the English beauty spots. Every English man and woman should realise the glory of our land.

35: GWR 'Cornwall' brochure 1934.

36: Official Guide to Penzance. 1908, P5. See also "Through The Window. Paddington To Penzance" GWR, 1924 and "Sunny Cornwall, England's Mediterranean Region". GWR, 1924, P19, for similar thematic focus.

37: GWR Holiday Haunts, 1936. P168.

38: Ibid P170.

39: See Wilkie Collins: Rambles Beyond Railways. Notes in Cornwall taken afoot, Richard Bentley, London, 1851 and the much earlier and highly acclaimed, A Journey To The Western Islands of Scotland And The Journal Of A Tour To The Hebrides, Samuel Johnson and James Boswell, 1775/1786, Penguin Classics ed, London. 1984. See esp. PPs 138-143.

40: GWR Holiday Haunts 1936. P168.

41: S.P.B. Mais. The Cornish Riviera, GWR 1928 ed, P75.

42: Ibid P75.

43: GWR Beautiful Brittany. La Belle Bretagne, May, 1909. This work drew close parallels between Cornish and

Breton landscape and culture. Subtitled: 'An Ideal New Holiday Ground' its comparisons included, for example, Pointe du Raz: "the resemblance of the Pointe du Raz to the English Land's End will at once be apparent. (P111). Likewise, Isle De Sein – "burial place of the Druids of Cornovaille ... the rugged coastline scenery reminds one forcibly of the Isles of Scilly" (P112). There were also the numerous instances of inundations – towns and villages lost to the sea – of mythopeoic creatures, numinous landscapes and personages definitive of Celtic mythology. Close comparisons here, served to enhance the differentiation of both locations from English metropolitan perspectives making Cornwall and Britanny equally mysterious and alluring but, vitally, accessible.

44: GWR Magazine June 1938. PPs 237-328.

45: Caroline Fox and Frances Greenacre. Artists Of The Newlyn School, 180-1900, Newlyn Orion Gallery, Newlyn, 1979 Caroline Fox. Painting In Newlyn, Newlyn Orion, Penzance, 1985. Caroline Fox. Stanhope Forbes And The Newlyn School, David and Charles, Newton Abbot, 1993.

46: Robert Hunt. Popular Romances Of The West Of England, (1871) Chatto and Windus, London, 1923. This collection was the basis and inspiration for the GWR's 'Legend Land' series published in four volumes from 1923.

47: Quoted: Caroline Fox, Painting In Newlyn, 1900-1930, Newlyn Orion, 1985. P14.

48: S.P.B. Mais. Isles Of The Island, Putnam, London, 1934. P266.

49: A.M. Broadley. Cornish Riviera, 1908 ed. P68:69.

50: S.P.B. Mais. Isles Of The Island. P256.

51: A.M. Broadley. Cornish Riviera, 1908 ed. P71.

52: A.M. Broadley. Historic Sites and Scenes of England, GWR (1904) 1910 ed P131.

Left: *The Golden Sands of Wales. The sense of the Celtic Westernland is evident here in the imagery of the cave, the deserted beach and the lonely sea. This plate was included in the GWR's Souvenir of the British Empire Exhibition at Wembley, 1924 and, as such, appealed to North American audiences who would, hopefully, respond to the high romance and sublime perspectives that characterised the 'Celtic' heritage.* Author's collection

Below: *Torquay. A very different seashore. Torquay was the focus of the English Riviera and was invariably described in terms of exclusive, superlative properties. Repeated identifications with Mediterranean resorts were common to both railway and non-railway-based guide books. The most fulsome praise came in SPB Mais' 'Glorious Devon', 1928, wherein classical perspectives were abundant.* Author's collection

Facing page: *Door to Door. Front cover for the second edition of the company's detailed handbook, 'Door to Door By Country Cartage Services'. From the early thirties and working under the shadow of the Depression, the GWR paid much greater attention to the promotion of its freight services. 'Door to Door' was one such enterprise, 'The Best Location' 1932 and 'Factory Sites' 1936 were further examples.* Courtesy G Baker

DOOR TO DOOR
BY
COUNTRY CARTAGE
SERVICES
GWR
RALPH MOTT
SCALES OF CHARGES &
LIST OF VILLAGES SERVED

CHAPTER FIVE

INDUSTRIAL INTERESTS

> The London area seems to be exceptionally popular with those contemplating the establishment of new industries and new factories ...[1]
>
> The gross receipts for the past two years from the docks at Newport, Cardiff and Penarth have not been sufficient to cover working expenses.[2]
>
> GWR AGM 27 February 1935

These two extracts from the company's Annual General Meeting at Paddington in the early stages of the Centenary Year indicate the disparate character and fortunes of the company's freight services in the early thirties. The collapse of the export market, especially in coal, had crippled the docks traffic in South Wales whilst the relatively prosperous region of South-East England flourished in its close association with new consumer-led light industries identified as being conspicuously modern and progressive. The G.W.R. embraced both the traditional and the contemporary structures of industry but, as the company's industrially-focused literature of the thirties revealed, its emphasis was increasingly with the latter.

There had been calls for greater interest and focus upon the promotion of freight services prior to the depression evident from 1930 onward. In 1929 - the acknowledged index as the best year for freight traffic between 1924 and 1939 - the Great Western Railway (London) Lecture and Debating Society[3] considered the issue of advertising. Mr. A.C. Pickford of the Goods Department argued that the company's promotional work on freight services were "unproductive". Whilst stressing, as he saw it, the fact of "serious decline in railway-conveyed tonnage, entirely due to advantages possessed by road motor concerns"[4] Pickford also emphasised that very little had been done to inform merchants, traders and the public generally of significant new developments in railway freight services. Listing railhead depots, the introduction of containers, accelerated freight trains and greater availability of storage accommodation, he called for "an interesting, informative booklet, brightly and succinctly setting out, among other features ... Goods train services to and from the district in which the booklet is distributed ... Also a list of railway telephone numbers instructing traders as to the number they should require ...[5] Pickford argued that such a book "not to be issued indiscriminately ... would be goods traffic advertising on right lines".[6]

Similarly founded criticisms and appeals for more extensive advertising were evident at both earlier and later Lecture Debating Meetings. In February 1925, for example,[7] there were calls for freight services to be publicised on a level commensurate with that devoted to passenger traffic. Almost a decade later, in October 1934, G.E. Orton, assistant to the Superintendent of the Line, considered that there were still many opportunities to increase publicity for freight services, poster work in particular[8] but progress from the early thirties was evident.

The creation of the Commercial Advertising Department, in January 1931, marked a necessary and significant development. Formed at a time of severe economic depression, nationally, this department headed initially by K.W.C. Grand and, in 1933, by G.E. Orton and, in 1934, by Major M. Dewar, was merged with the activities of the publicity agent (1932). All three personalities involved had extensive experience in advertising and, significantly, in overseas interests. The perspective for both passenger and freight traffic was therefore projected internationally, in a manner and level not evident previously.

'The Best Location', 1932,[9] was the company's co-ordinated statement on its freight services, its policies and amenities. Considered in some detail in the course of this chapter, its focus was international. It also worked in conjunction with a further new work at that time: 'GWR Door To Door Country Cartage Services.' As A.C. Pickford had advocated in 1929, this book was intended to promote and integrate the company's services and the customers' needs across the GWR network. Its message was clear.

> This new 52-page booklet giving full particulars of 142 lorry services, scales of charges and list of villages regularly serviced, should be in the hands of all Traders distributing goods in the area served by the GWR. Remote places and premises are brought in close touch with the centres of distribution.[10]

By the mid thirties, with the worst of the depression past, the GWR looked to the achievement of a modern, dynamic freight service, albeit, as the company recognised, that its industrial interests could never capture the public imagination in the manner that the holiday imagery had done.

'Holiday Haunts' for the centenary year, 1935, carried an explicit statement as to the company's popular identity: that its 'Holiday Line' image, "has completely overshadowed in the minds of the general public that of its extensive industrial interests."[11] Given that such a statement was surely an outstanding instance of the GWR's carefully considered promotional policy, it cannot be taken at face value and must be contextualised by reference to relative performances and to the commercial expediency of specific image-building.

The company's own records for revenue in 1934, as published in the January 1935 edition of the GWR Magazine declared its higher earnings from freight traffic than from the passenger business. Passenger Train Receipts: 46 weeks to Nov 18, 1934: £9,356,000. Overall freight traffic: 46 weeks to Nov 18, 1934: £12,798,000. Likewise, the statement in January 1938 for the previous year – to December 12: Passenger Receipts – £10,603,000 (+ £217,000 on 1936) Overall freight: £15,462,000 (+ £979,000).[2] Emphasis upon the would-be primacy of holiday-orientated imagery was seen as commercially expedient in terms of its traffic potential as a means of offsetting considerable losses in respect of the older, heavy industries, particularly coal, which, up to the early 1920s, had been a major revenue earner. Moreover, throughout the inter-war era, whenever possible and particularly in the thirties, the company presented industrial interests in dramatic imagery, as no less than the contemporary urban, industrial and, indeed, internationally orientated equivalent of the GWR's historical-cultural presentation. Paddington thereby ensured that the company was projected and perceived as constituting and fulfilling the identity of all things to all people. To this end, 'Glorious Devon' or 'Shakespeare Land' were effectively no more quintessentially Great Western than was the 'Black Country' or the docklands and coalfields of South Wales. The guiding principle was that of an integrated identity.

In many ways, the company employed the stylistically inspired characterisation definitive of so much of its tourist identity to dramatise and mythologise industrial and mercantile interests. Above all, the company was determined to present both a progressive and, specifically, an international context in

Front cover 'Factory Sites' 1936. Courtesy G. Baker

all its promotional activities, with particular emphasis upon Imperial identifications. This much was apparent in the 1924 publication, 'Commerce and the Great Western Railway', with its recognition of the fundamental structural changes that were taking shape at that time and of the need to accommodate them.

> The supreme importance of the area [GWR network] served does not lie so much in its constituting the present hub of British industrial life, as in the fact that, with its well-placed sites for new works, factories and warehouses, this part of Great Britain is naturally marked out as the home of the new and intense development of our commerce and history which must be forthcoming in the immediate future ... It will naturally follow that, if this country is to maintain its position as 'The World's Trader', manufacturers must give particular attention to the location of their works.[13]

Although the industrial identity, publicly, was of a lower key than that of tourism, works such as 'Through the Window. Paddington to Birkenhead', 1925, considered the 'Black Country', "as vital to England as the works are to a watch."[14] Heavy industry became, "commercial power stations of the Empire and the world",[15] essential to the overall English imperial representations. "Machinery", that which "makes the difference between barbarism and civilisation",[16] was the special creative achievement of 'Black Country' England – At night it was "the lurid glow of furnaces and blaze of light"[17] at West Bromwich that inspired the nocturnal traveller, offering challenging perspectives on vital industrial activity.

Mindful of the widest international context and of the commercial imperative of celebrating modern, dynamic perspectives, the Great Western produced a range of requisite promotional works. "Build Your Works on the GWR The Best Location',[18] was designed to attract industry to Great Western locations with their "valuable transport facilities for the delivery of raw materials and swift despatch of finished products."[9] Its designation, "Great Western Railway of England," indicated the direct appeal to prospective North American business. Particular emphasis was given to modern sites in the London area and to the modern concept of the factory site and means of production as exemplified in the Hoover building at Slough. Products from the new factory locations were listed to underline the modern character – "margarine, motor cars, radio equipment, dairy machinery and appliances, confectionery, tins for the canning industry, wallpaper, lamps etc."[20]

'The Best Location', 1932, stressed that the facilities and sites offered by the GWR appealed to the modern businessman and throughout this publication the focus was that of modernity, efficiency and service. Direct contrasts were drawn with the older nineteenth century industrial locations, emphasising, again, the modernity, the sense of transformation and direct reference to contemporary technology.

> Observers who have paid a first visit to the factory areas which have come into being in recent years in the western suburbs of London have been struck by the remarkable contrast between the cleanliness and brightness of these localities as compared with the grime and squalor associated with the older industrial areas of Great Britain. This attributable partly to the use of electricity instead of raw fuel and partly to other important factors which have contributed to the transformation.[21]

Amongst these contributing factors was that of the specially selected site "where the atmosphere is as free as possible from smoke and dirt which emanates from every large city."[22] Low rates were also essential and were forthcoming in Middlesex and, in consequence:

> Low rates attract not only factory promoters but also home seekers from the Metropolis; and the garden cities of the suburbs assure to the manufacturer a constant supply of labour of the best type.[23]

In an apparent reversal of the rural myth, 'The Best Location' commented upon the rapid transformation of the landscape, registering its endorsement of industrial enterprise.

> A passenger travelling by the Great Western Railway from Paddington to the West of England or by direct line to Birmingham, today sees from the carriage window modern factories pulsating with industrial energy, where a few years ago cows and sheep grazed placidly.[24]

The positive perspective on industry was fully consistent with established GWR practice in the pursuit of a collective identity. Modern industrial sites and conveniently-located contemporary suburban housing developments such as that advertised in 'Holiday Haunts', 1931, for Ritchings Park Estate, Iver, engaged progressive perspectives in social, economic and cultural terms, augmenting the concept of Englishness as the advertisement in 'Holiday Haunts' suggested.

> Live amid the Parklands of Buckinghamshire in a modern house with modern conveniences. Electric lighting, heating and cooking. Live healthy in a county well to the windward of London smoke and fog. Palatial cinemas, nine acres of Recreation Grounds, Hard Tennis Courts, Golf Links within easy reach, vicinity of Stoke Poges, Burnham Beeches, Windsor, Taplow and Maidenhead for the River.[25]

The GWR projected decidedly contemporary, fashionable imagery in its perceived close association with the British film industry. In an article from the company magazine in 1936, entitled, 'The British Film Industry Grows Around the Great Western Railway',[26] it portrayed itself as being in the vanguard of dynamic innovation by celebrating its direct identification with the Denham studio of the 'London Film Productions,' which the GWR proclaimed as "the biggest in the empire;"[27] with the newly opened Pinewood Studios at Iver Heath; the 'Associated Talking Pictures' studios at Ealing Common and the Gaumont-British Picture Corporation at Shepherds Bush. Thus, the unreserved statements of distinction and dynamic characterisation: the vital projection of image:

> The development of the [film] industry has been rapid, particularly so on the west side of London in the past twelve months, with the result that Paddington now finds itself in the very heart of Britain's Hollywood. With the growth of the film industry, Paddington has gradually and unconsciously assumed a film complex. Film stars, directors, employees, cameramen and buyers – those who scout around the world to bring the right atmosphere and properties to the set – are now part of its everyday life, passing to and fro between the terminus and the studio stations ...[28]

The West London locations at Denham and Iver were pronounced as offering film producers "as nearly ideal conditions as they are likely to get in this country"[29] ... and, in so doing, also spelled out the GWR's own definition of the contemporary ideal, in its complete and graduated form, of rural, aesthetic excellence in combination with the best of modern amenities to make access and availability no problem at all. The dialectic of country and city and all the cultural significance that this entailed was thus expressed through the film industry. Detailing "the ideal conditions" the GWR continued:

> .... beautiful surroundings, varied scenery at hand, quiet of the countryside, freedom from the suburbia, room to develop and complete isolation for their self-contained communities, yet within rapid communication with London – the main source of supply for artists and material, which now pass in increasing volume.[30]

Reporting the opening of the Pinewood Studios on 30

September 1936, the GWR offered every evidence stylistically of its association with the ethos and imagery of this potent symbol of modernity, celebrating its obviously exclusive, chic status.

> For the official opening of Pinewood Studios on September 30 last, a special train was run from Paddington to some of the 1,200 guests who attended the luncheon. In design, the studios are the most advanced yet seen in movie architecture. They stand in a hundred acres of grounds which includes a deer park, a swimming pool, acres of ornamental gardens, woods and the former residence of Colonel Grant Morden, which has been converted into Britain's most exclusive film club, having a limited membership confined to people with outstanding reputations in films.[31]

Progressive indicators such as these were intended to reflect the resolute achievement of a contemporary railway company claiming the vanguard of economic enterprise. Such developments were all the more welcome in view of the rapidly declining prospects for the company's hitherto lucrative trade in the export of coal from the South Wales field. The long-term and severe downturn in traffic hit hard at the docks trade.

Below: *Map concerning GWR docks and distribution from 'Commerce And The Great Western Railway, 1924.* Author's collection

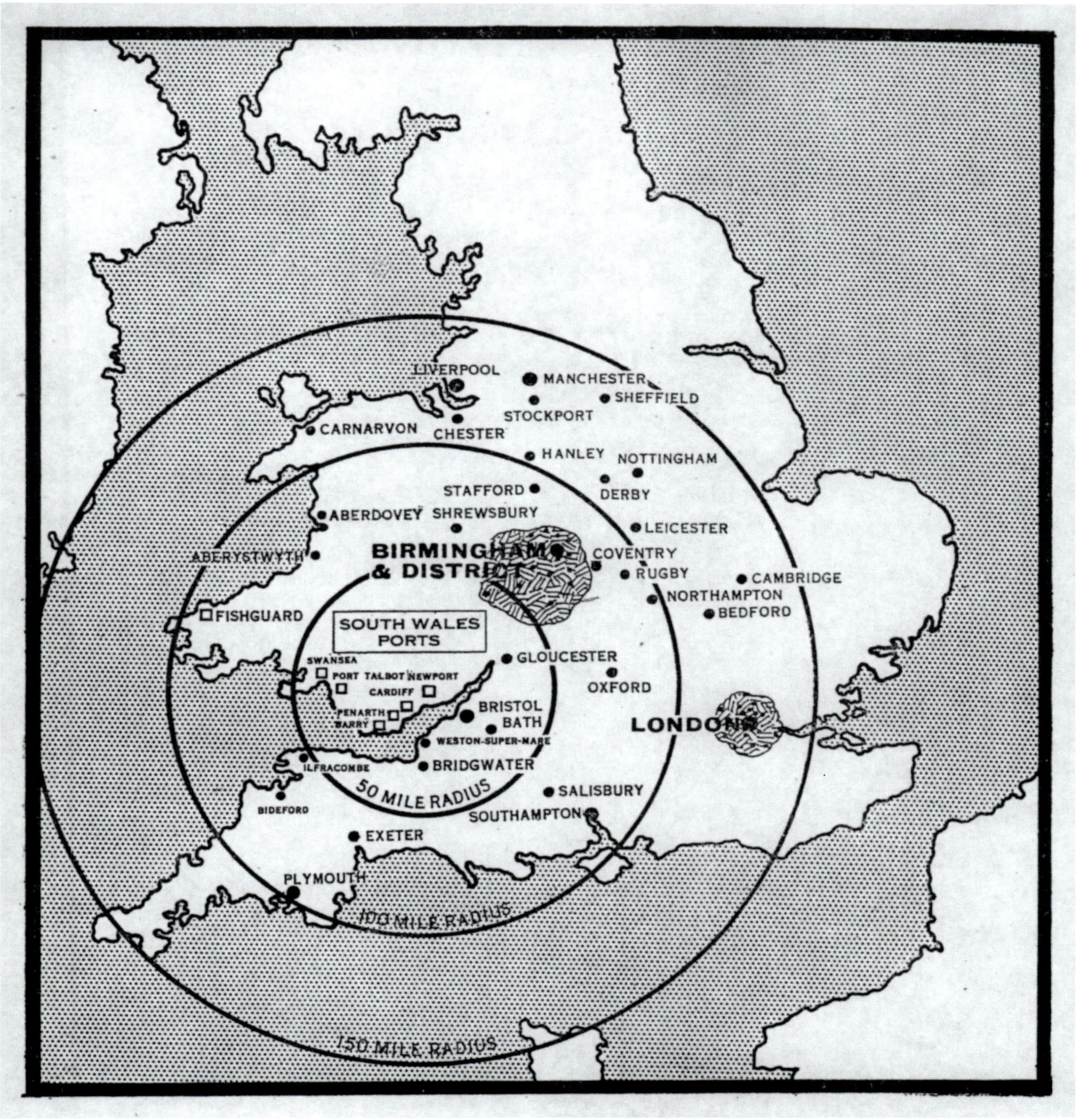

South Wales, in the thirties, was in the grip of a serious depression in trade and industry. Two detailed statements on the industrial crisis, principally related to the considerable decline of the export trade in coal, but also addressing wider, systemic problems, were presented in the company magazine in August 1936 and July 1938.[32] The former, relating the circumstances of the formation of the South Wales Trade Recovery and Expansion System, described South Wales as "a mere simulacrum of its previous self"[33]. Warnings of widespread social and political disaffection and "dangers to the interests of the State as a whole"[34] were given as a spur to action, thus, industrial enterprise in the form of new and diverse industries in South Wales was identified by the Great Western as a social and commercial imperative. This was the theme of 'New Industries for South Wales', 1938, an article underlining the necessary economic and social identification between Paddington and South Wales. The agenda was of development and change and of citizenship and common cause. It offered imagery of warfare – the conflict between prosperity and unemployment, "the country's greatest enemy"[35] - with its reference to a large-scale campaign and policy map indicating investment in South Wales, which was prominent in both the General Manager's office and that of the Chief Goods Manager at Paddington.

In working with the Special Areas (Development and Improvement) Act of 1934 and the Amendment Act of 1937, the GWR looked to the revitalisation and re-structuring of industrial activity in South Wales. Noting the social impact that characterised economic decline, the company recorded the ailing condition of the established heavy industries

> Most of the collieries were idle; the ironworks, if not entirely closed down, were working only part time; shops were closed and empty; in the valleys property was derelict; " men in their scores hung around street corners and – most depressing of all things – one could only see the older people and children; there seemed to be very few youths.[36]

It was stressed that the Chief Goods Officer's department had worked with potential business interests, nationally and internationally. Foreign investors were encouraged by the GWR's provision of linguists and with community-based strategies to find appropriate industrial sites, domestic housing, schools, religious and retail amenities. As a matter of policy the company looked to a new industrial structure – "For the first time in its history, South Wales is relinquishing its dependence upon coal"[37] – and, as in the London area, the new, light industries were identified with progress and prosperity. They also, significantly, broke with the close connection of the particular industrial traditions of coal and iron with recognised regionals; the new industries exemplified ubiquity.

The GWR article, identified "a new era for the region"[38] and included the familiar recital of wide-ranging products – 'sewing machines, glass, biscuits, paper, gloves, toys, electrical goods, sweets, chemicals, paints' and so on[39] – and, in conclusion, linked these directly with wider social and economic development: the context of community.

> When these attractive new industries become productive we shall see fewer idle men and women reflecting poverty and gloom in the valleys ... but as we hope, happy people, bright shops, crowded passenger trains, fully loaded goods trains, busy seaside resorts, well-nourished children and other signs of trade activity[40]

In cultivating a decidedly contemporary, dynamic representation, the GWR's industrial-orientated literature looked to concepts of regeneration and reinvention, in production, commodities and communities. Both large and small-scale industries were involved, particularly those dealing with merchandising and processing, as in the example of a newly commissioned flour mill and factory at Cardiff, featured in the GWR Magazine in March 1935. General merchandise traffic was the most lucrative within the freight sector and within this category the GWR outperformed the LMS, LNE and the SR throughout the inter-war period.[41] The numerous articles and press statements covering new factories emphasised the collectively inspirational properties inherent in design, function and image-building, as here, in the new mill in Cardiff.

> Impressions left upon the visitor are those of the dignity of modern large-scale industry when seen at its best, of skill and ingenuity in design of the buildings and of their equipment and efficiency, thoroughness and cleanliness in all the production processes.[42]

'Commerce and the Great Western Railway,' as mentioned, set trade in an international and imperial context and the company, therefore, made much of the role of its various docks, principally in South Wales – "Britain's Western Gateways." This was a policy carried through to the last days of the company in 1947.

> Britain to a very great extent lives by the sea-borne traffic that flows into and from her thriving ports. There is scarcely a trade that does not look out over the boundaries of these islands, either in viewing the markets that are to consume a portion of its industry or in search of the raw materials that go to the making of the finished products upon which its livelihood depends. It is therefore important to study in detail the actual facilities that the Great Western Railway has to offer on the quayside for that import and export trade which of necessity plays such an important part in the commercial life of our nation.[43]

The Centenary publication in association with the Baltimore and Ohio Railroad, 1927,[44] gave the GWR the opportunity for valuable promotionary work in the USA This volume informed American readers that by 1927 the GWR had invested over five million dollars in improvements with an overall predicted further investment in excess of fifteen million dollars.[45] Looking forward to 1945 and thereby indicating continuity of policy and practice, GWR publicity was directed immediately to economic recovery from World War Two. With foreign trade a priority, booklets in Russian, French and Spanish editions entitled 'The Ports of South Wales and Their Development, During And After The War' were issued in December that year.[46]

'Twixt Rail and Sea',[47] from 1927, was one of a series of books by W.G. Chapman dealing with various dimensions of Great Western engineering and commercial enterprise. The Foreword to this popularist expression of enterprise within the Docks Department was explicit.

> It seems fitting that as the Great Western Railway – this railway of records – now owns the largest and most important group of docks in the world, the next volume in the series should deal with that vital link in modern commerce between land and sea.[48]

Looking here for the character and imagery of this important dimension of GWR enterprise as opposed to specific details, we can refer to a general statement on the South Wales docks, reflecting the high levels of investment and ongoing achievement. The repetition of the word, "new" indicated something of the scale of modern development.

> Wherever we go in the South Wales docks we see signs of new works either recently completed or under construction – new joists, new power stations, miles of additional sidings, new machinery, new hydraulic mains, new transit sheds, new warehouses and new quayside cranes. All around us is evidence that the Great Western Railway Company has been very busy improving the docks since they became part of its vast undertaking.[49]

Elsewhere, Chapman consistently pointed the reader to the

dynamic, cosmopolitan context of Great Western trade and commerce. As a thriving passenger port, Plymouth has been proclaimed, 'the Gateway into England from the Atlantic.'[50] At Cardiff the context widened.

> Look at the names and signs over the (dockland) shop fronts. The names are those of the shopkeepers who are of many nationalities and the signs indicate that their customers speak a variety of languages - Greek, German, Italian, Spanish, Turkish, Chinese, Scandinavian, Dutch; in fact all the maritime countries are catered for. The people we now pass are largely men of colour – black, brown or yellow.[51]

This was an ethos far removed from the 'haunts of ancient peace' in deepest rural England, but it was a definitive dimension of Great Western enterprise. Chapman's delight in relating the scale and variety of goods, trade and activities – the commonplace commodities together with the more unusual and exotic – was clearly apparent. Inspecting Cardiff's Queen Alexandra Dock, Chapman described the contents of the transit sheds and cold stores with some relish, the range of goods and, equally, the cosmopolitan context, conferred a sense of glamour and confident achievement on the company.

> This great stack of cases contains butter from New Zealand. Nearby you can see veritable mountains of cheese and these are boxes of apples from Canada and the Antipodes. Now we come to oranges from Spain and Jaffa, dried fruits, sultanas, raisins, currants etc. from the Middle East and those chests containing tea from India, Ceylon and the Far East.[52]

Imperial and international perspectives, always important to the overall GWR identity, were always a feature of the company's promotion of commerce and trade, again asserting the Greater Britain identity. Consistent with the literature and film material promoted by The Empire Marketing Board, 1926-1933,[53] the GWR drew upon 'family' imagery in its reference to the Empire and, significantly, to the shifting perception away from militarist, territorial dimensions to those of the empire of trade and the expression and structural process of interdependence. This was evident in the company's endorsement of 'The Fellowship of the British Empire Association' featured in the Magazine in 1925.

> One of the main ideas is to encourage a 'family feeling' in all the peoples of the Empire and it is felt that this must go a long way towards the betterment of Empire trade and the promotion of Empire development.[54]

Similarly, the Foreword to 'Commerce and The Great Western Railway.'

> Every Business Man, whether from Overseas, or representing industry in this country, during his visit to the British Empire Exhibition, will have uppermost in his mind how he can best develop trade between Britain and Overseas in order to secure the fullest advantage of the great markets of the Empire.[55]

Above: *The Green Arrow registered freight service, introduced in 1928, was indicative of railway initiatives generally to promote a progressive image in freight handling. This was vital by the early thirties with the threat of rapidly increasing competition from road traffic. All four companies participated in the Green Arrow initiative, likewise, the Blue Arrow for consignments by passenger train, introduced in 1936.*

Right: *Advertisement 'GWR Docks', carried in 'Holiday Haunts' 1934.* Author's collection

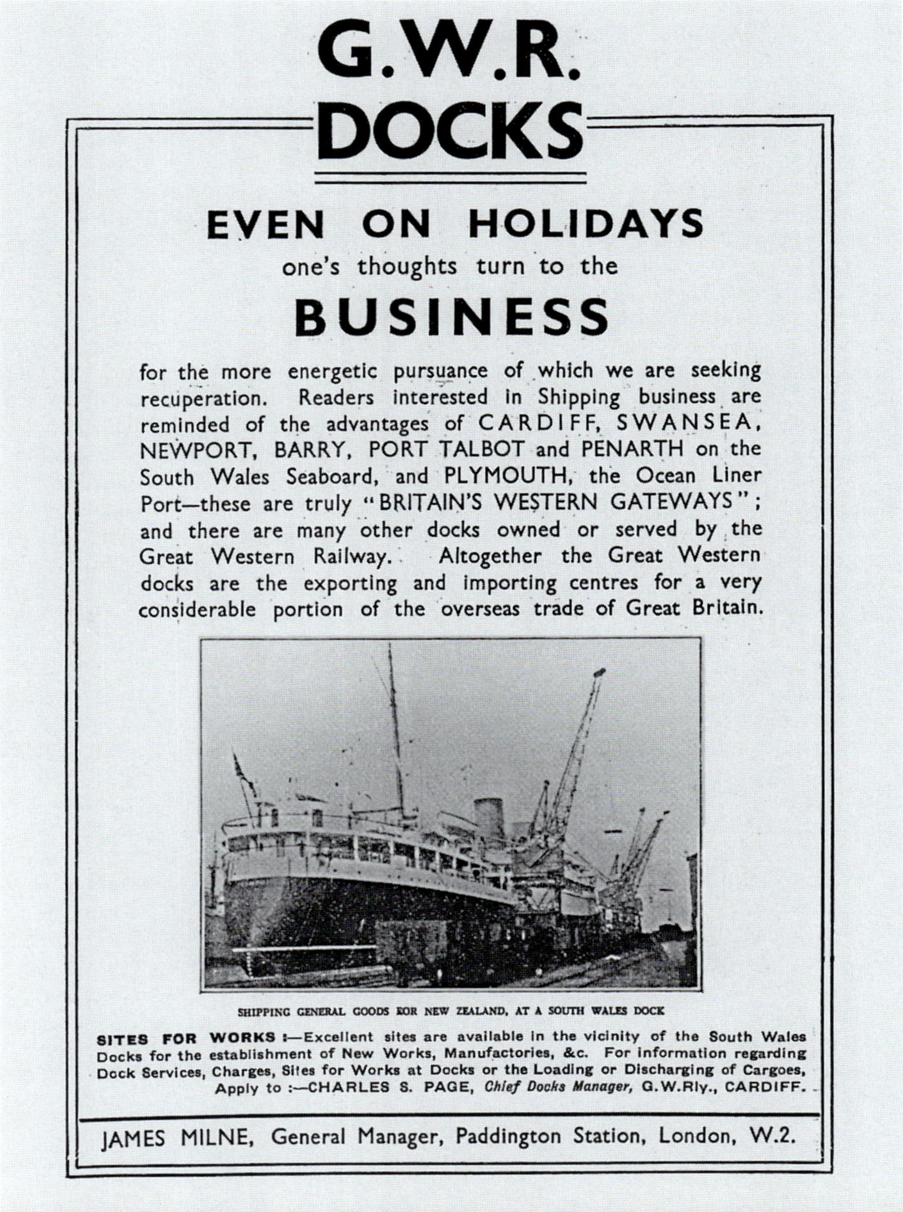

The 'family feeling' of the British Empire Association accorded with Stanley Baldwin's representation of Empire and Imperialism in terms of duties and ideas of a "Commonwealth of British Nations"[56] John Mackenzie, however, cautions that, within popular perceptions and for all its international idealism and economic harmony, "it was an Empire of stereotypes, climactic, national and racial, which bore little relation to the colonial reality of the thirties..."[57] But, he also recognises that "it seems to have won considerable support across the political spectrum."[58] Stephen Constantine, in developing Mackenzie's reference, also signals parallel perspectives on the part of the GWR in its identification with imperial interests.

> The business of extracting economic benefits for Britain from imperial connections involved British ministers in obsessive concern with migration, tariff and colonial development policies. Such an agenda, though with different emphases, was adopted by Labour and Liberal parties as well as by the Conservatives (and the British Union of Fascists) and was endorsed consistently by such organisations of industry and commerce as the Federation of British Industries and not infrequently by the Trades Union Congress. Moreover, the period shows no diminution but, if anything, an increase in the amount of propaganda, which pressed upon the British public through a wider range of media, the virtues and values of Empire.[59]

Considered in these terms of reference, the British Empire Exhibition of 1924-25 and the GWR's commemorative literature thereof, or events such as the ceremonial departure of 'The Cornish Riviera Express' from Paddington with the locomotive displaying the "Empire Marketing Board/Great Western Railway" commemorative headboard on Monday November 23, 1931,[60] suggested a popular, practical perception of empire, not that of an illusionary semblance of the "white empire on the cigarette cards and souvenir biscuit-tins," in children's scrap-books "and the minds of men" as argued by Correlli Barnett.[61] The Paddington ceremony, part of the "Buy British From The Empire At Home And Overseas Campaign," was attended by GWR dignitaries, The Secretary of State for the Dominions and Chairman of the Empire Marketing Board together with the Lord Mayor and Lady Mayoress of London. It was an unequivocal statement of imperial identification and orientation at both national and company levels, according directly with the GWR policy of the creative integration of commercial and cultural identities. This relationship was further reflected in the re-naming of 'The Travel Association of Great Britain and Ireland', itself, one part of the 'Come To Britain Movement' of 1926. From February 1932 The Travel Association became 'The Travel and Industrial Development Association of Great Britain and Ireland.'[62]

As with international, imperial perspectives, so similarly, 'Next Station', GWR, 1947,[63] celebrated the range of perishable produce once again originating from the various regional sources within its territory. The passage here from the chapter, 'The Freight Service', reinforced the sense of organic identity and considerably enhanced the Great Western's reputation through its close association with its many productive horticultural districts, resonant of the imagery of genial climate and the general sense of abundance. Urban/rural and cultural/commercial representations were again apparent.

> To people in London and other great cities, the flower expresses from Cornwall which ran again for the first time in April 1946, brought the pleasantest of reminders that peace had indeed returned to this hard-pressed land. In that year's season, express freight trains carried for distribution throughout the country 175,000 tons of fruit and vegetables – broccoli and early potatoes from West Wales, plums, apples, beans, peas, brussel sprouts, asparagus and other delicacies from the Vale of Evesham and tomatoes from the Channel Islands (over four-and-a-half million packages from Guernsey and Jersey were handled at Weymouth). To ensure that these highly perishable goods reached the market as soon after harvesting as possible, over a thousand special trains were run, not counting the fifteen special expresses which ran daily to distribute the plum crops of the short Worcester season.[64]

Such images had a long pedigree. Many years earlier, in 1904, no less than the GWR General Manager, James C. Inglis, presented a company article entitled, 'A New Railway Through the Garden of England.'[65] With reference to the new line linking Birmingham to Cheltenham, Inglis focused upon the horticultural trade centred around Toddington, again evoking the Great Western identity by association with the rich, rural and historical imagery of England and, therein, the commercial potential in traffic. Thus, again, the evidence for the commercial-cultural interaction.

> The cultivation of plums of all kinds received considerable attention. Plum trees adapt themselves to the soil in the situation while the space between the trees is utilised for strawberries, gooseberries and raspberries etc., as well as vegetables of all description ... The finer kinds of fruit – peach, nectarine, apricot, etc. – are grown under glass on a wholesale scale, the earliest peaches commanding high prices at Covent Garden market.[66]

Whilst these various forms of perishables were undoubtedly the most attractive and appealing of merchandise traffic, they also contributed substantially to the 56 per cent of mileage in freight run by the GWR on a weekly basis, as compared with 44 per cent for passenger trains.[67] Merchandise freight, as noted, had been one of the GWR's most sustained and lucrative sources of traffic during the inter-war years, thus progress was geared to efficient administration and considered marketing and investment. As expressed in the 'Next Station,' 1947. "It is object of the management to reap all the advantages of centralised control, but to combine them with the intimate grasp of local conditions...."[68]

Investment covered many dimensions, as particularly evident through the thirties. It include the provision of new goods depots for efficient handling, collection and dispersal, and modern containerised, refrigerated and ventilated freight vans, particularly for perishable traffic, many of them fitted for passenger train running. The company also invested in research projects as in the work carried out in horticulture in West Cornwall, particularly with the flower traffic.[69] Early anemones, for example, were displayed in London's Oxford Street and Charing Cross Road with the invitation to "See the Flower Fields." Publicity for the 'Cornish Riviera Express' was also incorporated into the enterprise[70]

Cornwall provided many such opportunities to correlate local, commercial interests – the flower fields, fruit and dairy produce and general horticulture – with the sense of special place. Flower field poster work and the numerous official company photographs of flower and potato harvesting, preferably with St. Michael's Mount or dramatic Isles of Scilly locations as a backdrop, or, indeed, those depicting milk lorries in deeply rural settings, clearly exemplified this strategy. The thematic interaction of directed railway enterprise and local-regional character instilled a sense of intended dramatic resonance which the GWR Magazine was ever keen to exploit, as in the feature, 'The Spring Harvest of the West Country', 1938.

> On a cold winter night many of those who have caught a glimpse of thousands of boxes of fresh Cornish flowers being unloaded at Paddington station for dispatch to Covent Garden Market must have felt a longing to travel West to the country where the narcissus blooms out of

A Sunday Penzance-Kensington milk train approaches Cowley Bridge Junction, Exeter, June 1959. Michael Mensing

doors before Christmas, and anenomes can be picked throughout the year.[71]

A similarly styled and thematically-led feature on Cornish milk traffic[72] highlighted the situation of "the early morning traffic of our city streets" in the form of the milkman and that of the GWR lorry negotiating "deep, narrow and winding Cornish lanes on [its] way to the farms."[73] In recording the work of the company in association with Nestle's milk concentration depot, 1932, at railside in the mid Cornish town of Lostwithiel, the GWR Magazine described the process of collecting, treating and despatching vast quantities of milk to Nestle's London depots and to other regional centres. Lostwithiel was the hub of the collection/distribution process, which saw the county partitioned into 24 collecting routes and regions with 9 other collection centres: Saltash, Liskeard, Looe, Bodmin, St. Austell, Truro, Helston, Falmouth and Newquay. Having initially emphasised the distance between London and Lostwithiel, that of 250 miles, the article simultaneously enhanced the sense of contrasts and integration by linking all the Cornish communities through the activities of the lorries converging on Lostwithiel and by the juxtaposition of key imagery. The modern, mechanised efficiency of the new depot where the milk was prepared and fed into "awaiting glass-lined tank wagons" was also set in sharp contrast with the image of the waiting farmer at his gate "carrying a lantern and accompanied by his dog."[74] The overall impact, however, was that of a closely co-ordinated, structured operation, clearly linking the country and the city, the urban and rural dimensions, by means of a dynamic railway enterprise.

Channel Islands traffic through Weymouth provided another such stimulus. With all their exotic associations underlined in GWR literature – the cast consignments of Guernsey tomatoes, Jersey potatoes and island flower traffic generally, together with that of French fruit, flowers and vegetables, not least, the considerable broccoli imports from the Roscoff district of Brittany–Weymouth harbour reflected a vibrancy that helped enhance the resort's overall appeal. It was also, of course, conducive to progressive imagery on the part of the railway company in its association with the Channel Islands generally. This was evident in the GWR's celebration of the new harbour facilities, of 1933, formally inaugurated by the Prince of Wales on 13 July that year. Under a joint scheme with Weymouth Corporation, a much enlarged, modern harbour complex was provided. A new pier built of reinforced concrete, 100 feet wide and almost a quarter of a mile long, replaced a much smaller timber structure of only 30 feet in width. The new development accommodated "one passenger, three cargo and two pleasure steamers simultaneously."[75] Six large electric cranes and railway facilities comprising two platforms to hold 36 coaches – where, formerly, there was room for only four – new baggage handling and customs amenities and a new refreshment room substantially improved services overall. Also incorporated, however, was a pedestrian promenade on the north side of the development that the GWR was evidently anxious to project as thematically integral to the whole project.

> On the promenade pier every effort has been made to provide for the needs of the public. Reinforced concrete shelters of pleasing design have been constructed with accessible (promenade-styled) flat roofs protected by ornamental railings; bathing facilities have been provided in the way of dressing accommodation and an elaborate diving stage; and stairways down to the water constructed at intervals along the pier for the use of small craft.[76]

The harbour development was described by the GWR as constituting "an admirable breadth of comprehension", a scheme that had "done justice to the claims of business and pleasure". As to the mutual interest of railway and town, the company reported that in 1928 it had paid harbour dues of £8,541, more than double the 1922 figure of £4,099 and that for the three years, 1929-1932, dues were in excess of £10,000 per annum.[77] This seasonal traffic, much expanded by the late thirties – as was also the case with the range of perishable produce from Cornwall – marked a valuable contribution to overall merchandise traffic. The latter, of course, was always central to the company's record in freight movements generally and, with carefully considered marketing, worked to the advantage of tourism generally.

An 'up' mixed freight, merchandise and china clay, between St Germans and Saltash in East Cornwall, July, 1959. Peter Gray

REFERENCES – CHAPTER FIVE

1: GWR Magazine March 1935 P130.

2: Ibid P131.

3: The Great Western Railway (London) Lecture and Debating Society No. 227 24 January 1929.

4: Ibid PPs 7-8.

5: Ibid P8.

6: Ibid P8.

7: GWR Lecture, Debating Society No. 179 5 February 1925. P16.

8: GWR Lecture, Debating Society No. 284 18 October 1934 PPs 14-15.

9: GWR Build Your Works on the GWR The Best Location. 1932.

10: GWR Door to Door Country Cartage Service Poster. The number of lorry services increased from 142 in 1932 to 184 by November 1937 – GWR Magazine January 1938 P9.

11: GWR Holiday Haunts. The Centenary of the Holiday Line. 1935. P33

12: GWR Magazine, January, 1935, P6. January, 1938, P4.

13: GWR Commerce and the Great Western Railway, April, 1924, P19

14: GWR Through The Window, Paddington To Birkenhead, P51

15: Ibid P51

16: Ibid P51

17: Ibid P51

18. GWR Build Your Works on the GWR The Best Location, 1932

19: Ibid P1

20: The Best Location, March, 1936 (Revised Edition)

21: The Best Location, 1932,. P2

22: Ibid P3

23: Ibid P3

24: Ibid P3

25: GWR Holiday Haunts. Advertisement: 'Ritchings Park', 1931, P66.

26: GWR Magazine, December, 1936. P575-77

27: Ibid P577

28: Ibid P577

29: Ibid P577

30: Ibid P577

31: Ibid P577

32: GWR Magazine, August 1936. The Problem of Restoring Prosperity to South Wales. PP 369-372 GWR Magazine, July 1938. New Industries for South Wales PP273-2

33: GWR Magazine. Problem ... Prosperity South Wales P369

34: Ibid P368

35: GWR Magazine. New Industries ... South Wales P273

36: Ibid P274

37: Ibid PP274

38: Ibid P275

39: Ibid PP274-275

40: Ibid P275 The Treforest Trading Estate was cited as a successful initiative in this context. Ibid PPs 7-8, 275.

41: John W.E. Helm. The Grouping Years (1923-1938). A comparative Study Of The Railways In Crisis. PART TWO. TRAFFIC RESULTS Back Track Vol XI P19, February, 1997 P75-76

42: GWR Magazine, December 1935 P147. See also for example, GWR Magazine, Oct 1924, P385, 'The Chocolate

Traffic'. (Fry's at Bristol with its imagery of "truck loads of chocolate" and the context of "the River Avon with its willow-hung banks [which] flows very near." Likewise, 'The World's Largest Milk Depot.' GWR Magazine, Feb. 1935, P75. "Equipped with the most modern plant for processing by pasteurization, homogenisation and sterilization and with a laboratory for bacteriological and chemical control, the depot is one of the marvels of the milk industry." The depot at Wood Lane in West London was the focus for milk traffic from all parts of the company's system. The article included a structural reference indicative of the metropolitan perspective and city-country dialectic. Noting "the scattered farms" – the first stage – the milk was then transferred to 'concentration depots' in Cornwall, Devon, Dorset, Wiltshire, Somerset and West Wales, for example, the intermediate stage, and thence to London's Wood Lane in the specially designed glass-lined tankers, for its treatment – the final stage. Thus, again, the organic, interactive structure is expressed. Other such intended wholesome identifications came with the fruit, vegetable, flower and fish traffic from the various representative regions of the GWR This 'wholesome' imagery was also utilised in several instances of poster work.

43: GWR Commerce and the Great Western Railway. 1924. P9

44: GWR Great Western Railway of England 1837-1927, Souvenir published by GWR of England in connection with the Centenary Exhibition and Pageant of the Baltimore and Ohio Railroad, Baltimore, Maryland, USA Sept 24 – Oct 8, 1927.

45: Ibid P23

46: GWR The Ports of South Wales And Their Development During And After The War. Acknowledged Chief Docks Manager, Leslie Ford GWR Cardiff. December 1945. This was a policy closely linked with that of the British Travel Association's initiative begun earlier, in 1937: British Travel Association 1929-1969, British Travel Authority, London. 1970. P10.

47: W.G. Chapman. Twixt Rail And Sea, GWR 1927

48: Ibid Foreword

49: Ibid P73

50: GWR Great Western Railway Ports. (Plymouth), 1937, P71

51: Chapman Twixt Rail And Sea, P61

52: Ibid P64. Chapman's general reference here drew upon an extensive literature of the celebration literature of the celebration and interaction of empire, trade and cultural identity. From Classical representations of Alexandria or Ostia or the sixteenth and seventeenth century geo-political relation ship of Europe to the Orient and the New World in the art and literature of Portugal, Italy, Spain and the Low Countries; likewise, the colonial-mercantile interests of Britain and France in the eighteenth century and through the self-conscious Crown-Imperial perspectives of Britain in the late nineteenth and early twentieth centuries, cultural authority was paramount. The Baedeker Guides to Britain through the later nineteenth and early twentieth centuries likewise reflect the international, cosmopolitan credentials of political, economic and cultural authority. See also Alain Corbin. Lure Of The Sea. Chapter Seven: The Visit To The Harbour, PP187-97

53: See John M. Mackenzie, ed. Imperialism And Popular Culture, Chapter Nine, Stephen Constantine. 'Bringing The Empire Alive.' The Empire Marketing Board And Imperial Propaganda, 1926-33, Manchester University Press, Manchester, 1986

54: GWR Magazine April, 1925. P147

55: GWR Commerce And The Great Western Railway P3

56: Stanley Baldwin. On England, Penguin ed. 1939 PPs 187-88 Philip Wilkinson 'Stanley Baldwin' P264.

57: John M. Mackenzie, ed. Imperialism And Popular Culture. In Touch with the Infinite, P186

58: Ibid P186

59: Stephen Constantine. Bringing the Empire Alive, John Mackenzie ed. Imperialism And Popular Culture P192 See also Raphael Samuel. Island Stories. Unravelling Britain. Versa, London, 1998. Empire Stories: The Imperial and the Domestic. PPs 84-93 London Underground. London Guide No. 3, 1924. P133. Kew Gardens in context of commercial welfare of Empire.

60: GWR Magazine, December, 1931. P507

61: Correlli Barnett. The Collapse Of British Power, Alan Sutton Publishing, Stroud, 1984 P211. Barnett's sustained critique of what he considered the disingenuous 'Little England' perceptions of Empire are evident in his chosen imagery and, specifically, in his representation of Stanley Baldwin (PP65-68). This, together with what he considered was Britain's misplaced faith in any Anglo-American 'special relationship', indicated something of his impatience and barely concealed contempt for the domesticated, commercial perspectives and sentimentally inspired imperial policies that he derides throughout his work.

62: GWR Magazine, February, 1932, P96

63: Christian Barman. Next Station. A Railway Plans For The Future, George Allen and Unwin, London for the GWR 1947.

64: Ibid P19

65: James C. Inglis. 'A New Railway Through The Garden of England', G.,W.R. Magazine, October 1904. Inglis also incorporated a considerable historical-cultural dimension in this work, celebrating perspectives of landscape, tradition and cultural identity.

66: Ibid P168

67: John W.E. Helm. The Grouping Years (1923-1938 P74:75)

68: Christian Barman. Next Station, P18

69: GWR Magazine. The Spring Harvest of the West Country, April, 1938 PPs 141-143

70: Ibid Cornish Anemones Come to Town December 1938. P493

71: GWR Magazine April, 1938 P141.

72: GWR Magazine February, 1933 PPs 63-66.

73: Ibid PPs 63:65.

74: Ibid PPs 65:66.

75: GWR Magazine July, 1933 P283.

76: Ibid P284.

77: Ibid P281.

CHAPTER SIX

THE HOLIDAY LINE: POST-WAR PERSPECTIVES

Great Western post-war Summer services began on Monday 6 May 1946, two months earlier than was the case with pre-war timetables. Three months later, on 15 August, the company's first excursion train, 'The Kiddies Express', to Weston-Super-Mare, left Paddington with 500 children on a day's outing to the seaside.[1] This was the beginning of the last great era in railway holiday travel, peaking in the mid fifties and falling into rapid decline a decade later. The GWR related 'Next Station', 1947, reported the greatly increased scale of post-war holiday traffic:

> In 1946 the number of workers enjoying holidays with pay was roundly fifteen million – nearly four times the pre-war figure.[2]

Comparative figures for 1938 and 1946 revealed that the number of passengers leaving Paddington in the third week of August had almost doubled from 104,595, pre-war, to 202,270, post-war.[3]

There were considerable problems, however, in meeting demand given the legacy of six years of war. Sir James Milne, General Manager, GWR, wrote in the Midsummer edition of the Company Magazine, 1947, of the obstacles to the summer train service for that season. Under the direction of the Minister of Transport, the summer timetable was reduced by ten per cent on the 1946 figure in order to save coal supplies which were 25 per cent below pre-war production levels. It was also emphasised that there would be severe waiting times and queues at stations, together with unavoidable and extensive overcrowding during journeys themselves with the prospect for many passengers of standing in corridors for entire journeys. Speed restrictions from increased loadings to compensate for reduced timetables, from the deterioration of the permanent way and from the priority given to coal and freight traffic, extended journey times and compromised published timekeeping schedules. Heavy arrears in the maintenance of rolling stock and locomotives also meant detailed shortages. On coaching stock, Milne revealed that in 1947 there were 6,000 fewer vehicles in service than in 1939. Moreover, of the 1,350 new coaches anticipated for service generally, it was anticipated that only 570 would enter traffic.[4]

A particular blow to GWR prestige and to the Cornish holiday business was the enforced, albeit temporary withdrawal of 'The Cornish Riviera Express' from 15 March 1947 to 16 June that year. Withdrawal was imperative in order to conserve previous coal stocks. Major Dewar, on behalf of the Publicity Department, put the company's position to the Newquay Chamber of Commerce at the March meeting.

> I ask you to believe that it is a matter of the utmost regret to the GWR. The need is obvious and we act under Government instructions in taking off our old friend, 'The Limited'. It is obvious that under the circumstances obtaining at the present juncture of our history, no railway can do anything to attract visitors to any resort and if I have nothing more than a very barren message it is because of the very unfortunate conditions which have been brought on us after six years of war which make it necessary for us to draw into our shells.[5]

This summary of some of the principal operating problems in the immediate post-war period offers a useful reminder of the circumstances in which the GWR and early Western Region were required to work, despite being faced by the much increased demand for holiday train services on the part of the public, anxious to enjoy the various pleasures of the seaside.

Looking to the post-war holiday literature, the 1947 edition of 'Holiday Haunts' was the final volume under GWR management prior to Nationalisation, introduced from 1 January 1948. This publication reflected detailed differences from the 1939 edition, mainly in terms of its content and perspective which was much more attuned to an all-inclusive, popularist approach, subtly derided in the company's pre-war work as that of the "carefree democracy".

Maxwell Fraser edited the 1947 'Holiday Haunts' as she had in 1939, thereby creating a sense of continuity, but the 1947 edition, although similar in format, was reduced in size to 688 pages as against 968 in 1939. A definite shift in character and approach was evident. The lavish pre-war perspectives of received historical and rural imagery and all it symbolised were largely removed in post-war publications, being replaced by a more economical and factually-based style, more akin to that of the other three companies of the inter-war years. Overall the post-war focus was that of the popular, openly democratic character of both the seaside and rural-historic landscapes, also the emphasis, especially at the seaside, being upon more organised entertainment and convenience, the perspective of a decidedly family-orientated experience.

The stylistic and thematic contrasts, pre and post-war, can be appreciated by reference to various representative locations. Looking first to the seaside resorts, it is clear that there was much greater continuity of content and style between the GWR work of 1947 and British Railways 1959 edition of 'Holiday Haunts' than was evident for the GWR's 1939 and 1947 publications.

Torquay, for example, was presented in much less exclusive manner. The pre-war emphasis upon favourable comparisons with Mediterranean resorts was dropped for an evidently more egalitarian image. "Torquay provides all, and more than all, the entertainment and sports demanded by modern holiday-makers, all through the year, with hundreds of hotels to suit every purse".[6] Neighbouring Paignton's popular 'family' resort image was enhanced in 1947 and, as with Torquay, the British Railways Western Region 'Holiday Haunts' entry for 1949 was unaltered. By 1959, however, the handbook's entry for the resort was substantially increased with much greater detail on recreational facilities. Paignton also warranted the most extensive coverage by that time of all the resorts served by the Western Region.[7]

Ilfracombe, in North Devon, was likewise re-invented in 1947. Its entries in 'Holiday Haunts' from, for instance, 1936 and 1947, were transformed. Post-war Ilfracombe was 'the largest and gayest seaside resort on the north coast of Devon."[8] The "pretty tree-shaded, countrified lanes and cliff walks [were] within a few minutes walk of the High Street."[9] In an atmosphere of comfortable convenience, the 1947 Holiday Haunts summarised Ilfracombe as "an ideal place for a happy family holiday."[10] Gone were the pre-war comparisons with the Spanish town of San Sebastian; likewise the celebration of lanes and roads "leading to fascinating villages and historic buildings,"[11] in the pre-war context of dynamic landscape and the sense of adventure into deep rural, coastal locations. The Southern Region edition of 'Holiday Haunts', 1960 – perpetuating the GWR title – characterised the contemporary character of the resort and of the tourist industry generally in even more explicit manner.

> Ilfracombe has its history. Its harbour dates at least from Saxon times, but its laudable ambition today is to ensure that its holiday-makers get such a welcome and such enjoyment that a return visit becomes an automatic certainty.[12]

Above: *Holiday Guide, South West , 1954.* Author's collection

Left: *Front cover, British Railways, Western Region, 'Holiday Guide' 1949.* Author's collection

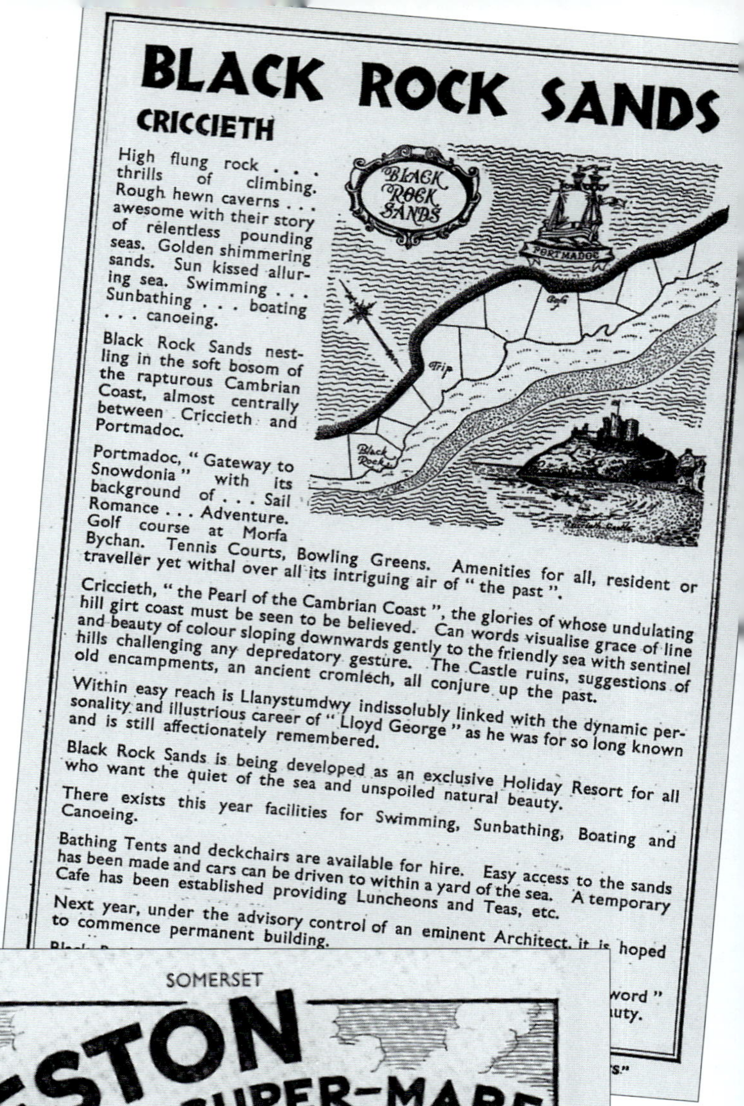

Above, left: *Advertisement from 'Holiday Haunts' for Butlins Holiday Camp at Pwllheli, opened in 1947.*

Above, right: *Advertisement for development at Black Rock Sands, Criccieth, carried in Holiday Haunts, 1947.*

Right: *Advertisement from 'Holiday Haunts' 1959: Weston-Super-Mare.*

Further west, Penzance lost its detailed comparisons with Mediterranean resorts. References characteristic of the town from 1904 and the initial publication of 'The Cornish Riviera' celebrating favourable identifications with Monte Carlo, Paris, Algiers or Madeira,[13] were replaced in 1947 by much less ambitious or potentially intimidating characterisation. For 1947, Penzance offered "an equable climate", and was "the centre of a great flower-growing district" [where] a collection of sub-tropical trees and flowers grow to perfection in the open air".[14] It is also significant that this 1947 entry for Penzance was virtually unchanged when used in the Western Region's 1959 edition.

In South Wales, Tenby provided a decisive example of re-writing. The town's dramatic aesthetic and historical perspectives, detailed in chapter one, were replaced by a much cosier, domesticated representation. Tenby, in 1947, had "exceptional attractions as a family resort where the tastes of each individual member of the family can be gratified".[15] Once again, emphasising the all-round, comprehensive character of the town, the 1947 handbook declared:

> There are splendid sands, rocks, caves and islands for the children, all kinds of sports, cinemas, dances and entertainments for the adults, quiet nooks on the cliffs or among sand-dunes for those in need of a restful holiday, an outstanding interesting 13th century parish church, 14th century city walls, a Tudor house and the remains of a medieval castle for the historically minded.[16]

The historical dimension was incorporated, albeit much reduced, on pre-war works but the literary flourish and commitment that was so definitive of the pre-war era was gone. In effect, scenery replaced challenging aesthetic experience; the gratuitous pleasures of the promenade and beach ousted the former studies and protocols of the seashore in their variously related educationalist perspectives, whilst romantically-inspired legend and mystery largely took the place of the GWR's evident historical focus.

The changes evident in the company's rural-historical interests can be appreciated by reference to various key locations. The extended history lesson that comprised the GWR's entry for Monmouth in 1936, for example, was much reduced by 1947 to only a third of its former self.[17] Hereford was similarly treated.[18] Here, the strong sense of its Anglo-Saxon inheritance was, like that at Monmouth, substantially reduced to a compact, summative statement. Both communities in the 1947 handbook had, effectively, lost their rich historical and cultural resonances in favour of a more factually informative approach.

Changes in style and theme were especially evident in the GWR's rural coverage, as two examples, one from the Wye Valley and one from Devon, will indicate. Symonds Yat was one of the GWR's set-piece locations as the literature of the inter-war era demonstrates.

The pre-war celebration of landscape, in colour, elevation, shape, contrasting distances and historical association, was replaced in 1947 by a bland entry of three sentences, factually-based, but emotionally unengaged.

> Like many of the beauty spots of the Wye Valley, Symonds Yat is seen at its best from the train. A footpath from the end of the down platform climbs the wooded hillside to the Yat Rock, a famous view-point, and from the up platform another path runs beside the river to the Ferry across the Wye. The high, densely wooded cliffs with their great bastions of rock, on each side of the river, make Symonds Yat the most famous of all the glorious reaches of the Wye.[20]

Tintern, in the Wye Valley, was given similar treatment in 1947. From a site of "sublime beauty that is forever a thing apart in the memory of all who have been there," the post-war perspective was that of "one of the most popular tourist resorts in the Wye Valley."[21] From the former entry of sixteen lines of superlatives, the post-war statement was reduced by almost two thirds.[22]

The most stark of comparisons, however, is probably that relating to Newton Ferrers and Noss Mayo in South Devon. Again, from a detailed paragraph of intense romanticaly-charged imagery and associations of deepest rural England, in the pre-war works, that of 1947 – retained for the 1959 British Railway's edition – was effectively unrecognisable. A total transformation in character and theme was evident.

> Newton Ferrers and Noss Mayo face each other across the upper reaches of the Yealm estuary and are so closely linked with Plymouth by bus that they are rapidly developing as a residential district for business people of that city. There are field and woodland paths on both sides of the river, which also offers excellent boating, bathing, fishing and sailing.[23]

The paramount suburban ethos and its emphasis upon amenities and convenience generally exemplifies the substantial shift in focus and theme and, in many respects, was very similar to the pre-war Southern Railway approach evident in its "Rambles"[24] series as it applied to the Home Counties, metropolitan experience. The GWR's pre-war celebration of rural-historical Britain and the conspicuous identification with imagery and associations of this tradition were no more. It was also significant, however, as a recurrent feature here, that the 1947 GWR 'Holiday Haunts' set the literary pattern for the Western Region's editions thereafter until 1963, as from that year the handbook ceased to be a railway-based publication.

REFERENCES – CHAPTER SIX

1: Christian Barman Next Station. George Allen and Unwin Ltd. 1947 P14.

2: Ibid P10.

3: Ibid P11.

4: GWR Magazine. Midsummer 1947 Vol. 59 No. 5 PPs 101-102.

5: Newquay Guardian. The Newquay Chamber of Commerce. Report Thursday 20 March 1947. P2.

6: GWR Holiday Haunts, 1947. P255.

7: British Railways W.R. Holiday Haunts 1959, P78.

8: GWR Holiday Haunts 1947 P248.

9: Ibid P248.

10: Ibid P248.

11: GWR Holiday Haunts 1936 P333.

12: British Railways S.R. Holiday Haunts 1960. P315.

13: GWR The Cornish Riviera. A.M. Broadley 1926 (Fifth edition) P54.

14: GWR Holiday Haunts 1947 PP133-134.

15: Ibid P589.

16: Ibid P589.

17: Ibid P583.

18: Ibid P653.

19: GWR Holiday Haunts 1936 P949.

20: GWR Holiday Haunts 1947 P584.

21: GWR Holiday Haunts 1936 P854.

22: GWR Holiday Haunts 1947. P584.

23: Ibid P251; Holiday Haunts, 1936. P337.

24: S.P.B. Mais. Southern Rambles For Londoners. Southern Railway 1931. Walking At Weekends. S.R. 1936. See also Southern Homes Series – anon.

LOADS FOR POTATO TRAINS—WORKED BY STEAM LOCOMOTIVES.

The following are the maximum engine loads for complete trains of Potato traffic shewn in this Notice. Any " Siphons " or other heavily " tared " wagons (except Cattle Wagons) to be calculated 1 equals 2 ordinary wagons.

	Maximum Number of Wagons for Headcode and Type of Engine shewn.		
Headcode ...	" C "	" D "	" E "
Type of Engine ...	" Castle " " County " " Hall " " Grange."	" Castle " " County " " Hall " " Grange."	" Manor " and " 43XX "
Penzance to Camborne...	32	32	29
Camborne to Tavistock Junction ...	35	35	32
Tavistock Junction to Newton Abbot (assisted from Tavistock Junction to Hemerdon and from Totnes to Dainton)	35 †22	44 †22	38 †19
Newton Abbot to Taunton ...	50	55	50
Taunton to Bristol and Cardiff (assisted Stapleton Road to Filton and Pilning to Severn Tunnel Junction)	*50 †30	55 †35	50 †32
Taunton to Paddington (assisted Castle Cary to Witham)	50 †43	55 †43	50 †40
Newbury to Didcot (via Compton) ...	‡45	‡48	‡45
Reading or Didcot to Banbury ...	50	55	50
Maindee Junction to Shrewsbury (assisted Abergavenny to Llanvihangel)	45 —	48 †35	45 †32
Shrewsbury to Saltney ...	45	45	43
Bristol to Bordesley Junction via Yate and Standish Junction (assisted Stapleton Road to Filton and Stratford-on Avon to Wilmcote)	45 —	48 †35	45 †31
Gloucester to Crewe via Honeybourne or Ashchurch and Wombourn (assisted Stourbridge Junction to Kingswinford Junction)	45 —	48 †35	45 †31
Bordesley Junction to Oxley Sidings. (Not to be stopped at Moor Street) ...	45	46	43

*—Assisted Stapleton Road to Filton only. †—Unassisted loads.
‡—" Castle " and " County " Class Engines not authorised.

Any train which does not conform with these instructions must be dealt with in accordance with the standard arrangements as set out in the Working Time Tables.

The actual loads of trains must not exceed the " Working Loads " as set out in the Working Time Tables.

LOADS FOR BROCCOLI TRAINS— WORKED BY STEAM LOCOMOTIVES.

The following are the maximum steam engine loads for complete trains of Broccoli traffic shewn in this Notice. Cattle wagons to be calculated for loading purposes, as Vanfits.

	Maximum Number of Wagons for Headcode and Type of Engine shewn.		
Headcode ...	" C "	" D "	" E "
Type of Engine ...	" Castle " " County " " Hall " " Grange "	" Castle " " County " " Hall " " Grange "	" Manor " and " 43XX "
Penzance to Camborne...	40	40	36
Camborne to Tavistock Junction ...	45	45	40
Tavistock Junction to Newton Abbot (assisted from Tavistock Junction to Hemerdon and from Totnes to Dainton)	50 †27	54 †27	48 †24
Newton Abbot to Taunton ...	50	67	62
Taunton to Bristol and Cardiff (assisted Stapleton Road to Filton and Pilning to Severn Tunnel Junction)	50 †43	65 †43	62 †38
Taunton to Paddington (assisted Castle Cary to Witham)	†50	67 †53	62 †48
Westbury to Didcot North Junction (via Swindon) ...	50	62	57
Newbury to Didcot (via Compton) ...	‡50	‡53	48
Maindee Junction to Shrewsbury (assisted Abergavenny to Llanvihangel) ...	†50	53 †45	53 †40
Shrewsbury to Saltney ...	50	55	50
Bristol to Bordesley Junction via Yate and Standish Junction (assisted Stapleton Road to Filton and Stratford-on-Avon to Wilmcote) ...	50 †43	67 †43	63 †38
Reading or Didcot to Bordesley Junction (assisted Warwick to Hatton North) ...	50	67 †58	64 †54
Gloucester to Crewe via Honeybourne or Ashchurch and Wombourn (assisted Stourbridge Junction to Kingswinford Junction) ...	50 †43	59 †43	54 †39
Bordesley Junction to Oxley Sidings. (Not to be stopped at Moor Street) ...	50	58	54

†—Unassisted loads.

‡—Castle and County Class Engines not authorised.

Any train which does not conform with these instructions must be dealt with in accordance with the standard arrangements as set out in the Working Time Tables.

The actual loads of trains must not exceed the " Working Loads " as set out in the Working Time Tables.

Instructions for Broccoli and Potato traffic from Marazion eastward, 1960/61 season

TRAIN SCHEDULES FOR BROCCOLI AND POTATO TRAFFIC.

Number of Special ...	1		2		3	
	11.20 a.m. Marazion to Cardiff.		†11.20 a.m. Penzance to Paddington Goods.		12.10 p.m. Penzance to Cardiff. (See Note k.)	
DAYS CONCERNED: BROCCOLI ...	Tues., Weds. and Thurs.		Mondays to Thursdays.		Saturdays.	
POTATOES ...	Nil.		Mondays to Fridays.		Nil.	
Headcode	"D" to Truro, "C" beyond.		"D" to Truro, "C" beyond.		"D" to Truro, "C" beyond.	
	arr. a.m.	dep. a.m.	arr. a.m.	dep. a.m.	arr. p.m.	dep. p.m.
Penzance Goods ...	...	...	—	11 20	—	12 10
Marazion ...	—	11 20	11 25	11 40	12 15	12 45
St. Erth ...	11 28	11 42	11 48	12 0	12 53	1 10
Hayle ...	— a	—	— a	—	— a	—
		p.m.	p.m.	p.m.		
Gwinear Road ...	11 56	12 11	12 14	12 49¶	1 24	1 51
Camborne...	— b	—	— b	—	— b	—
Drump Lane ...	p.m. 12 26		1 4		2 6	
Truro ...	12 50	1 8	1 22	1 40	2 24	2 53
Par ...	1 46		2 18		3T32	3T35n
Bodmin Road ...	2 3		2 35		3 53e	
Liskeard ...	2 26		2 58		4 16	
Menheniot ...	— c	—	—	—	—	—
Saltash ...	2 49X		3 26X		4 37	
Royal Albert Bridge ...	2 51		3 28		4 39	
North Road ...	2 59		3 37		4 52	
Tavistock Junction ...	3EL12	3EL AE30	3EL47	4EL 0	5EL 5 k	6EL 0
Plympton Loop ...	—	—	4 5	4AE27	6 5	6AE23
Hemerdon ...	3 42		4 40		6 36	
Brent ...	3 55		4 53		6 49	
Totnes ...	4* 8	4AE*54	5* 6	5AE*12	7* 1	7AE*24
Dainton Siding ...	5AE 7	5 10	5AE25	5 28	7AE37	7 40
Aller Junction ...	—	—	—	—	—	—
Newton Abbot ...	*5 20d		5 37d		7*T50	8*T 1
Dawlish Warren ...	5 40 *	5 55	—	—	—	—
Exeter ...	6T20	6T25	6 5		8* 40	
Cowley Junction ...	—	—	—	—	—	—
Sampford Peverell ...	—	—	—	—	—	—
Whiteball ...	7 12		6* 49		9* 25	
Taunton ...	M7 35L		7EL10 M	L 7EL30	9T44	9T49
Creech Junction ...	R L		M L		m R L	—
Castle Cary ...	...	...	8 15	8 26		
Witham ...	For continuation see page 16.		8 41		For continuation see page 16.	
Blatchbridge Junction ...			8 49			
Clink Road Junction ...	...	...	8 52		...	...
Fairwood Junction ...	...	...	8 56		...	...
Heywood Road Junction ...	...	...	9 0		...	...
Patney & Chirton ...	...	...	9 23		...	...
Savernake (Low Level) ...	...	...	9 41		...	...
Bedwyn ...	...	...	9 47		...	...
Enborne Junction ...	...	...	—	—	...	...
Newbury ...	...	...	10 2J		...	...
Theale ...	...	...	—	—	...	...
Southcote Junction ...	...	...	10 22		...	...
Oxford Road Junction ...	...	...	10T26	10T31	...	...
Reading General ...	...	...	M10 35L		...	...
Twyford ...	...	...	10 42		...	...
Maidenhead ...	...	...	10 51		...	...
Slough ...	...	...	10 59		...	...
West Drayton ...	...	...	—	—	...	...
Southall West Junction ...	...	...	—	—	...	...
Southall ...	...	...	11 15	11 45	...	...
Acton Main Line ...	...	...	11 57		...	...
Ladbroke Grove Junction ...	...	...	R L		...	...
Portobello Junction ...	...	...	G L		...	...
Paddington Goods ...	...	...	a.m. 12 10	—	...	...

J—8.5 p.m. Westbury to Hayes to be kept clear. 9.30 p.m. Newbury to Reading to be kept clear at Thatcham W. a—Hayle traffic to be worked to St. Erth by local arrangement. b—Camborne traffic to be worked to Gwinear Road by local arrangement. c—12.45 p.m. St. Blazey to Tavistock Junction to be kept clear. d—2.10 p.m. Tavistock Junction to Swindon to be held to follow. e—3.5 p.m. St. Blazey to Tavistock Junction to be kept clear. k—When conveying less than 15 wagons to terminate at Tavistock Junction and connect with 7.30 p.m. (**SO**) Tavistock Junction to Cardiff. m—8.25 p.m. Taunton to Bristol to be held to follow from Durston. n—2.5 p.m. Burngullow to Tavistock Junction to be kept clear. †—This train to run for a minimum of 10 wagons. When fewer than 10 wagons are available the traffic to be attached instead to the 4.10 p.m. Meat, Penzance to Acton, traffic to be cleared promptly to Paddington Goods as arranged by Control. ¶—Ten minutes later from Gwinear Road to Tavistock Junction when 12.5 p.m. **Q** Flowers Penzance to Swindon runs.

LOCAL FREIGHT TRAINS AND SHUNT ENGINES.

The following to run at "**Q**" times shewn in Working Time Tables:—

5.30 p.m. (**SX**) Marazion to Drump Lane.

5.50 p.m. (**SX**) Drump Lane to Hayle.

9.10 a.m. (Q SX) Falmouth to Truro—to run at amended times shewn below:—

	S X arr. a.m.	dep. a.m.
Falmouth ...	—	9‖10
Penryn ...	9‖20Y	12 0
	p.m.	p.m.
Perranwell ...	12 14X	12 27
Penwithers Jc.	12 40	
Truro ...	12 43	—

Y—Shunt as required.

11.10 a.m. Special Nancegollan to Gwinear Road (FSX Broccoli; SX Potato Seasons).

	arr. a.m.	dep. a.m.
Nancegollan ...	§	11 10
Praze	**D**	—
Gwinear Road	11 30	—

§—Train engine to leave Long Rock 9‖30 a.m., arr. Gwinear Road 9‖50 a.m. and work special thence (dep. 10.15 a.m.) to Nancegollan (arr. 10.36 a.m.). Engine to shunt at Gwinear Road 11.30 a.m. to 6.0 p.m. (or finish), then to Shed.

5.0 p.m. Helston to Gwinear Road.
Retimed **TWThO.**
Applies during peak of potato season only.

	arr. p.m.	dep. p.m.
Helston ...	—	5 45
Nancegollan ...	5 57	6 12
Stop Board ...	— **P**	—
Gwinear Road	6 30	**Y**

Y—L.E. to Long Rock at 6‖45 p.m.

Broccoli and Potato shunt engines to be provided daily as follows:—

At	From a.m.	To p.m.
Marazion ...	9 0	5 0
St. Erth ...	11 0	6 0
Gwinear Road	1§30	6 0

§—11‖0 a.m. ex Long Rock. (Applies **FSO** Broccoli, **SO** Potato Season).

LOCAL WORKING, PENZANCE GOODS AND MARAZION.

A transfer trip to leave Ponsandane punctually at 4.25 p.m. (**SX**) for Marazion with traffic for the 5.5 p.m. and 5.30 p.m. services thence.

Running and Maintenance Department to provide an additional Bank Engine at Tavistock Junction when both the 12.45 p.m. and the 1.35 p.m. Marazion run.

Train Schedules for Broccoli and Potato Traffic—continued.

Number of Special ...	4		5		6		—	
	12.45 p.m. Marazion to Cardiff. (See Note k.)		1.25 p.m. Penzance to †Crewe. via Yate.		1.35 p.m. Marazion to Oxley Sidings via Yate. (See Note d.)			
DAYS CONCERNED: BROCCOLI ...	Tues., Weds. and Thurs.		Saturdays (York)		Tues., Weds. and Thurs.			
POTATOES ...	Tues., Weds. and Thurs.		Saturdays (Crewe)		Mondays to Fridays.			
Headcode ...	"D" to Truro, "C" beyond.		"D" to Truro, "C" beyond.		"D" to Truro, "C" beyond.			
	arr. p.m.	dep. p.m.	arr. p.m.	dep. p.m.	arr. p.m.	dep. p.m.		
Penzance Goods ...	...	...	—	1 25	...	...	...	...
Marazion ...	—	12 45	1 30	1 50	—	1 35	...	...
St. Erth ...	12 53	1 10	1 58	2 42	1 43	1 58	...	...
Hayle ...	— a	—	—	—	— a	—	...	...
Gwinear Road ...	1 24	1 51	2 56	3 10	2 12	2 35	...	...
Camborne ...	— b	—	—	—	—	b	...	...
Drump Lane ...	2 6		3 25		2 51		...	...
Truro ...	2 24	2 53	3 43	4 5	3 10	3 25	...	...
Grampound Road ...	—	—	—	—	— c	—	...	...
St. Austell ...	—	—	4 37 c	4R44	—	—	...	...
Par ...	3T32	3T35	4T54	4T56	4T 4	4T 7	...	...
Lostwithiel ...	— n	—	—	—	— n	—	...	...
Bodmin Road ...	3 53e		5 15		4 26e		...	...
Liskeard ...	4 16		5 42		4 49		...	...
Saltash ...	4 37		6 5X		5 10		...	...
Royal Albert Bridge ...	4 39		6 7		5 12		...	...
North Road ...	4 47		6 15		5 32		...	...
Tavistock Junction ...	4EL55	5EL20	6EL25	6EL48	5EL45	6EL0	...	...
Plympton Loop ...	5 25	5AE47	—	—	6 5	6AE23	...	...
Hemerdon ...	5 59		7 0		6 36		...	...
Brent ...	6 12		7 15		6 49		...	...
Totnes ...	6 25	6AE30	7*27	7AE*44	7* 1	7AE*24	...	...
Dainton Sidings ...	6AE43	6 46	7AE57	8 0	7AE37	7 40	...	...
Aller Junction ...	—	—	—	—	—	—	...	...
Newton Abbot ...	6T56	7T 5	8 10		7T51	7T57	...	...
Hackney ...	—	—	—	—	—	—	...	...
Exeter ...	7 40*		8T41	8T46 ...	8 40*		...	...
Sampford Peverell ...	— z	—	—	—	—	—	...	...
Whiteball ...	8 13		9 32*		9 25*		...	...
Taunton ...	k8T29	8T34	9 55*		9T44	d 9T49	...	...
Creech Junction ...	R L g		R L m		R L m		...	...
Bridgwater ...	8 54		10 17 j		10 6 j		...	...
Highbridge ...	9 4		10 25		10 16		...	...
Brent Knoll ...	—	—	10*32	10*45	—	—	...	...
Uphill Junction ...	9*15	9*25	10 55		10 25		...	...
Worle Junction ...	—	—	11 1		10*30	10*51	...	...
Yatton West ...	9 37		11 8		11 2		...	...
Claverham ...	9 39		—	—	—	—	...	...
West Depot ...	9 52		11EL22	11EL50	11 15		...	...
Pylle Hill ...	—	—	—	—	—	—	...	...
Bristol West ...	9 55		—	—	11 19		...	...
Temple Meads ...	—	—	—	—	—	—	...	...
St. Philip's Marsh ...	10 0	10T35	—	—	11EL23	11EL55	...	...
Marsh Junction ...	10 39		11 59		11 58		...	...
Dr. Day's Bridge Junction ...	10 43		SUNS. 12	2RL a.m.	R12	1L a.m.	...	...
Stapleton Road ...	10 48	10AE51	12 6	12AE 9	12 4	12AE 7	...	...
Filton Junction ...	11 0 X		12 18		12*17	12*20	...	...
Patchway ...	11 12						...	...
Pilning Junction ...	11Z8	11 18	for continuation see page 17.		for continuation see page 16.		...	...
Severn Tunnel East ...	—	12* 1					...	...
Severn Tunnel West ...	12 18 a.m.		...	...	...	...	...	...
Severn Tunnel Junction ...	12 23	1* 3	...	...	...	...	...	...
Newport (High Street) ...	1*23 v	1*25	†—Destination York Broccoli Season only.		...	...	...	...
Ebbw Junction ...	—	—			...	...	...	...
St. Brides ...	1 33				...	...	...	...
Cardiff Goods ...	1 47	3* 5 p	For continuation see page 17.		...	...	...	...
Cardiff General ...	3 10				...	...	...	...
Bridgend ...	3 57		...	...	...	...	...	...
Pyle West Junction ...	4 12		...	...	...	...	...	...
Port Talbot (General) ...	4*22	4*32	...	...	...	...	...	...
Court Sart Junction ...	4 40		...	...	...	...	...	...
Neath General ...	4 45	5W8 q	...	...	...	...	...	...
Lonlas Junction ...	5* 30		...	...	...	...	...	...
Felin Fran ...	5*34	6* 0	...	...	...	...	...	...
Morlais Junction ...	6 20		...	...	...	...	...	...
Llandilo Junction ...	6 27	—	...	...	...	...	...	...

a—Hayle traffic to be worked to St. Erth by local arrangement. b—Camborne traffic to be worked to Gwinear Road by local arrangement. c—2.25 p.m. Truro to St. Blazey to be kept clear. d—When conveying less than 10 wagons to terminate Taunton and connect with 11.20 p.m. Taunton to Wolverhampton Parcels. (Scottish Region traffic to connect with 5.5 p.m. Marazion to Crewe.) e—3.5 p.m. St. Blazey to Tavistock Junction to be kept clear. g—8.25 p.m. Taunton to Bristol to be held to follow from Taunton. j—4.5 p.m. Exeter to Swindon to be kept clear. k—When conveying less than 15 wagons to terminate at Taunton and connect with 11.45 p.m. (**SX**) Taunton to Cardiff. m—8.25 p.m. Taunton to Bristol to be held to follow from Durston. n—2.5 p.m. Burngullow to Tavistock Junction to be kept clear. p—To be extended to Llandilo Junction for a minimum of 5 wagons. q—Port Talbot traffic to connect with 8.0 a.m. Neath to Port Talbot. Swansea (High Street) traffic to connect with 5.30 a.m. Neath to Swansea (High Street). v—12.5 a.m. (**MX**) Severn Tunnel Junction to Cardiff to be regulated. **X**—3.5 p.m. Hackney to be kept clear. z—2.10 p.m. Tavistock Junction to Swindon to be held to follow.

Acknowledgements

I would like to thank all those who have helped in the preparation of this book. Professor Colin Divall of the Institute of Railway Studies, York, has been central to the project overall in offering advice and expertise in terms of structure and theme, and for helping to initiate and develop the work in this form. Likewise, Stephen Mourton at Runpast Publishing for his interest and enthusiasm for the project in terms of publication and the development of railway history into wider social and cultural perspectives. Terry Knight, Principal Librarian, Kim Cooper and Joanne Laing at the Cornish Studies Library, Redruth, and Sherryl Healey, Librarian at the Railway Studies Library, Newton Abbot, have, as always, been extremely helpful in making essential source materials available. I would also thank Gerald Baker for his particular contribution in working with me on valuable primary sources and for his interest throughout preparation. In this context I would also acknowledge Tony Rivers at the Great Western Trust, Didcot. Peter Gray has, again, provided the best in photographs for the final years of steam working; likewise, Roger Venning for his contribution in terms of the immediate pre-and post-war periods.

Front Cover: *2800 class, No.3841, heads a class 'H' freight on the climb to Dainton Tunnel – between Newton Abbot and Totnes – on the South Devon main line. Banked by 5100 class 2-6-2T, No.5153, this westbound train was tackling gradients which, at their fiercest, were down to 1 in 36. 11 March 1960.* P. Gray.

Back Cover: *The final edition, 1947, of 'Holiday Haunts' under GWR ownership. Colour covers were introduced in 1929.* Author's Collection.

Published by Runpast Publishing,
10 Kingscote Grove, Cheltenham, Gloucestershire GL51 6JX

Typesetting and reproduction by Viners Wood Associates – 01452 812813
Printed in England by The Amadeus Press Ltd., Cleckheaton

ISBN 1 870754 55 7